*Oratory and Rhetoric
in the
Nineteenth-Century South*

Oratory and Rhetoric in the Nineteenth-Century South

A Rhetoric of Defense

W. Stuart Towns

PRAEGER

Westport, Connecticut
London

Library of Congress Cataloging-in-Publication Data

Towns, W. Stuart, 1939–
    Oratory and rhetoric in the nineteenth-century South : a rhetoric
of defense / W. Stuart Towns.
        p.   cm.
    Includes bibliographical references and index.
    ISBN 0–275–96223–7 (alk. paper)
    1. Speeches, addresses, etc., American—Southern States—History
and criticism.   2. Oratory—Southern States—History—19th century.
3. English language—Southern States—Rhetoric.   4. English
language—19th century—Rhetoric.   I. Title.
PS407.T69   1998
815'.309975—DC21   98–13544

British Library Cataloguing in Publication Data is available.

Copyright © 1998 by W. Stuart Towns

Library of Congress Catalog Card Number: 98–13544
ISBN: 0–275–96223–7

First published in 1998

Praeger Publishers, 88 Post Road West, Westport, CT 06881
An imprint of Greenwood Publishing Group, Inc.

Printed in the United States of America

The paper used in this book complies with the
Permanent Paper Standard issued by the National
Information Standards Organization (Z39.48–1984).

10 9 8 7 6 5 4 3 2 1

This book is lovingly dedicated to my parents, Homer and Evelyn Towns, who instilled in me a life-long love of learning, a curiosity about my world, and a love of the South. I also owe a large debt of gratitude to Ralph T. Eubanks, my career-long mentor, who is a classic model of a gentleman and a scholar, and who first whetted my appetite to study the history of southern public address.

Contents

Photo essay follows page 100

CHAPTER 1

Introduction

ORATORY AND THE SOUTH

Historians have long acknowledged the important role of public speaking in the history of the United States. Daniel Boorstin, writing about the period from the Revolution to the Civil War, points out that the "orator—the man speaking to or for or with his community—acquired a mythic role." He goes on to say that oratory became "the main form of American public ritual."[1] William G. Carleton reminds us that, "throughout most of American history, the folk hero has been the jury lawyer, the hortatory minister, and the political orator. Until the turn of the century the most important American folk art was oratory." Public speakers who were nationally acclaimed were as famous in their day as modern Hollywood stars are in our era.[2]

Nowhere in nineteenth-century America was the effective orator more respected than in the South. Waldo W. Braden, writing about the southern oral tradition, says the "masters of the oral medium became folk heroes."[3] The South was an oral society, and "the opportunity to exchange ritual words or hear them eloquently pronounced was deeply cherished."[4] William G. Brown wrote that "it was the spoken word, not the printed page, that guided thought, aroused enthusiasm, made history." He went further, claiming that "it is doubtful if there ever has been a society in which the orator counted for more than he did in the Cotton Kingdom."[5] Clement Eaton refers to the "passionate addiction of Southern people to florid and emotional oratory."[6] Wilbur J. Cash pointed out that rhetoric flourished in the South "far beyond even its American average; it early became a passion . . . a primary standard of judgment, the *sine qua non* of leadership."[7]

Many observers and historians of southern life have helped to create and perpetuate a descriptive and stereotypical myth of the "Southern orator." He is often portrayed as a huckster, a charlatan, a demagogue, or a con man selling "snake oil." There have been many examples of this demagogic genre, just as there have been many spokesmen and spokeswomen who were genuinely seeking humane and tolerant solutions to the various problems of race, poverty, and defeat which the southern region has endured. This anthology documents this positive side of southern public communication as well as the negative impact of public address on the southern mind.

One of the distinguishing features of the South has been its traditional conservatism and its love of tradition and heritage. This collection of public speeches delivered by southerners in the nineteenth century illustrates that tradition-bound culture, but it also reflects the changes that began to touch the region late in the century. So that we can better understand the audiences these speakers addressed and see more clearly the regional values with which they identified and the foundations onto which they anchored their rhetorical appeals, we should define and describe the South.

CHARACTERIZING THE SOUTH

Defining the region may be a daunting task, as many non-southerners, newly-arrived residents, and life-long southerners find it difficult to really understand "The South." It is an entity that has formed the way generations of Americans have identified themselves. It is a concept that is known by all who identify themselves as southerners and by those hundreds of journalists, historians, economists, sociologists, and rhetoricians who have examined it closely. It is an idea or a state of mind that is recognized by the thousands of non-southerners who have read about the region and who seek out information and interpretation about it. Whatever it is, southerners believe their region is unique in American history, and many of them hold to that uniqueness with a fervent intensity. As many of our speakers show clearly, southerners are often without interest in changing, and they are especially not interested in being told by "outsiders" that something is wrong with the region's lifestyle or folkways.

Can we define the South by its people? From the beginning, there have been many contrasting dichotomies in the South: urban-rural, planter-yeoman, white-black, Piedmont-delta, merchant-agrarian; these examples only begin to suggest the list. When one attempts to characterize the South, immediately one is faced with the great variety of people that make up what is termed a "southerner": Louisiana oil field worker, Appalachian millhand, Saturn car plant skilled technician, Nashville song writer, migrant farm worker, Orlando businesswoman, media evangelist, Gulf Coast shrimper, cotton farmer, urban professional, Ozark "hillbilly." All these types and many more make up the South historically and today.

Can the South be defined geographically? The Mississippi Gulf Coast certainly has little in common with the Smoky Mountains of Tennessee and

North Carolina. The bayou country west and south of New Orleans shares little with the fertile cotton fields of the river valley only a few hundred miles to the north in the so-called delta country of western Mississippi and eastern Arkansas. What similarities are there between the orange groves of central Florida and the rice fields of central Arkansas, or the Ozark foothills and the Okefenokee? Is there commonality between the Tidewater of Virginia and Maryland and the Piedmont of Georgia and South Carolina?

Can the South be defined economically? Again, there are many Souths: the highly rural and agricultural base of the southern economy still exists, alongside the Mercedes-Benz assembly line in Alabama, the Saturn plant in Tennessee, the vast Huntsville, Alabama, space center, the Kennedy Space Center at Cape Canaveral, the Research Triangle in North Carolina, and Disney World in Orlando. Even the South's agriculture is widely diversified, with rice, peaches, soybeans, citrus, sugar cane, cattle, hogs, and poultry successfully challenging King Cotton. The South can no longer be considered genuinely rural with the presence of Atlanta, Houston, Dallas, Orlando, Tampa, Miami, Birmingham, Memphis, Charlotte, and a dozen other major cities. In fact, almost three out of four southerners lived in urban areas in the 1990s.

Perhaps Quentin Compson in William Faulkner's *Absalom, Absalom!* begins to get at the heart of "southernness" when he tells his college roommate, "You cant understand it. You would have to be born there."[8] Or when Richard Weaver writes that being a southerner is "definitely a spiritual condition, like being a Catholic or a Jew."[9] Let us examine some of these "spiritual condition[s]," these elements that illustrate that perhaps one does have to be "born there" in order to know and understand the South.

Many observers and students of the southern scene have commented on several characteristics of the region that seem to define it. Perhaps the most important one is the intense ties to place, the land, the soil, the family—in short, a sense of locale. There is a love of the soil and the growing of things that doubtless goes back even further than the early statement of Thomas Jefferson that, "Those who labor in the earth are the chosen people of God" or James Henry Hammond's romantic assessment that rural life "promotes a generous hospitality, a high and perfect courtesy, a lofty spirit of independence . . . and all the nobler virtues and heroic traits."[10] Certainly many southerners in the late 1990s still nourish a deep and abiding love of the land.

A corollary of this relationship to the land is the southerners' tie to the place they call home and the family relationship to that place. While the South is certainly much more mobile and not nearly so place-bound as just a generation or two ago, the place called "home" is still a powerful magnet for both black and white southerners.[11] Many, like myself, left their homes and struck off for other places to earn their fortunes and fame. Many groups, especially blacks and poorer whites, left the region entirely, headed for Detroit, Chicago, New York, Philadelphia, and other northern metropolises where they thought jobs would be easier to find. They hoped for better pay and believed there would be less concern over skin color. They left in the 1930s and 1940s to work in the automobile factories of Detroit; today the automobile plants are in South Carolina, Alabama, Georgia, or Tennessee. Beginning with the decade of the 1970s, many of these southerners have come back to the South to better jobs and much more livable conditions. For many of us, even those of us who stayed in the South, there has always been a small sense of guilt because we felt we had to leave home in the first place.[12]

Another often-cited characteristic of the South is its conservative religiousness and the crucial role the church plays in the life of the southerner. John Shelton Reed shows clearly that there are "substantial differences between white southerners and other white Americans in religious beliefs and practices."[13] According to Reed's surveys, southerners are more likely to attend church, listen to religious programming on television and radio, and name a religious leader when asked whom they most admire.[14] This conservative, orthodox religion (90 percent are Protestant, with about 50 percent claiming membership in a Baptist church, and with a large Methodist minority), provides many anchors for the persuasive rhetoric of the speakers in this anthology. We will see a reflection of the South's skepticism about human perfectibility; a thread running through southern religion and southern rhetoric is the Biblical concept that "all are guilty and fall short of the glory of God." Violence, sin, evil, Satan, and unrighteousness are all part of the human condition and cannot be eradicated by the mere efforts of men (and, especially, the ventures of government).

Yet another distinguishing characteristic of the South is the presence of the nation's largest concentration of African-Americans. For almost the entire history of the American nation, the relationship and interactions of white and black have dominated southern history. The historian Carl Degler has written that this interaction, "more than anything else," makes the South different and sets it apart from the rest of the nation.[15] William G. Carleton points out that, "In some attributes and values the white culture and the Negro culture have interacted very little; but in others they have interacted very much, and what we call 'Southern' is to a considerable degree the result of that interaction."[16]

While these ingredients—love of the land, place, family, conservative Christianity, and the large presence of African-Americans—go far to define the region and the southerner, another and darker side of the southern psyche must be an important part of this description of the South. Over the generations, southerners have developed a siege mentality, a paranoid and defensive outlook on life that shows itself clearly in many southern speeches. Many groups and individuals have been seen as "the enemy" by passing generations of southerners. In the nineteenth century the enemy included abolitionists and northern politicians who attacked southern institutions and lifestyles beginning as early as the debates that produced the Missouri Compromise; the northern armies during the Civil War; the occupying army, carpetbaggers, and Freedman's Bureau of the reconstruction years. In the twentieth century the enemy has included the "liberals," the "Commies," the "outside agitators," and even the federal government. Black southerners have also accepted this defensive mentality. A black North Carolina furniture plant worker said in 1976 that he would vote for Jimmy Carter for president because he was "tired of listening to all those slick Yankees who think they know everything and have all the answers."[17] For generations, southerners have felt looked down upon, humiliated, dominated, and attacked verbally and militarily. Southerners often have practiced a defensive rhetorical stand: defending their way of life, culture, and very existence against those from the "outside" who they felt would destroy what they held dear. Many of the speeches in this book are built largely on that premise. Indeed, as Francis Butler Simkins has pointed out, oratory "was the main weapon of defense in the controversies over Southern institutions."[18]

There are many other elements of the stereotype of the South, the southerner, and southernness: food, music, language patterns, a "laid back" lifestyle, the cult of chivalry and its respect for womanhood, the relationships of black and white (which doubtless affects most of the other elements of the South), and the widespread and pervasive poverty of the region. All are frequently cited as southern traits and most of these foundations were laid in the nineteenth century. There is, however, more to the South than these characteristics.

Lillian Smith writes about "memories that are never quite facts but sometimes closer to the 'truth' than is any fact."[19] Above all, shaping the South, the southern audience and the southern speaker, there is the traditional memory of the South which has configured the way southerners have lived for generations, regardless of whether it was "truth" or not: the moonlight and magnolias, mint juleps on the veranda, and Scarlett O'Hara of *Gone with the Wind* fame; the days of slavery and oppression for a quarter of the population; the almost cultic worship and reverence of the Old South, the Confederacy, and the Lost Cause; the unpleasant memories of Reconstruction and the bitter and harsh Jim Crow laws of segregation days; the last stand for white supremacy and the difficult battles of the civil rights era; and the sudden prosperity and the knowledge of being in the national spotlight—in a positive sense for a change—during the "Sunbelt" years of the 1980s and 1990s. All this cultural memory, and more, is the South. The speeches in this anthology clearly reflect that culture and help to define the region, its people, and its shared memories.

THE DEFENSIVE SOUTH

As early as the 1820s, the wary and protective mode of the region begins to evolve and is fully developed within a decade as southern spokesmen defend the region, and particularly its peculiar institution, against the first waves of "outsider" attacks first by those who would limit slavery, then later, by those who would abolish it. Throughout this period, the region and its spokesmen looked at the world from a defensive posture, and its rhetoric became a "rhetoric of desperation,"[20] beginning with the Congressional debates over the admission of Missouri in 1820. William Smith and William Pinkney clearly defined the South's defense in that debate and set the tone of a great deal of southern oratory for the next eighty or more years.

A decade later in South Carolina, debate over the right of a state to nullify a federal law took center stage and the defensive posture of the South was delineated by James Hamilton, Jr., and the South's intellectual leader, John C. Calhoun. While state rights was a cogent Constitutional issue, slavery was the emotional rock that eventually split the nation. Increasingly, as the fateful election of 1860 and its aftermath in the winter and spring of 1861 drew closer, southern speakers grew more and more defensive and paranoid. They saw their region and themselves as different from and superior to their adversaries in the North who seemed bent on destroying everything that constituted the South and "southernness." By the mid-to-late 1850s, southern spokesmen like Robert Toombs and James Henry Hammond were defending the indefensible, human bondage, and at the same time creating and defending the image of an idealistic southern "way of life." The leadership of the South saw their society as an elite culture based on a "mudsill" of hewers of wood, drawers of water, and choppers and pickers of cotton; their rhetoric was designed to preserve that eliteness—at the expense of the unified nation, if need be. In 1860–1861 it came to that, and William L. Yancey, Benjamin Morgan Palmer, and Jefferson Davis were among the leaders who persuaded the South to leave the nation.

All of the major issues of this era focused essentially on the debate about the nature of the government that had been created such a short time before, the role of minorities within that government, and the relationship of states to the national government. Southerners debated northerners on these issues from a defensive posture; public communication finally failed, however, and the sections settled their differences on the fields of the Civil War. Though the war may have resolved issues of the nature of government, the South for generations never gave up a direct link to that antebellum era. As Wilbur Cash expressed it, "The South, one might say, is a tree with many age rings, with its limbs and trunk bent and twisted by all the winds of the years, but with its tap root in the Old South."[21]

After Appomattox, the defensiveness continued, but with a different flavor—accommodation by much of the South to the demands of Reconstruction and the newly freed slaves. Alfred Moore Waddell and Benjamin H.

Hill addressed these demands in the 1870s, but their oratory simply deepened the problem and helped create the atmosphere for continued bitterness. There were some, however, who did try to create and enhance national reconciliation; Lucius Q. C. Lamar and Henry W. Grady were recognized in both North and South as leading contributors to reunification. Perhaps the most tragic era of southern history, this post-war "New South" marked little change or transition to identify it as truly new. Racial segregation, perhaps as brutal in some respects as the slavery it replaced, was developed as a means of racial control. Zebulon B. Vance, Benjamin R. Tillman, and Booker T. Washington contributed their points of view to the debates over the "racial problem," all of which solidified the segregated relationships between the races. While the bitterness continued and the South looked back to the past to forge the myths of the Lost Cause and of White Supremacy, the era did have the optimism and positive outlook of the New South spokesmen. Their vision was of the future, which was the most positive approach the South had so far seen in its history and was not to see again until the 1970s and 1980s. While the bitterness of the war years lasted for decades—and in the minds of some, until well into the twentieth century—the South desired to rejoin the Union and did so largely under its own terms. The Old South legend was created, Jim Crow segregation laws defined the new relationships between the races, and since the North needed new markets and new locations for industry, railroads, and new sources of labor, the South was essentially welcomed back into the Union with open arms.

The vision of the New South did not materialize as Henry Grady and other New South advocates had hoped. Instead, the darker side of man's nature prevailed and Jim Crow, lynch law, and the Ku Klux Klan dominated the section. The South remained defensive and suffered from a continuing crisis of self-confidence.[22] The suppression of hope and a region-wide poor self-image fostered the milieu that led to Franklin Roosevelt's assessment of the South as the nation's number one economic problem nearly half a century later. The Populists and some early versions of the Progressives tried to break the pattern, but their changes were superficial and short-lived. Atticus G. Haygood strongly advocated a more humane treatment of black southerners and Ida Wells-Barnett fought lynching from platforms across the country and abroad, but their words fell on rocky soil and the problem festered for another three-quarters of a century.

CONCLUSION

Southern public address scholarship has been a productive line of research since Dallas C. Dickey's ground-breaking 1947 essay, "Southern Oratory: A Field for Research."[23] Dickey and his doctoral students at the University of Florida, followed by Waldo W. Braden and his students at

Louisiana State University built an impressive platform of research which continues strong in the 1990s.

While this scholarship has opened many doors to the rhetorical history of the American South, there is still no modern collection of speeches by southern speakers on themes that have shaped the history and life of the region. This anthology fills part of that gap and provides future students and persons interested in the South with some of the important texts on many of the major topics which reflect and have conditioned southern collective memory.

A thorough reading of these speeches will help the student of the South better understand the region. For example, it is much easier to comprehend the conflicts of the civil rights era if one has read the speeches of some of the builders of the Jim Crow system of segregation and the creators of the Lost Cause mythology. In short, these speeches, while often little known today, affected the immediate audiences of their times, and by creating part of the southern collective consciousness they also influenced audiences concerned with important issues in the twentieth century.

For the most part, these addresses are published in full—just as the original source had printed them. Due to the nineteenth century proclivity to orations that lasted for hours,[24] I have eliminated portions that do not seem germane to the major ideas of the speaker's theme. In these cases, I have indicated this extensive editing using ellipsis at the end of a paragraph. In some few cases, the original texts I had available had eliminated portions of the speech and had indicated these parts with standard ellipsis marks. With the exception of modernizing the spelling and punctuation in some cases, these texts are faithful to the original sources.

The speeches anthologized here were selected, not on the basis of "greatness" or notoriety, but because from my point of view they were representative of the hundreds I have read on the major issues that have shaped the South. Other issues and certainly other speeches could have been selected (those anthologized were selected from over 600 speeches in the editor's collection), but these concerns and this set of nineteenth century speeches have certainly shaped the history and life of the American South.

NOTES

1. Daniel J. Boorstin, *The Americans: The National Experience* (New York: Random House, 1965), 308, 312.

2. William G. Carleton, "The Celebrity Cult of a Century Ago," *The Georgia Review* 14 (Summer 1960), 133.

3. Waldo W. Braden, *The Oral Tradition in the South* (Baton Rouge: Louisiana State University Press, 1983), 42.

4. Bertram Wyatt-Brown, *Southern Honor: Ethics and Behavior in the Old South* (Oxford: Oxford University Press, 1982), 330.

5. William G. Brown, *The Lower South in American History* (New York: P. Smith, 1930 reprint of 1902 ed.), 125.

6. Clement Eaton, *The Mind of the Old South*, rev. ed. (Baton Rouge: Louisiana State University Press, 1967), 275.

7. Wilbur J. Cash, *The Mind of the South* (New York: Alfred A. Knopf, 1941), 53.

8. William Faulkner, *Absalom, Absalom!* (New York: Random House, 1936), 361.

9. "The South and the American Union," in *The Southern Essays of Richard M. Weaver*, George M. Curtis, III and James J. Thompson, Jr., eds. (Indianapolis, IN: Liberty Press, 1987), 251.

10. Both the Jefferson and Hammond quotations are found in James McPherson, *Battle Cry of Freedom: The Civil War Era* (New York: Oxford University Press, 1988), 98.

11. While many black southerners left the region seeking a better life, many expect to retire to the South and to "inherit a house or a bit of land from a parent or other relative." William G. Carleton, "The South's Many Moods," *The Yale Review* LV (October 1965), 640.

12. The case of the author, I submit, is typical of many persons who call themselves southerners. While I have spent my professional career in the South, I am not at "home." I deeply cherish the family farm back on Crowley's Ridge in eastern Arkansas—the acreage that I constantly implore my parents not to sell, because I want to return there when I retire and I want to be buried there when I die. That locale is home for me, and that area is home, as well, for the scores of persons who come back to that small town on holidays, driving cars with license plates from Ohio, Michigan, Indiana, Illinois, and other far-away places.

13. John Shelton Reed, "Southerners," in *Harvard Encyclopedia of American Ethnic Groups*, Stephen Thernstrom, ed. (Cambridge, MA: Belknap Press, 1980), 945.

14. Ibid., 946.

15. Carl N. Degler, *The Other South: Southern Dissenters in the Nineteenth Century* (New York: Harper Torchbooks, 1975), 6.

16. Carleton, "South's Many Moods," 640.

17. As told in John Shelton Reed, "The South's Mid-Life Crisis," *Southern Humanities Review* 25 (Spring 1991), 134–135.

18. Francis Butler Simkins, *A History of the South*, 3rd ed. (New York: Alfred A. Knopf, 1963), 178.

19. Lillian Smith, *Killers of the Dream*, rev. ed. (Garden City, NY: Anchor Books, Doubleday & Co., 1963, originally published in 1949), 3.

20. See Ralph T. Eubanks, "The Rhetoric of the Nullifiers," in *Oratory in the Old South, 1828–1860*, Waldo W. Braden, ed. (Baton Rouge: Louisiana State University Press, 1970), 19–72, quotation on page 21.

21. Cash, *Mind of the South*, x.

22. As Gaines Foster has pointed out, "Defeat in battle and the exigencies of the war's aftermath wounded southerners' confidence in their righteousness, honor, and manliness." *Ghosts of the Confederacy: Defeat, the Lost Cause, and the Emergence of the New South, 1865 to 1913* (New York: Oxford University Press, 1987), 35.

23. *Quarterly Journal of Speech* 33 (December 1947), 458–463.

24. Richard M. Weaver discusses this characteristic of nineteenth-century oratory in his essay, "The Spaciousness of Old Rhetoric," in *The Ethics of Rhetoric* (Chicago: Henry Regnery Co., 1953), 164–185.

CHAPTER 2

The Missouri Compromise: The Firebell in the Night

And provided also, That the further introduction of slavery or involuntary servitude be prohibited . . . and that all children of slaves, born within the said state, after the admission thereof into the union, shall be free, but may be held to service until the age of twenty-five years.[1]

When presented to the United States House of Representatives on February 13, 1819, these words galvanized one of the most intense and time-consuming debates in the country's brief history. For the next year, the discussion of this Tallmadge Amendment to the Missouri statehood bill overshadowed all other business before the Congress. More important, this issue set the stage for the next forty years of acrimonious sectional debate that finally culminated in the Civil War. Over the next twelve months, Senators and Congressmen put forth most of the major arguments for and against slavery, and thoroughly debated the issues concerning the powers of Congress to control that institution.

Henry Clay, who was later credited with engineering a compromise solution, wrote to John J. Crittenden on January 29, 1820: "The Missouri subject monopolizes all our conversations, all our thoughts and for three weeks at least to come, will all our time."[2] What was the issue and the problem?

Several northern Congressmen, led by James Tallmadge of New York, saw the admission of Missouri as an opportunity to limit the spread of slavery. While abolition of the peculiar institution was not the rabid issue it became in the 1830s and 1840s, there was abolition support in both North and South. The northern states had abolished slavery by this time, and there were numerous southerners who, privately at least, denounced the practice. In these debates, for example, Robert Reid, a Congressman from Georgia, remarked on February 1, 1820, that slavery, "is an unnatural state; a dark cloud which obscures half the luster of our free institutions."[3]

In these debates from February 1819 through March 1820, southerners did not really defend slavery so much as they argued that Congress did not have the right to control the institution in the individual states. In the eyes of southern Congressmen and Senators, if a state wanted to free the slaves within its boundaries, it was perfectly able to do so, but they believed that Congress had no right to interfere with privately held property within a state. They argued that all states must be equal and that Congress could not impose limitations on one state that had not been imposed on other states at the time of their admissions into the Union.

The northern spokesmen argued from the moral stand that slavery was wrong and should be abolished—or, at least, not allowed to expand beyond its present boundaries. Some asserted that Congress could control slavery, but many northerners who were opposed to slavery would not go so far. John Quincy Adams, a staunch abolitionist and long-time foe of slavery, wrote to the governor of Indiana at the end of the Congressional debate that, "The abolition of slavery where it is established must be left entirely to the people of the state itself."[4] Clay, a Kentuckian who opposed slavery, "vigorously supported" the southern view that it was a state's matter to deal with, not the role of Congress.[5]

Northern support for restricting slavery in Missouri was based not just on anti-slavery impulses, but also on the political fear of increased southern power in Congress. At the time the Missouri admission bill was presented, there was a balance between the number of slave and free states, and hence, a balance in the Senate. Due to the so-called three-fifths compromise which counted a slave as three-fifths of a free person, southern states had more representation in the House of Representatives than the North was now willing to accept. Northern Congressmen feared that if the door were opened to slavery expansion throughout the lands included in the Louisiana Purchase, the Northeast would lose even more relative power in Congress; the altruistic motive was mixed with the political.[6]

Finally, after a year of consideration, Congress reached a compromise in which Maine was paired with Missouri and admitted as a free state, with Missouri admitted as a slave state. In addition, opponents agreed that slavery would be prohibited in all other Louisiana Purchase territory above the 36 degree, 30 minute parallel.

Although it seemed that the issue was settled, John Quincy Adams voiced what some wise Americans predicted when he asserted that the debate was merely the "title-page to a great tragic volume."[7] Thomas Jefferson, himself a slave-owner, wrote just after the compromise:

> But this momentous question, like a firebell in the night, awakened and filled me with terror. I considered it at once as the knell of the Union. It is hushed, indeed, for the moment. But this is a reprieve only, not a final sentence.[8]

Jefferson was correct.

WILLIAM PINKNEY

While the debates went on for many weeks during the fifteenth and six-teenth Congresses, not all of the speeches are extant. For example, Henry Clay spoke for four hours on February 8, 1820, but his speech is not published in the *Annals of Congress*, and neither is a three-hour speech made by John Randolph on February 2. The most outstanding available speech for the southern side was given on February 15, 1820, by William Pinkney, a Senator from Maryland. Pinkney had also spoken over a two-day period on January 21 and 24, but that speech was not recorded.

Pinkney had a fine reputation as a speaker. He was recognized as perhaps the nation's foremost lawyer, arguing many cases before the Supreme Court and having the most lucrative private practice in the country.[9] He had a long career in public life, starting with his election as a delegate to the Maryland convention that ratified the Constitution (Pinkney voted against ratification).

While a member of the Maryland House of Delegates in 1788, Pinkney spoke twice in opposition to a bill that would prevent manumission of slaves upon the owner's death. In these speeches, he defended the right of states to deal with slavery, as he did thirty-two years later in the debates on Missouri.[10]

He was, at various times, a member of the Maryland House of Delegates, a member of the Executive Council of Maryland, a member of Congress, a commissioner to England, a minister to Russia and envoy to Italy, and Attorney General in President Madison's cabinet. During the War of 1812, Pinkney served as a Major in the Maryland militia and was wounded at the battle of Bladensburg. In 1819 he was elected to serve the unfinished term of a Senator from Maryland. He retained that seat until his death in 1822.[11]

After Pinkney's death, Judge Joseph Story, before whom Pinkney had argued many cases, wrote, "never do I expect to hear a man like Pinkney. He was a man who appears scarcely once a century." About his courtroom speaking, Story remarked, "Pinkney is vehement, rapid, and alternately delights the fancy and seizes on the understanding . . . [he] hurries you along with him, and persuades as well as convinces you . . . you must move rapidly or you lose the course of his argument."[12]

Comments regarding the speaker and speech depend largely on the partisanship of the reporter. Pinkney's biographer, his nephew, remarked about the speech included here: "This speech gratified to the full the highest expectations of the audience. It was a surprising combination of eloquence and argument, beauty and strength, amplitude and condensation."[13] On the other hand, an opposition observer, Congressman William Plumer, Jr., had a more unflattering view of Pinkney's January 21 and 24 address:

As a public speaker, his manner appears to me very bad—he is alternately loud & low, like some of our methodist preachers, impetuous, theatrical, & overbearing—His language however is elegant, forcible & commanding—& I have no doubt his speech [*sic*] will read much better than it appeared when delivered. As to his arguments, I hardly dare give an opinion respecting them. To those who are opposed to the restriction, they appeared unanswerable—that is to say—he succeeded perfectly in convincing those who were before of his opinion—But to me, they appeared perfectly inconclusive—It was throughout the speech of an able *lawyer*, & I could not help thinking . . . he might, with equal ease, have argued the other side quite as well, &, I have no doubt, much better.[14]

Regardless of Plumer's opinion, Pinkney's speech laid out many of the major positions advocated by the South for the next forty years. His major arguments are that the Congress does not have the power to limit or control in any way the expansion of slavery in the territories or in planned new states. According to Pinkney, the right to legislate regarding slavery rests in the various states, not the federal government.

SPEECH ON THE MISSOURI QUESTION[15]

Slavery, we are told in many a pamphlet, memorial, and speech, with which the press has lately groaned, is a foul blot upon our otherwise immaculate reputation. Let this be conceded—yet you are no nearer than before to the conclusion that you possess power which may deal with other subjects as effectually as with this. Slavery, we are further told, with some pomp of metaphor, is a canker at the root of all that is excellent in this republican empire, a pestilent disease that is snatching the youthful bloom from its cheek, prostrating its honor and withering its strength. Be it so—yet if you have power to medicine to it in the way proposed, and in virtue of the diploma which you claim, you have also power in the distribution of your political alexipharmics to present the deadliest drugs to every territory that would become a State, and bid it drink or remain a colony for ever. Slavery, we are also told, is now "rolling onward with a rapid tide towards the boundless regions of the West," threatening to doom them to sterility and sorrow, unless some potent voice can say to it—thus far shalt thou go and no farther. Slavery engenders pride and indolence in him who commands, and inflicts intellectual and moral degradation on him who serves. Slavery, in fine, is unchristian and abominable. Sir, I shall not stop to deny that slavery is all this and more; but I shall not think myself the less authorized to deny that it is for you to stay the course of this dark torrent, by opposing to it a mound raised up by the labors of this portentous discretion on the domain of others—a mound which you cannot erect but through the instrumentality of a trespass of no ordinary kind—not the comparatively innocent trespass that beats down a few blades of grass which the first kind sun or the next refreshing shower may cause to spring again, but that which levels with the ground the lordliest trees of the forest, and claims immortality for the destruction which it inflicts.

I shall not, I am sure, be told that I exaggerate this power. It has been admitted here, and elsewhere, that I do not. But I want no such concession. It is manifest, that as a discretionary power it is every thing or nothing—that its head is in the clouds, or that it is a mere figment of enthusiastic speculation—that it has no existence, or that it is an alarming vortex ready to swallow up all such portions of the sovereignty of an infant State, as you may think fit to cast into it as preparatory to the introduction into the Union of the miserable residue. No man can contradict me when I say, that if you have this power, you may squeeze down a new-born sovereign State to the size of a pygmy, and then taking it between finger and thumb, stick it into some niche of the Union, and still continue by way of mockery to call it *a State in the sense of the constitution*. You may waste it to a shadow, and then introduce it into the society of flesh and blood, an object of scorn and derision. You may sweat and reduce it to a thing of skin and bone, and then place the ominous skeleton beside the ruddy and healthful members of the Union, that it may have leisure to mourn the lamentable difference between itself and its companions, to brood over its disastrous promotion, and to seek in justifiable discontent, an opportunity for separation, and insurrection, and rebellion. What may you not do by dexterity and perseverance with this terrific power? . . .

We are told that admitting a State into the Union is a compact. Yes—but what sort of a compact? A compact that it shall be a member of the Union, as the constitution has made it. You cannot new fashion it. You may make a compact to admit, but when admitted, the original compact prevails. The Union is a compact, with a provision of political power and agents for the accomplishment of its objects. Vary that compact as to a new State—give new energy to that political power, so as to make it act with more force upon a new State than upon the old—make the will of those agents more effectually the arbiter of the fate of a new State than of the old, and it may be confidently said that the new State has not entered into *this Union*, but into another Union. How far the Union has been varied is another question. But that it has been varied is clear. . . .

One of the most signal errors with which the argument on the other side has abounded, is this of considering the proposed restriction as if levelled at the *introduction or establishment of slavery*. And hence the vehement declamation, which, among other things, has informed us that slavery originated in fraud or violence.

The truth is, that the restriction has no relation, real or pretended, to the right of *making slaves of those who are free*, or of introducing slavery where it does not already exist. It applies to those who are admitted to be already slaves, and who (with their posterity) would continue to be slaves if they should remain where they are at present; and to a place where slavery already exists by the local law. Their civil condition will not be altered by their removal from Virginia, or Carolina, to Missouri. They will not be more slaves than they now are. Their abode, indeed, will be different, but their bondage the same. Their numbers may possibly be augmented by the diffusion, and I think they will. But this can only happen because their hardships will be mitigated, and their comforts increased. The checks to population, which exist in the older States will be diminished. The restriction, therefore, does not prevent the establishment of slavery, either with reference to persons or place; but simply inhibits the removal from place to place (the law in each being the same) of a slave, or make his emancipation the consequence of that removal. It acts professedly merely on slavery as it exists, and thus acting restrains its present lawful effects. That slavery, like many other human institutions, originated in fraud or violence, may be conceded: but, however it *originated*, it is established among us, and no man seeks a further establishment of it by new importations of freemen to be converted into slaves. On the contrary, all are anxious to mitigate its evils by all the means within the reach of the appropriate authority, the domestic legislatures of the different States.

It can be nothing to the purpose of this argument, therefore, as the gentlemen themselves have shaped it, to inquire what was the origin of slavery. What is it now, and who are they that endeavor to innovate upon what it now is (the advocates of this restriction who desire change by unconstitutional means, or its opponents who desire to leave the whole matter to local regulation), are the only questions worthy of attention. . . .

Of the Declaration of our Independence, which has also been quoted in support of the perilous doctrines now urged upon us, I need not now speak at large. I have shown on a former occasion how idle it is to rely upon that instrument for such a purpose, and will not fatigue you by mere repetition. The self-evident truths announced in the Declaration of Independence are not truths at all, if taken literally; and the practical conclusions contained in the same passage of that Declaration prove that they were never designed to be so received.

The Articles of Confederation contain nothing on the subject; whilst the actual constitution recognizes the legal existence of slavery by various provisions. The power of prohibiting the slave trade is involved in that of regulating commerce, but this is coupled with an express inhibition to the exercise of it for twenty years. How then can that constitution which expressly permits the importation of slaves, authorize the national government to set on foot a crusade against slavery?

The clause respecting fugitive slaves is affirmative and active in its effects. It is a direct sanction and positive protection of the right of the master to the services of his slave as derived under the local laws of the State. The phraseology in which it is wrapped up still leaves the intention clear, and the words "persons held to service or labor in one State under the laws thereof," have always been interpreted to extend to the case of slaves, in the various acts of Congress which have been passed to give efficacy to the provision, and in the judicial application of those laws. So also in the clause prescribing the ratio of representation—the phrase, "three-fifths of all other persons," is equivalent to *slaves*, or it means nothing. And yet we are told that those who are acting under a constitution which sanctions the existence of slavery in those States which choose to tolerate it, are at liberty to hold that no law can sanction its existence! . . .

But let us proceed to take a rapid glance at the reasons which have been assigned for this notion that involuntary servitude and a republican form of government are perfect antipathies. The gentleman from New-Hampshire has defined a republican government to be that in which all the *men* participate in its power and privileges: from whence it follows that where there are slaves, it can have no existence. A definition is no proof, however; and even if it be dignified (as I think it was) with the name of a maxim, the matter is not much mended. It is Lord Bacon who says "that nothing is so easily made as a maxim;" and certainly a definition is manufactured with equal facility. A political maxim is the work of induction, and cannot stand against experience, or stand on anything but experience. But this maxim, or definition, or whatever else it may be, sets fact at defiance. If you go back to antiquity, you will obtain no countenance for this hypothesis; and if you look at home you will gain still less. I have read that Sparta, and Rome, and Athens, and many others of the ancient family were republics. They were so in form undoubtedly—the last approaching nearer to a perfect democracy than any other government which has yet been known in the world. Judging of them also by their fruits, they were of the highest order of republics. Sparta could scarcely be any other than a republic, when a Spartan matron could say to her son just marching to battle, RETURN VICTORIOUS, OR RETURN NO MORE. It was the unconquerable spirit of liberty, nurtured by republican habits and institutions, that illustrated the pass of Thermopylae. Yet slavery was not only tolerated in Sparta, but was established by one of the fundamental laws of Lycurgus, having for its object the encouragement of that very spirit. Attica was full of slaves—yet the love of liberty was its characteristic. What else was it that foiled the whole power of Persia at Marathon and Salamis? What other soil than that which the genial Sun of Republican Freedom illuminated and warmed, could have produced such men as Leonidas and Miltiades, Themistocles and Epaminondas? Of Rome it would be superfluous to speak at large. It is sufficient to name the mighty mistress of the world, before Sylla gave the first stab to her liberties and the great dictator accomplished their final ruin, to be reminded of the practicability of union between civil slavery and an ardent love of liberty cherished by republican establishments.

If we return home for instruction upon this point, we perceive that same union exemplified in many a State, in which "Liberty has a temple in every house, an altar in every heart," while involuntary servitude is seen in every direction. Is it denied that those States possess a republican form of government? If it is, why does our power of correction sleep? Why is the constitutional guaranty suffered to be inactive? Why am I permitted to fatigue you, as the representative of a slaveholding State, with the discussion of the *nugae canorae* (for so I think them) that have been forced into this debate contrary to all the remonstrances of taste and prudence? Do gentlemen perceive the consequences to which their arguments must lead if they are of any value? Do they reflect that they lead to emancipation in the old United States—or to an exclusion of Delaware, Maryland, and all the South, and a great portion of the West, from the Union? My honorable friend from Virginia has no business here, if this disorganizing creed be any thing but the production of a heated brain. The State to which I belong, must "perform a lustration"—must purge and purify herself from the feculence of civil slavery, and emulate the States of the north in their zeal for throwing down the gloomy idol which we are said to worship, before her senators can have any title to appear in this high assembly. It will be in vain to urge that the old United States are exceptions to the rule—or rather (as the gentlemen express it), that they have no *disposition* to apply the rule to them. There can be no exceptions, by implication only, to such a rule; and expressions which justify the exemption of the old States by inference, will justify the like exemption of Missouri, unless they point exclusively to them, as I have shown they do not. The guarded manner, too, in which some of the gentlemen have occasionally expressed themselves on this subject, is somewhat alarming. They have no *disposition* to meddle with slavery in the old United States. Perhaps not—but who shall answer for their successors? Who shall furnish a pledge that the principle once engrafted into the constitution, will not grow, and spread, and fructify, and overshadow the whole land? It is the natural office of such a principle to wrestle with slavery, wheresoever it finds it. New States, colonized by the apostles of this principle, will enable it to set on foot a fanatical crusade against all who still continue to tolerate it, although no practicable means are pointed out by which they can get rid of it consistently with their own safety. At any rate, a present forbearing disposition, in a few or in many, is not a security upon which much reliance can be placed upon a subject as to which so many selfish interests and ardent feelings are connected with the cold calculations of policy. Admitting, however, that the old United States are in no danger from this principle—why is it so? There can be no other answer (which these zealous enemies of slavery can use) than that the constitution recognizes slavery as existing or capable of existing in those States. The constitution, then, admits that slavery and a republican form of government are not incongruous. It associates and binds them up together, and repudiates this wild imagination which the gentlemen have pressed upon us with such an air of triumph. But the constitution does more, as I have heretofore proved. It concedes that slavery may exist in a new State, as well as in an old one—since the language in which it recognizes slavery comprehends new States as well as actual. I trust then that I shall be forgiven if I suggest, that no eccentricity in argument can be more trying to human patience, than a formal assertion that a constitution, to which slave-holding States were the most numerous parties, in which slaves are treated as property as well as persons, and provision is made for the security of that property, and even for an augmentation of it, by a temporary importation from Africa, a clause commanding Congress to guarantee a republican form of government to those very States, as well as to others, authorizes you to determine that slavery and a republican form of government cannot coexist.

But if a republican form of government is that in which *all* the men have a share in the public power, the slave-holding States will not alone retire from the Union. The constitutions of some of the other States do not sanction universal suffrage, or universal eligibility. They require citizenship, and age, and a certain amount of property, to give a title to vote or to be voted for; and they who have not those qualifications are just as much disfranchised, with regard to the government and its power, as if they were slaves. They have civil rights indeed (and so have slaves in a less degree); but they have no share in the government. Their province is to obey the laws, not to assist in making them. All such States must therefore be forisfamiliated with Virginia and the rest, or change their system: for the constitution being absolutely silent on those subjects, will afford them no protection. The Union might thus be reduced from an Union to an unit. Who does not see that such conclusions flow from false notions—that the true theory of a republican government is mistaken—and that in such a government, rights political and civil, may be qualified by the fundamental law, upon such inducements as the freemen of the country deem sufficient? That civil rights may be qualified as well as political, is proved by a thousand examples. Minors, resident aliens, who are in a course of naturalization—the other sex, whether maids or wives, or widows, furnish sufficient practical proofs of this.

Again; if we are to entertain these hopeful abstractions, and to resolve all establishments into their imaginary elements in order to recast them upon some Utopian plan, and if it be true that all the *men* in a republican government must help to wield its power, and be equal in rights, I beg leave to ask the honorable gentleman from New Hampshire—and why not all the *women*? They too are God's creatures, and not only very fair but very rational creatures; and our great ancestor, if we are to give credit to Milton, accounted them the "wisest, virtuousest, discreetest, best;" although to say the truth he had but one specimen from which to draw his conclusion, and possibly if he had had more, would not have drawn it at all. They have, moreover, acknowledged civil rights in abundance, and upon abstract principles more than their masculine rulers allow them in fact. Some monarchies, too, do not exclude them from the throne. We have all read of Elizabeth of England, of Catharine of Russia, of Semiramis, and Zenobia, and a long list of royal and imperial dames, about as good as an equal list of royal and imperial lords. Why is it that their exclusion from the power of a popular government is not destructive of its republican character? I do not address this question to the honorable gentleman's gallantry, but to his abstraction, and his theories, and his notions of the infinite perfectibility of human institutions, borrowed from Godwin and the turbulent philosophers of France. For my own part, Sir, if I may have leave to say so much in the presence of this mixed uncommon audience, I confess I am no friend to female government, unless indeed it be that which reposes on gentleness, and modesty, and virtue, and feminine grace and delicacy; and how powerful a government that is, we have all of us, as I suspect, at some time or other experienced! But if the ultra republican doctrines which have now been broached should ever gain ground among us, I should not be surprised if some romantic reformer, treading in the footsteps of Mrs. Wolstoncraft [*sic*], should propose to repeal our republican law salique, and claim for our wives and daughters a full participation in political power, and to add to it that domestic power, which in some families, as I have heard, is as absolute and unrepublican as any power can be.

I have thus far allowed the honorable gentlemen to avail themselves of their assumption that the constitutional command to guarantee to the States a republican form of government, gives power to coerce those states in the adjustment of the details of their constitutions upon theoretical speculations. But surely it is passing strange that any man, who thinks at all, can view this salutary command as the grant of a power so monstrous; or look at it in any other light than as a protecting mandate to Congress to interpose with the force and authority of the Union against that violence and usurpation, by which a member of it might otherwise be oppressed by profligate and powerful individuals, or ambitious and unprincipled factions.

In a word, the resort to this portion of the constitution for an argument in favor of the proposed restriction, is one of those extravagances (I hope I shall not offend by this expression) which may excite our admiration, but cannot call for a very rigorous refutation. I have dealt with it accordingly and have now done with it.

WILLIAM SMITH

William Smith was a successful South Carolina lawyer who followed a typical path from local courtrooms to the United States Senate. His first political office was the state Senate, where he served from 1802 to 1808, including a term as president of the Senate. In 1808 he was elected judge of the court of appeals and in 1816, the state legislature sent him to the United States Senate.

Although Smith was a leading South Carolina political figure, he often incurred the enmity of John C. Calhoun for his early defense of state rights and his opposition to the tariff and internal improvements long before Calhoun came to that position. Having lost his bid for reelection in 1823, he returned to South Carolina and worked to organize those in the state who opposed Calhoun's nationalism. He was elected to the state legislature for two terms, during which he helped push through resolutions advocating the unconstitutionality of tariffs and internal improvements of Henry Clay's American System. In 1826 the legislature again returned Smith to the United States Senate to fill an unexpired term. During this second period in the Senate, Smith adamantly attacked internal improvements and the tariff as unconstitutional. He was, however, opposed to nullification, a stand which led to his defeat in 1830. He remained a bitter opponent of Calhoun and in 1833 moved to Louisiana, then to Alabama, where he was elected to the state legislature in 1836, a post he held until his death in 1840.[16]

Senator Smith's speech is notable for his argument that slavery has been a condition of human history since the times of the ancient Greeks and Romans, which were both model governments and societies for the South in the nineteenth century. He also asserts that slavery is a condition in which the slaves are comfortable and happy and are well taken care of by their masters, and finally, that the practice of slavery is supported and defended by no less an authority than the Bible and the Judeo-Christian faith.

THE MISSOURI QUESTION[17]

Mr. Smith, of South Carolina, observed, that, after the Senate had heard from the honorable gentleman from Maryland (Mr. Pinkney) a speech of five hours in continuance, not less distinguished for its logical and unsophisticated reasoning, and its pure, classical style, than for its unrivalled eloquence and brilliancy of fancy, and which had been preceded by a number of eloquent speeches from other gentlemen, on the same side of the question, he could hardly indulge a hope that the Senate would believe, at this late hour of the discussion, any further light could be shed upon it. But, as he believed this to be a more important subject than any which had agitated the public mind since this Government had been established, if the Senate would have the goodness to give him their attention, he would beg leave to present his humble views. He knew many gentlemen thought the subject already exhausted; and he would, therefore, that he might not contribute further to weary the patience of the Senate, carefully avoid touching those points which had already been so ably treated, and so luminously explained by others. If he should, it would be to give them a different construction, and from reasons different from those which had as yet been applied.

The first clause of the ninth section of the first article of the Constitution of the United States, in the following words, "the migration or importation of such persons as any of the states now existing shall think proper to admit, shall not be prohibited by Congress prior to the year 1808, but a tax or duty may be imposed on such importation, not exceeding ten dollars for each person," has received a different construction by different gentlemen on both sides of this question; and he would beg leave to give it his construction. The Constitution of the United States is the supreme law of the land, and, like all other laws, when any doubts arise as respects its meaning, some fixed rules must be resorted to by which these doubts can be solved. The rule laid down by one of the greatest jurists known to us (Judge Blackstone) is, to ascertain, by the fairest and most rational means, the intention of the law-giver at the time the law was made or enacted. This is done in various ways; either by the words of the law, by the subject-matter, the context, the effects and consequences, or the reason and spirit of the law itself. . . .

Those gentlemen who pressed the principle of restriction, did it on the authority of the words migration or importation. They say the slaveholding States refused to subscribe to the Federal Constitution, unless it should be conceded to them by the non-slaveholding States, that they should be permitted to continue the further importation of slaves from Africa until the year 1808; and in compromising the principles upon which the Constitution should be framed, they yielded to the General Government the right, after that period, to restrain the migration of slaves from one State to another, and hence they pretend to derive the power vested in Congress to inhibit the admission of slavery into the State of Missouri. They have some other grounds, which they deem auxiliary, and which he [Smith] would examine presently, but the preceding was their strong ground. For this construction they offer no reasons but that it comports with the general principles of free government, and the spirit of the Declaration of Independence.

On the other hand, gentlemen who oppose the right of restriction have given a different construction, and think that the word "migration" is coupled with the word "importation," and is synonymous, and that the import of it is entirely foreign; that it does not relate to our domestic relations, and could never be intended to regulate the internal-distribution of our slaves. Some other constructions had been presented, and enforced by strong arguments. These grounds of construction had been in abler hands than his, and he would not disturb them; but he would repose his solution of these words on a ground which had not yet been presented to the Senate, by any gentleman on either side. He would draw it from the Declaration of Independence itself; and for that purpose, would beg leave to read the first clause of that declaration, in these words:

> When in the course of human events, it becomes necessary for one people to dissolve the political bands which have connected them with another, and to assume, among the powers of the earth, the separate and equal station to which the laws of nature and of nature's God entitle them, a decent respect to the opinions of mankind requires that they should declare the causes which impel them to a separation.

It then speaks of a long train of abuses and usurpations imposed on us by the King of Great Britain, whose yoke we were then about to shake off; to prove which a number of facts are submitted. In the specification of these facts, distinctly and separately set forth and enumerated in that declaration, there are none more conspicuous than the following. In alluding to these usurpation and abuses, it says: "He has endeavored to prevent the population of these States; for that purpose, obstruction the laws for the naturalization of foreigners; refusing to pass others to encourage their migration hither, and raising the conditions of new appropriations of lands." This is the only State paper in which the word migration has been used, until the Constitution was formed. This stamps upon it a character which cannot be doubted; that it was among the primary objects of the United States, in the commencement of their career, to increase their population by migration from what was then called the mother country and which has been denied them. The whole population of the United States at the time they declared their independence, was between two and three millions only. This gave rise to the great defection which prevailed among the inhabitants in many of the States. They believed all the physical force which the United States could oppose to Great Britain was totally inadequate and therefore they marshalled themselves on the side of His Majesty. During a seven years' war migration was entirely suspended, and a constant waste of the native population ensued. The war terminated late in 1783, and early in 1787 this Constitution was formed; and here, for the second time, in which it is to be traced in any public act of the Government, you will find the word migration settled down in the Constitution. At that time, too, many of the States had but a very small population, scattered over a wide extended surface, and particularly so in the Southern States. By reason of this thin population their frontiers were greatly exposed, and constantly harassed by the inroads and butcheries of the savages, which even the Government of the United States were unable to repress for many years after the adoption of the Constitution. Your Northern posts, stipulated to be surrendered by the treaty which terminated your Revolutionary war, were detained by the British

Government in defiance of good faith; and your population was too feeble to afford you an army to enforce the stipulations of the treaty; and you were obliged, in 1794, to have recourse to negotiation, to enable your Government to gain possession of the posts; and obtained them by a bargain not very much to the advantage of the United States. Does there exist a doubt as to the object for which the Convention introduced into the Constitution that word migration, joined with the word importation? The word *importation* is agreed, on all hands, to mean nothing more than to authorize such States as thought fit, to import Africans. The necessity and desire for the migration of foreigners was much greater. This is made more than manifest by the prompt manner in which the First Congress acted upon the subject of naturalization. This word is coupled with that of migration; and in the same specification of injuries and usurpations, complained of in the Declaration of Independence against the King of Great Britain. The word "naturalization," as it stands in the Constitution, required Congress to give it efficacy by a law. This Congress did early in the second session of the First Congress. The word "migration" required no such aid from Congress. These two Constitutional provisions were clearly intended to aid each other. Migration, to authorize the States to admit foreigners, and naturalization to make them citizens. The power of naturalizing was given by Congress to the courts under the State jurisdiction so anxious were they to encourage the growth of population from migration.

But, sir, if a doubt could yet exist, as to the true construction of this word "migration," it must be completely obviated by considering what was the situation of the several States in regard to this species of population, at the time the Constitution was entered into by the several States. At this time all the States in the Union held slaves except Massachusetts. All the States north of Maryland were desirous of selling their slaves, and found a ready market in the Southern States, whither they sent them in ship loads, about that time, and after, until they relieved themselves of the greater part of their slaves by sale. Would the Northern States have ever consented to such a power in the Constitution, that would have enabled Congress to cut off so desirable a traffic, by preventing slaves from going beyond the boundary of their respective States? But it is not till after they have sold their slaves from among themselves, that they have made the discovery that Congress can restrain their migration.

It is said, by all, that the slaveholding States would have refused to come into the Union, if the right of importing had not been yielded to them until the year 1808. Were not the reasons infinitely stronger to resist such a power in Congress, to prevent their removal immediately after they had possessed themselves of them by importation, together with every other part of that species of population? That they must be fixed to the soil, when the immense tracts of the most fertile lands of Tennessee, Kentucky, and the vast extent of uninhabited lands now forming the States of Alabama and Mississippi, were without population, or nearly so; and holding out the fairest prospects to the inhabitants of the Atlantic States, to migrate there with their slaves. It is impossible that men can believe it for a moment.

That part of the Constitution which is found in the second clause of the third section of the fourth article, which says "the Congress shall have power to dispose of and make all needful rules and regulations respecting the territory or other property belonging to the United States," has been relied upon as giving the power to Congress to impose such rules as Congress might deem necessary, and therefore could inhibit slavery. This clause of the Constitution gave to Congress a right to dispose of the territory, or to make rules and regulations respecting it, but it gives no right over anything but the territory and other property of the United States. Slaves are not territory. And it would be just as proper to say that slaves were territory, as to say that it gives Congress power to dispose of slaves, because it has power to make all needful rules and regulations respecting the territory. By what principle, or by what rule, do you apply the power over slaves, that is given over the territory only? It is said that the United States Government is the domestic government of the territory; but the Constitution reserves to the States, or to the people, all power which is not given to the United States; and it can assume no government without express power. The Constitution is a delegation of powers only; and where there is no delegation of power, there is no government. It is a legal principle, never to be departed from, when a law gives a power over a greater subject, it does not include a lesser one.

It has been said that this power is given by that part of the Constitution which vests in Congress the right to regulate commerce among the several States. How would our Eastern friends relish it, if Congress should undertake to regulate the trade for one of their own States, and interdict their commerce with all the other States? Would they not cry aloud, and say the power was given to regulate commerce among all the several States, and not of any one State? And would they not say justly? Here, then, you are regulating what you would call commerce, for Missouri alone. . . .

The most opprobrious epithets have been lavished upon those who hold slaves; calling the practice cruel, derogatory to the character of the nation, opposed to the Christian religion, the law of God, pagan in its principles, and everything else that can be called up, by which to reproach us. Let us compare, on particular occasions which have fully manifested the temper of both parties, those who hold slaves, with those who do not, and see who have been most honest in their endeavors to put a stop to the slave trade. In 1818 a committee was appointed by this Senate to report a bill, the better to prevent the smuggling of African slaves into the United States. On that committee were three gentlemen from the slaveholding States and two from non-slaveholding States, as they are pleased to call them (Mr. Roberts and Mr. Burrill). These two gentlemen were told to make the penalty death, upon all who should be detected in this trade; the Eastern members of the

Senate opposed every thing like corporal punishment—even whipping, because they said it would never do to whip a respectable merchant. They were willing to compromise the sin, for a fine and imprisonment, and here it ended; and their ships are yet engaged in carrying slaves under every flag and for every nation that indulges the trade. . . .

We are told that our representation, by the three-fifths of the slaves, amounts to twenty members, and gives us an undue weight in the Government, and gives us twenty votes in the Presidential elections. And an honorable gentleman, who was now of the Senate, had said, upon this question, last year, "This inequality in the apportionment of Representatives was not misunderstood at the adoption of the Constitution; but no one anticipated the fact that the whole of the revenue of the United States would be derived from direct taxes, but it was believed that a part of the contribution to the common treasury would be apportioned among the States by the rule for the apportionment of Representatives." Let us examine who fixed this apportionment. It was done by members of the convention from the Eastern States. Mr. Randolph, of Virginia, proposed that the rights of suffrage ought to be proportioned to the quotas of contribution. Mr. Madison, of Virginia, made a proposition for an equitable ratio; Mr. Rutledge, of South Carolina, made a proposition; none of which embraced the black population. It was then proposed by Judge Wilson, of Pennsylvania, that it should be "in proportion to the whole number of white and other free citizens and inhabitants of every age, sex, and condition, including those bound to servitude for a term of years, and three-fifths of all other persons, except Indians not paying taxes." This was followed by a proposition from Mr. Patterson, of New Jersey, of the same import. Upon revising this proposition, among other, the committee of revision was Mr. Johnson, of Connecticut, Mr. Hamilton of New York, Mr. Morris, of Pennsylvania, Mr. Madison, of Virginia, and Mr. King, of Massachusetts. This committee adopted the proposition of Judge Wilson and Mr. Patterson, and formed that clause of the Constitution which regulates the representation and direct taxes, now so much complained of. The Eastern members of the convention proposed it; they supported it; and they modelled it to their mind. It was good and righteous whilst the Government was supported by direct taxes. There were no complaints in the years 1798 and 1799, when it was necessary to resort to a direct tax to support the war then waged against France. There were no complaints during the late war with England. It has afforded you a revenue to carry on these two wars; in the latter of which six hundred thousand dollars were annually raised upon slaves. It was taken and applied to public uses without any compunction. But, when direct taxes are no longer necessary, its great deformity presents itself. Is this a time to complain and to wish to change the system of representation when the burden is gone. If it was founded in compromise, are you to give up its equivalent? No, you hold the equivalent, and complain of the compromise when you think it can be no longer useful. This is the spirit of amity with which you present us.

One gentleman from Massachusetts (Mr. Otis), in the course of this discussion, has spoken of the policy of excluding slavery from Missouri and says the slaveholding States will be too numerous. But how is this fact? There are one hundred and eighty members in the House of Representatives; of them, there are one hundred and four belonging to the States which wish, and have abolished slavery, and seventy-six to other States. With all this difference you complain that there are twenty votes for slave population, which ought to be corrected. Why is the complaint made now? If Missouri can be played off another year and Maine admitted, the Presidential election will take place before Missouri can have a voice in that election; but Maine will have her two Senators, and of course two more Presidential votes to the Eastern States. If we look to the balance of power, as that gentleman would wish, this is its true complexion.

The subject of slavery, as it now presented itself, was one of serious import to the Southern and Western States. It was matter of mere calculation with the Eastern States, since they pressed their own to the South. Gentlemen had different feelings on it. Since this question had been agitated, he had looked into the history of slavery, and he found it had been the lot of man, in this shape or that, to serve one another from all time. At least, slavery has prevailed in every country on the globe, ever since the flood. All the nations of the East held slaves in abundance. The Greeks and the Romans, at the most enlightened periods of those republics. Athens, the seat of the Muses, held slaves. They were often chained at the gates of the rich, as porters, and were treated very different from ours; yet Demosthenes is made to say, "that the condition of a slave at Athens was preferable to that of a free man in many other countries." The Spartans approached nearer to a pure democracy than any other people ever did; yet they held slaves in abundance too. It prevailed all over the Roman Empire. Julius Caesar sold at one time fifty thousand slaves, yet Caesar was never held to be a cruel or barbarous man. He would, no doubt, be thought a great sinner by the Eastern States, who hold but a few: for even the States of Pennsylvania and Rhode Island had their slaves yet. This was a small sin and could be repented of after these few should die off. . . .

These people (the slaves) are so domesticated, or so kindly treated by their masters, and their situations so improved, that Marcus and all his host cannot excite one among twenty to insurrection. They are able to compare their comforts and their labor, and are fully sensible that their comforts are as great, and their labor not more arduous, than any other class of laboring people. The owners of these people can place arms in their hands, if necessary. In the late war they played a manly part in defence of their masters, in many instances. They were among the defenders of the country at Orleans, as well as at other places. . . .

There is no class of laboring people in any country upon the globe, except the United States, that are better clothed, better fed, or are more cheerful, or labor less, or who are more happy, or, indeed, who have more liberty and indulgence, than the slaves of the Southern and Western States. . . .

It has been sung in every town and village of the States which call themselves non-slaveholding States, that slavery is opposed to our holy religion. . . . Mr. Smith said he had taken the liberty, two years ago, to admonish his honorable friend from New Hampshire (Mr. Morril) on this subject, as it respected our religion. . . . He would point him now, as he had done before, to the 25th chapter of Leviticus, which, after describing who should be held as hired servants, and when the hired servants should go free, it then, with a direct allusion to this very people, in the 44th, 45th, and 46th verses, says in these words:

> 44. Both thy bond-men and thy bond-maids, which thou shalt have, shall be of the heathen that are round about you; of them shall ye buy bond-men and mold maids.

> 45. Moreover, of the children of the strangers that do sojourn among you, of them shall ye buy, and of their families that are with you, which they begat in your land; and they shall be your possession.

> 46. And ye shall take them as an inheritance for your children after you, to inherit them for a possession; they shall be your bond-men forever.

These are the divine words of the Lord himself, delivered to his holy servant Moses, as a law to his holy people.

Mr. President, the Scriptures teach us that slavery was universally indulged among the holy fathers. The chosen people of God were slaves; and that, by His divine permission, Joseph was sold by his brethren to the Egyptian merchants, who carried him into slavery. There was no vengeance of Heaven upon this people for holding them in slavery. They were not relieved until God in His wisdom saw fit. . . .

When Mr. Smith had concluded the Senate adjourned.

NOTES

1. *Journal of the House of Representatives*, 15th Cong., 2nd Sess., 272.

2. Cited in Glover Moore, *The Missouri Controversy, 1819–1821* (Lexington: University of Kentucky Press, 1953), 90.

3. *Annals of Congress*, 16th Cong., 1st Sess., 1024.

4. Quoted in *The Annals of America, 1797–1820*, vol. 4 (Chicago: Encyclopaedia Britannica, 1968), 589.

5. Cited in Moore, *Missouri Controversy*, 94–95.

6. See Charles S. Sydnor, *The Development of Southern Sectionalism: 1819–1848* (Baton Rouge: Louisiana State University Press, 1948), 126–127.

7. *Memoirs of J. Q. Adams*, IV, 502. Cited in Moore, *Missouri Controversy*, 339.

8. Jefferson to John Holmes, April 22, 1820, quoted in *Annals of America*, 603.

9. Robert M. Ireland, "William Pinkney: A Revision and Re-emphasis," *The American Journal of Legal History*, XIV (July 1970), 236 and 238.

10. Rev. William Pinkney, *The Life of William Pinkney* (New York: Da Capo Press, 1969, reprint of the 1853, D. Appleton and Company edition), 17–18.

11. Much of this biographical sketch is from John J. Dolan, "William Pinkney," in *Dictionary of American Biography*, vol. XIV, Dumas Malone, ed. (New York: Charles Scribner's Sons, 1934), 626–627. There are also useful entries on Pinkney in "Attorney General: William Pinkney," *The Vice Presidents and Cabinet Members*, vol. I, Robert I. Vexler (Dobbs Ferry, NY: Oceana Publications, 1975), 67–69; and Lawrence S. Kaplan, "William Pinkney" in *The Encyclopedia of Southern History*, David Roller and Robert Twyman, eds. (Baton Rouge: Louisiana State University Press, 1970), 980.

12. Quoted in Pinkney, *Life of William Pinkney*, 84.

13. Pinkney, *Life of William Pinkney*, 290.

14. William Plumer, Jr., to his father, January 30, 1820. Cited in *The Missouri Compromise and Presidential Politics 1820–1825, From the Letters of William Plumer, Jr.*, Everett S. Brown, ed. (St. Louis: Missouri Historical Society, 1926), 4.

15. Pinkney, *Life of William Pinkney*, 292–337. Another version can be found in *Annals of Congress*, 16th Cong., 1st Sess., 389–417.

16. Most of this biographical material comes from J. G. DeR. Hamilton, "William Smith," in *Dictionary of American Biography*, vol. XVII, Dumas Malone, ed. (New York: Charles Scribner's Sons, 1935), 359–361. There is also a biographical sketch by Major L. Wilson in *The Encyclopedia of Southern History*, 1120; and *Who Was Who in America* (Chicago: A.N. Marquis Co., 1963), 494.

17. *History of Congress*, 16th Cong., 1st Sess., January 26, 1820 (Washington: Gales and Seaton, 1855), 259–275. This speech by Smith is reported in the third person by Gales and Seaton.

FOR FURTHER READING

Freehling, William W. *The Road to Disunion, Secessionists at Bay, 1776–1854*. New York: Oxford University Press, 1990. See especially chapter eight, "The Missouri Controversy."

CHAPTER 3

Nullification: South Carolina Versus the Union

During the second decade of the nineteenth century, the new American nation struggled to preserve its independence. The War of 1812 helped to reaffirm America's political freedom, but its economic independence was far from assured. In 1816, Congress first adopted the concept of a protective tariff, as part of Henry Clay's American System, in order to nurture the newly developing industries in the northeast. At first, much of the leadership in the southern states warmly endorsed the concept, and the South, indeed the whole nation, strongly accepted the idea of nationhood.

Even that early, though, there were some southern voices crying out against the concept of protectionism. John Randolph of Roanoke asserted during the debates in 1816, that he "will not agree to lay a duty on the cultivators of the soil to encourage exotic manufactures; because, after all, we should only get much worse things at a much higher price, and we, the cultivators of the country, would in the end pay for all."[1]

The economic panic of 1819 led to calls for increased protection of the North's newly emerging industries. The following year, a higher tariff on imported manufactured goods was defeated. Pressure continued, and in 1824 the higher tariff gained sufficient support to move through Congress. Southern members of Congress argued that the national government could only tax to raise revenue—in their view, protective tariffs were therefore unconstitutional.

In 1828, Congress enacted the so-called Tariff of Abominations and the South truly felt financial pressure. Some argued that the tariff caused southern plantations to pay an average of 40 percent more for manufactured goods such as woolens for slave clothes, sugar, and iron products. In a famous speech, George McDuffie of South Carolina asserted that forty bales of cotton out of every 100 went to pay for increased costs to the southern cotton-grower, for the sole benefit of northern industry.

Urged on by his South Carolina colleagues, Vice President John C. Calhoun wrote the "Exposition and Protest" which defined the concept of state interposition. Calhoun argued that a tariff must be designed to collect revenue only and not to benefit one section of the country or one industry at the expense of others. He attacked the tyranny of majority rule and said that a state's interposing itself between the national government and the citizens of the state was the only solution. The South Carolina legislature printed and circulated 5000 copies of the document. Carolinians opposed to nullification were still in the majority in the legislature, however, and they did not accept William C. Preston's call for implementing immediate interposition against the tariff. They did, however, pass a strong protest against the tariff, which they sent to the United States Senate.

During the next two years, those supporting Calhoun and the Nullifiers set out to educate South Carolinians and other southerners on the need for nullification. Their arguments considered not only the evils of the tariff but focused also on the issue of the federal government's power to override states' rights and their perception that Congress had gone beyond the Constitution. They largely failed in their efforts to spread their doctrines beyond the borders of South Carolina, however, and this failure to gain widespread southern support was one of the major reasons the nullification movement did not succeed.

South Carolinians elected a state legislature in 1830 which passed a strong set of state rights resolutions, but they could not yet get a two-thirds vote in order to call a state convention to deal with the issue.

Congress in 1832 passed a new tariff that kept most of the protectionist features of the 1828 tariff, while at the same time reduced some nonprotective duties. It was set to go into effect March 2, 1833; this date became a deadline for South Carolina's action on nullification. It was not long in coming.

That fall voters elected a new state legislature and the States Rights Party won overwhelmingly. Governor James Hamilton, Jr., called a special session on October 22, and the newly elected legislators immediately voted for a state convention to meet on November 19.

The Convention adopted an Ordinance of Nullification on November 24 by a vote of 136 to 26. The Ordinance nullified both the tariffs of 1828 and 1832, as being "unauthorized by the Constitution of the United States. . . . [They] violate the true meaning and intent thereof, and are null, void, and no law, nor binding upon the State, its officers or citizens."[2] Nullification was to become effective on February 1, 1833, one month before the Tariff of 1832. The Convention also passed a Test Oath Act, which required state officials to support nullification. The Union Party deeply opposed this measure and some South Carolinians began to arm in anticipation of conflict.

While no shots were fired in this crisis, the nullification issue stirred the emotions and led thinking southerners to realize that war *could* result from sectional differences. A South Carolinian wrote to a friend in December 1832, at the height of the crisis:

> I had the pleasure & the *pain* of hearing Gov. Hayne's Inaugural address on Tuesday.... It was violent & *inflammatory* in the extreme.... There was a show of patriotism & daring, an apparent honesty & a *real* eloquence, which gave it *prodigious power*. I never saw a greater excitement. I actually saw several of the legislators shedding *tears*. It made *me* feel solemn, for it seemed as if that awful scourge—civil war must *soon* come.[3]

In December, Unionists under Joel Poinsett met in Charleston and passed a strong resolution opposing the Ordinance of Nullification. The Carolina Legislature elected Calhoun to the Senate and he quickly resigned as Vice President. President Andrew Jackson's annual message to Congress on December 4 referred to the tense situation, and on December 10 he issued a proclamation to the people of South Carolina denying the right to nullify a federal law and stated that he would execute the laws, with force if necessary. Jackson believed nullification to be "incompatible with the existence of the Union," and that with the national government, not the states, was where sovereignty lay.[4]

Governor Hamilton and the legislature continued to defy Jackson and military preparations proceeded. Jackson placed General Winfield Scott in command of federal troops in South Carolina and the president sent reinforcements and supplies to the forts in Charleston harbor. Two armed revenue cutters patrolled off the coast from Charleston to aid federal forces in collecting the tariff if force were needed.

Early in 1833, the South Carolina legislature modified the effective date of the Ordinance of Nullification so that Congress could have time to revise the Tariff. On February 12, Henry Clay presented a compromise that provided for a gradual reduction of the tariff rates to 20 percent over a nine year period. Calhoun supported it, and both Houses of Congress passed the measure.

President Jackson had asked Congress for enlarged powers to deal with the situation and this so-called Force Bill passed Congress on March 1. Congress authorized the president to use the military to enforce the revenue laws and to put down the nullification movement. Jackson signed both the compromise tariff and the Force Bill on March 2.

On March 11, the South Carolina Convention reconvened and rescinded the Nullification Ordinance by vote of 153 to 4. In an apparent face-saving measure, they adopted a measure nullifying the Force Bill. State interposition, or nullification, would not be heard from again to any important degree, until it resurfaced in support of the Massive Resistance Movement during the 1960s integration crisis. After almost a half-century of national existence, Americans saw that majority rule would govern the nation. The issue was not dead, as the bloody Civil War would prove, but the strength and the proactive leadership of Andrew Jackson, coupled with South Carolina's inability to gain widespread southern support—not to mention the strong Unionist support in the Palmetto State itself—doomed nullification as a workable alternative. Perhaps the key meaning of the crisis was summed up by James Petigru in a letter to Hugh S. Legare, both staunch Unionists: "But nullification has done its work, it has prepared the minds of men for a separation of the States."[5] Nullification was one more issue about which the South thought it had lost to the majority North and southern defensiveness was reinforced.

JAMES HAMILTON, JR.

James Hamilton, Jr., was apparently the first South Carolinian to publicly advocate nullification when he spoke at Walterboro, South Carolina, on October 21, 1828. From that point forward, he was the leading proponent of the policy in the state, and he was elected governor in 1830 due to his strong stand on the issue. His Walterboro speech, included in this collection, is said to have set the tone for the crisis over the tariff, and as Ralph Eubanks has written: "Four more years of debate would contribute little to the basic analysis he had offered at Walterboro."[6]

Hamilton was not a single-issue man, however, as he had a long and distinguished career in South Carolina politics. He was born in Charleston in 1786 and after being admitted to the bar, began practicing law in 1810. He served as a major in the army during the War of 1812, and in 1820 served in the state House of Representatives. In 1822, his constituents moved him to the United States House of Representatives, where he served until 1829, when he resigned and returned home to be elected governor the following year.

By the mid 1820s, Hamilton had shifted his views from an ardent nationalism to a devoted advocacy of state rights and an equally fervid opposition to the protective tariff. His constant agitation on the issue helped bring John C. Calhoun into the public limelight as the key architect of the nullification papers in South Carolina.

While serving as governor, Hamilton was largely responsible for securing passage of the Nullification Act, as he had organized the state-wide nullification clubs, called the States Rights and Free Trade Society, lobbied for the state convention, was elected to it, and served as its president. After leaving the governor's office in 1832, he led the 27,000 South Carolina militia forces which were raised to oppose President Jackson in the final showdown over nullification. Like most of the nullifiers, Hamilton was not eager for war or the breakup of the Union, so he supported the compromises that lowered the tariffs. Later in his career, he was involved in various banking and farming operations and served as a diplomat from the Republic of Texas to various European nations. During his life, he earned a reputation as a duelist—the concept of honor, as for many South Carolinians, was more important to him than life. He fought fourteen duels, in each one successfully wounding his opponent, but never shooting to kill. He died in an accident in the Gulf of Mexico in 1857 when the ship on which he was a passenger collided with another vessel and sank.[7]

In this speech at Walterboro, Hamilton argues that Congress had passed the bounds ascribed to it by the Constitution; the majority can now run roughshod over the minority; and the sovereign states have been swallowed up in a consolidated government. Furthermore, he asserts that the taxes designed to protect the northeast's industries hit the hardest on the southern producers of the cotton that drives the northern mills.

SPEECH AT THE WALTERBORO DINNER[8]

About this time, forty years since, Gentlemen, the Constitution of the United States was subscribed by the delegates from South Carolina, and from that day to this, the conduct of her people has not only been marked by a devoted fidelity to that instrument, but by an almost superstitious attachment to the Union, which it was its purpose to form and perpetuate. Yes, our delegates thought they had assented to a scheme of government calculated "to form a more perfect Union, to establish justice, to ensure domestic tranquility, to provide for the common defence and general welfare, and to secure the blessings of liberty to ourselves and to our posterity;" and this belief has hitherto been common to our whole people, until, by the wanton violations and gross perversions of this compact, "the Union" so far from being "perfect" is in danger—"justice" not "established," but its principles outraged-domestic dissentions substituted for "domestic tranquility"—sectional interests promoted at the expense of "the common defence and general welfare"—and the very "blessings of liberty to ourselves and our posterity," put in awful peril by the unmeasured strides of a Government which has already passed the very barriers of the Constitution to which it owes its existence, and which now lies at the mercy of a majority who seem to acknowledge no other canons for its interpretation than their own selfish and misguided interests.

That man must have been a very inattentive observer of the history of all Governments, and very little have considered the philosophy of our own, who could not have predicted, and cannot now foresee that no General Government formed of separate and confederate sovereignties, can sustain the shock of the abuses of internal legislation among its members—that, to such legislation, there will always be incident partiality and injustice on the one hand, and distrust and jealousy on the other—that money, raised by unequal taxation in one section, would be expended in unequal proportions in another, and the moment such a Government quits the exclusive guardianship of "the common defence and general welfare" to provide for the domestic interests of its members, that moment its foundation would be sapped and its existence endangered. And why? Because a Confederacy, thus degenerating, loses its fundamental and distinctive character, and becomes a consolidated Government.

The events which surround us, in language too true, tell us that our Government has reached this crisis. For, when in a confederacy of States professing to retain separate sovereignties, its common head, in spite of all limitations, determines that the labor of one member of the league shall pay tribute to nourish and reward the labor of another: or, to state the exact case, when it is decided that the agriculture and trade of South Carolina shall be taxed two millions and a half to foster the manufactures of New England, this is consolidation in its most potent form; and the separate existence of a State, as a sovereign member of a confederacy of limited powers, is destroyed and swallowed up in one great and undivided empire. And, Gentlemen, how can it be otherwise? In a Confederate Government, when internal legislation is pushed into the sphere of domestic interests and duties, representative responsibility is, in fact, destroyed? For, what sort of responsibility have you over a member from Vermont, who, nevertheless, in the domestic legislation which Congress has usurped, votes that your imports, which form the only medium of exchange for the purchase of your exports, shall be taxed one hundred and twenty per cent—For what? For any of the legitimate purposes for which this Government was formed? To build fortifications for the protection of your coast from the incursions of an enemy? To construct those beautiful emblems of our prowess, which have borne our infant flag in triumph and glory through every sea? To redeem the national faith by paying the national debt, contracted for the prosecution of that just and honourable war, in which the South had not a single interest at stake, but into which she, nevertheless, flung the tributes of her generous and devoted chivalry? No, not for one of these purposes; but to pay base tribute to a craving monopoly—to make an industry profitable in which we have not the slightest interest, at the cost of sacrificing our own, and at once to be taxed, not for "the common defence and general welfare," but for purposes the most odiously sectional, and the most detestably unjust.

Gentlemen, when such a confederate Government as this, acting over a region, having such dissimilar interests, the diversity itself created by the laws of God, which cannot be surmounted by the laws of man—when I say it comes down from "its high estate," from taking care that the Republic is tranquil at home, and respected abroad—to huckster and traffic for paltry gains by pitiful means—when it enters your cotton fields and granaries, and with the insolent officiousness of a Turkish Pacha, prescribes both the amount and the profit of your labor, which is to be borne to some more favorite Province, depend upon it, it is a state of things which cannot last, in spite of the religious veneration which a people may cherish for the forms of their ancient polity. For a selfish majority, exercising in a confederacy domestic and sectional legislation, in violation of a solemn bargain between the parties, must, in the end, form the most loathsome Government on the face of the earth—because your task-master must soon become a tyrant, from the very abuses and corruptions of the system, without the bowels of compassion, or a jot of human sympathy. . . .

It is undeniable, therefore, that from 1816, down to the present time, the South has been drugged by the slow poison of the miserable empyricism of the prohibitory system, the fatal effects of which we could not so long have resisted, but for the stupendously valuable staples with which God has blessed us, and the agricultural skill and enterprise of our people. But the work of death has already commenced, and he must be insensible and stupefied by poverty and degradation who cannot perceive it. And, Gentlemen, can it be otherwise? In proportion to the aggregate income of the country, my lamented predecessor, Mr. Lowndes, in 1820, said we were the highest taxed people on the face of the earth. This declaration, borne out by the most irrefutable statistics, was made when our duties did not average more than 20 per cent; now they have reached an average of upwards of 60 per cent, and on the articles which more especially enter into the consumption of the South, and furnish the medium of exchange for its staples, in some instances have attained the enormous range of 160 per cent, and the very point of prohibition itself.

The very form of the taxation is so deceptive, that it is impossible, except by a minute and somewhat complicated analysis, to measure it. It can only be done by separating the original cost of an article from the impost; when this is done, the result of the base tribute which we pay, is altogether astounding. There is no man in the South, whose expenditure amounts to four thousand dollars per annum, who does not pay at the smallest calculation, one thousand dollars, in the shape of a clear tax to the Government and the monopolists, which they divide in pretty equal proportions between them. Great as this burden is, it might indeed be borne if it had not a double operation. For the tax of one thousand dollars, being the duty on the articles consumed, has a direct tendency to exclude from our market those exchangeable values, by which the price of our products is enhanced, and they themselves are to be bought. To the Cotton growing States, this last consequence is incomparably the most serious of all, for it may be taken as a fact, beyond all dispute, that the value of their staple depends on the unshackled freedom of our foreign trade. This staple, which throughout the United States stands in the place of the precious metals, by enabling us hitherto, on advantageous terms, to conduct our commerce with other nations, is burdened nevertheless with nearly the whole amount of the duties on imports; which falls with almost unmitigated severity on those who are engaged in its production. This result is obvious from the fact that the imposts, or as they falsely and fraudulently called "the American System," operates almost exclusively on the staple manufactures of the greatest and best customer for this staple product of Southern Agriculture, and the trade between Great Britain and the United States, in the article is, in effect, burdened with a tax of $10,000,000, to enable the cotton and woollen manufacturers of other portions of the Union to realize a profit of five. Of the fifty-eight millions of exports of domestic products the last year, at least thirty-five millions were the growth of the five plantation States, and it is a fact which the Treasury documents will sustain, that at least fourteen millions of tax was levied on the articles of foreign merchandize with which those thirty-five millions of home products were purchased, which might as well have been levied on the home products themselves in the form of an export duty.

With these burdens, have we no just cause to complain when we see one of the most munificent products with which God ever blessed the industry of man threatened with almost certain ruin—not by his inscrutable dispensations, not from the blight of unpropitious seasons, not from the ravages of Egyptian locusts, not by the stinted fertility of an overburdened soil, but by the grasping avarice, and unconquerable injustice of those whom we have hitherto regarded as brothers of one family, hitherto bound to us by the natural ties of a common origin, by the association of united labors and confederate triumphs, by all that can consecrate and endear the sympathies of a common country—one people and one home! . . .

We are equally destitute of hope when we consider the peculiar character of the manufacturing spirit. There is in it an unrelenting avarice and selfishness that admits of no propitiation. It is not alone fortified by the appetite for gain, but by the insulting arrogance with which it vaunts a peculiar and exclusive patriotism—upon the insolent presumption that a man who makes a yard of cloth under an enormous bounty, created by a tax on the rest of the community, has higher claims to the consideration of his country than the honest yeoman who raises a bushel of corn without this bounty. . . .

Gentlemen, I fear I have tried you, I am sure I have myself, in passing through this miserable and fruitless waste, where not a salutary hope takes root. I am sick at heart of these poor sums in arithmetic, which tell us how much we are ruined, but tell us not how our wrongs are to be redressed. Are we, indeed, without remedy? None, I again repeat, which is to be found in the justice or the mercy of our opponents. But, thanks be to God, we have a remedy full of security and honor in ourselves—in the sacred Aegis of the Constitution itself—in the sovereignty of this State—in the high and insuperable obligation of our Legislature to protect each and all of its citizens from the injustice and oppression of an unconstitutional law,—and lastly, (shall we count it as nothing?) in the spirit of a gallant people, reared amidst those memorials which tell them they were once free, and educated by a Constitution which instructs them that they have an imprescriptible claim still to do so.

Our scheme of civil freedom would, indeed, be a miserable mockery, if there was a conservative principle no where; if a solemn compact between coequal sovereigns could be violated at will by a corrupt or despotic majority—if we had a resource no where except in a base acquiescence in its will, by virtue of the long-exploded, degrading and ignominious doctrine of "passive obedience and non-resistance," our situation would, indeed, be one of disgrace and misery, which would admit of no extenuation. But this is not our situation. On the reserved rights of this State you may build as upon a rock upon which the tempest and billows may beat, but cannot shake. Do I find this security in the revolutionary enthusiasm, in the treasonable aspirations of some political incendiary, who wishes in the madness or the fury of his crime to pull down this beautiful political edifice, on whose altars we have hitherto hoped the fires of liberty would be eternal? No, Gentlemen, I do not go to such apostles for this faith: I find it resting on the authority of names venerated and endeared to you by associations connected with every thing that has been proud, valuable and consoling to our country—resting upon the authority of Jefferson and of Madison, sustained by the findings of the almost unanimous votes of the Legislatures of Virginia and Kentucky, canonized, at once, by the Catholic faith of the great republican party of our country.

Our reliance, then, is on the Virginia and Kentucky Resolutions of '98—and upon these we put our citadel where no man can harm it. It is, perhaps, the most fortunate circumstance for us in the world, that the passage of the Alien and Sedition Laws, (which rest on the same implied powers on the part of Congress, on which the Tariff finds its authority) furnished the occasion both to Mr. Jefferson and Mr. Madison, to give, as they have done, in the resolutions in question, their luminous and unanswerable commentary on the reserved and ultimate rights of the States. This commentary covers the whole ground for us. And what is it? Mr. Madison says—"in case of a deliberate, palpable and dangerous exercise of powers not granted by the compact, the States who are parties thereto, have the right, and are in duty bound to interpose for the purpose of arresting the progress of the evil, and for maintaining, within their respective limits, the authorities, rights and liberties appertaining to them." Is it necessary I should stop to inquire whether the Tariff is "a deliberate, palpable and dangerous exercise of power, not granted?" Is this not the universal sense of the South, with as near an approach to unanimity as the diversity of the human understanding, under any circumstances, will permit? Is not this opinion founded on the position which we assume, that the right to raise taxes is restricted to the obligations of paying the debts of the Union, and providing for the common defence and general welfare? And further, do we not find the power to encourage the useful arts by bounties, whether by imposts or not, positively inhibited to Congress by an express decision of the Convention? And, in a word, is the exercise "not determined and dangerous?"

But how are we to interpose for the purpose of "arresting the progress of the evil?" Let Mr. Jefferson answer this question, who, in the memorable resolutions he prepared for the Kentucky Legislature, (which were adopted almost unanimously) by that State in '98, thus speaks—"That the several States who formed the Constitution being sovereign and independent, have the unquestionable right to judge its infractions; and that a Nullification by those sovereignties of all unauthorized acts, done under color of that instrument, is the rightful remedy."

"A nullification," then, "of the unauthorized act," within our respective limits, is the "rightful remedy." But the question arises, who is to determine whether the act is unauthorized? Mr. Madison says, "That when resort can be had to no tribunal higher than the parties themselves, the parties themselves must be the rightful judges"; in other words, the State itself, under its ultimate reservation of sovereignty. The judiciary, he very properly determines, has no constitutional competency for this high province; that it has the power merely to decide in relation to acts growing out of the authority of the departments of government, not as to questions involving the sovereignties of the high contracting parties themselves. This opinion of the absolute unfitness of the Supreme Court to decide between the States and the General Government has obtained irresistible confirmation, by the doctrine which it has more recently avowed, "that it will not inquire into the motives of the Legislature," although a fraud may be perpetrated in the very title of a law, and that it will feel it its duty, to give, if possible, such a construction to a law as will sustain the measures of the Government. I quote from memory, Gentlemen, but believe that I have not mistaken the consoling dictum of this metropolitan court.

Now one word as to the mode by which the State of South Carolina should "interpose for the purpose of arresting the progress of the evil," and "nullifying the unauthorized act." This must be left to the sound discretion of the Legislature, in what manner it shall exonerate our citizens from all obligations to laws enacted under a "deliberate, palpable and dangerous exercise of power not granted!" To our trustees, to the guardians of our rights and liberties, we may with undoubting confidence devolve this high trust.

I know, Gentlemen, that various remedies have been proposed, which are designed to come somewhat short of an appeal to the reserved sovereignty of the State; that State Excises are in favor with many intelligent and patriotic men, whose opinions are entitled to great respect. I must confess that I regard them as worse than inefficient, that they are in effect a sort of domestic tariff of our own enactment, of indiscriminate and injurious operation against our friends as well as our foes, and heaping still greater and more aggravated burdens on our own consumption, to say nothing of the legal as well as moral risk which we shall run of redressing one infraction of the Constitution, by perpetrating another. This policy would also be attended by much heart-burning and discontent at home, from the fiscal inquisition which must be established to enforce it, whilst among our best friends abroad, it would often bear with a severity which it would not be in our power to mitigate. With this view of the subject, I am not sure that the war which this State seemed disposed to wage with Kentucky, is not to be deprecated, because I believe that that part of her people engaged in the rearing of domestic animals for our market, are decidedly anti-tariff; that the tariff there finds its support in the hemp-growing interest, almost exclusively. But of one thing I am certain, although this gallant, generous and patriotic people have been led astray on this subject, by the cunning deception and profligate ambition of him who was once their idol, but who is now rapidly becoming the object of their unmingled scorn and detestation; that they will soon, under a kind and social intercourse, understand that their interests are ours, and that they cannot be more injurious to themselves than by consenting to be unjust to us. That to oppress the South, is to impoverish their best customers, and that as we stuck to them when they were deserted by their present northern political allies, on the free navigation of the Mississippi, we have some right, if our "hour of utmost need" should come, to count on their sympathy and support. . . .

My friends, the approaching dusk tells me that I have too long taxed your patience. Let me in reiterating my gratitude for all the proofs of your generous attachment and devoted confidence, bid you an affectionate farewell. Perhaps it is the last time I shall ever address you as your Representative. On the 4th of March next, my stewardship will be at an end—I shall then surrender to my friend (Mr. Barnwell) who sits at my side, this invaluable trust. Your unanimous choice permits me without indelicacy to say, I know that in his hands it will be safe. I promise not more than he will perform when I tell you, that in his genius you will have pride, in his honor confidence, in his patriotism safety, and in his courage the assurance that if it becomes necessary he will "nail your colors to the mast."

In conclusion, permit me to offer for your pledges, a Toast which I believe to be in harmony with your wishes, your hopes, and your sentiments—because I know you venerate the Constitution of your country, and that you yet cherish a confidence that this instrument carries a sanative principle within itself, by which the corruption and injustice which have been fastened upon it, will be shaken off, and that it will come forth again in all "the beauty of truth and holiness"—I therefore, Gentlemen, give you—The Constitution of the United States—"Whilst there is life there is hope." Let us not abandon this work of our fathers until the only alternative left us is to abandon it or Liberty itself.

JOHN C. CALHOUN

John C. Calhoun was perhaps the most important southern political figure in the three decades preceding the Civil War. His thinking, speaking,
and writing set the intellectual tone for the South's political and social views
during those fateful years. Calhoun was an optimistic and ardent nationalist during his terms as a young "War Hawk" Congressman. By the 1830s,
however, Calhoun was a pessimistic sectionalist, who clearly foresaw the
coming of the Civil War. Never wanting to see that vision realized, Calhoun
for years as vice president, United States senator, and private citizen
worked diligently to devise a method by which any minority in the nation—but especially his beloved South, and, even more, South Carolina—could successfully seek redress for ills imposed by the majority. He
called his solution "interposition," and he believed it to be a Constitution-
ally sanctioned means to protect a minority in a democracy. It was soon la-
beled "nullification" and was seen by many, even some in South Carolina
and around the South, as being illegal, unconstitutional, and leading
straight to disunion and even civil war.

Calhoun was born in Abbeville, South Carolina, in 1782, attended Yale
College, and read law at Judge Tapping Reeve's law school in Connecticut.
He began his Congressional career in 1810, and two years later he helped
guide through the House the declaration of war against Great Britain. Until
he left Congress in 1817 to become President Monroe's secretary of war, Calhoun advocated protective tariffs and internal improvements—a position
that would later haunt him. From 1817 to 1825, Calhoun was secretary of war,
a position from which he strongly supported internal improvements to increase the nation's defensive capabilities. In 1825, he was elected vice president, resigning in 1832, when he took his seat in the United States Senate.

As senator, Calhoun led the fight for state rights and against the growing
abolition crusade. In 1842, he resigned from the Senate and began to seek the
1844 Democratic Party nomination for president. He failed in this quest, but
John Tyler selected him to serve as his secretary of state. He filled this position for only two years, as South Carolina once again sent him to the Senate.
Calhoun died in office, shortly after his remarks on the 1850 Compromise issues.[9]

In this speech on the Force Bill, Calhoun asks the question: "Has the Government a right to impose burdens on the capital and industry of one portion of the country, not with a view to revenue, but to benefit another?" His
answer, of course, is "No," and he and his state consider that action an "unconstitutional exercise of power." He also argues that sovereignty does not
reside in the people, but in the states, and that the general government has
consolidated into a government that no longer allows the states to provide a

check on its actions. Calhoun's means of limiting the power of this consolidated government is by a state's interposing its authority between the general government and the citizens of the state.

SPEECH ON THE FORCE BILL[10]

Mr. President—I know not which is most objectionable, the provision[s]
of the bill, or the temper in which its adoption has been urged. If the extraordinary powers with which the bill proposes to clothe the executive, to the utter prostration of the Constitution and the rights of the States, be calculated
to impress our minds with alarm at the rapid progress of despotism in our
country; the zeal with which every circumstance calculated to misrepresent
or exaggerate the conduct of [South] Carolina in the controversy, is seized
on with a view to excite hostility against her, but too plainly indicates the
deep decay of that brotherly feeling which once existed between these
States, and to which we are indebted for our beautiful federal system, and
by the continuance of which alone it can be preserved. It is not my intention
to advert to all these misrepresentations, but there are some so well calculated to mislead the mind as to the real character of the controversy, and to
hold up the State in a light so odious, that I do not feel myself justified in per-
mitting them to pass unnoticed.

Among them, one of the most prominent is the false statement that the
object of South Carolina is to exempt herself from her share of the public
burdens, while she participates in the advantages of the government. If the
charge were true—if the State were capable of being actuated by such low
and unworthy motives, mother as I consider her, I would not stand up on
this floor to vindicate her conduct. Among her faults, and faults I will not
deny she has, no one has ever yet charged her with that low and most sordid
of vices—avarice. Her conduct, on all occasions, has been marked with the
very opposite quality. From the commencement of the Revolution—from its
first breaking out at Boston till this hour, no State has been more profuse of
its blood in the cause of the country, nor has any contributed so largely to the
common treasury in proportion to wealth and population. She has in that
proportion contributed more to the exports of the Union, on the exchange of
which with the rest of the world the greater portion of the public burden has
been levied, than any other State. No: the controversy is not such as has been
stated; the State does not seek to participate in the advantages of the government without contributing her full share to the public treasury. Her object is
far different. A deep constitutional question lies at the bottom of the controversy. The real question at issue is, Has the Government a right to impose
burdens on the capital and industry of one portion of the country, not with a
view to revenue, but to benefit another? and I must be permitted to say that,
after the long and deep agitation of this controversy, it is with surprise that I
perceive so strong a disposition to misrepresent its real character. To correct

the impression which those misrepresentations are calculated to make, I will dwell on the point under consideration for a few moments longer.

The Federal Government has, by an express provision of the Constitution, the right to lay duties on imports. The State has never denied or resisted this right, nor even thought of so doing. The government has, however, not been contented with exercising this power as she had a right to do, but has gone a step beyond it, by laying imposts, not for revenue, but for protection. This the State considers as an unconstitutional exercise of power—highly injurious and oppressive to her and the other staple States, and has, accordingly, met it with the most determined resistance. I do not intend to enter, at this time, into the argument as to the unconstitutionality of the protective system. It is not necessary. It is sufficient that the power is nowhere granted; and that, from the journals of the Convention which formed the Constitution, it would seem that it was refused. . . .

There is another misstatement, as to the nature of the controversy, so frequently made in debate, and so well calculated to mislead, that I feel bound to notice it. It has been said that South Carolina claims the right to annul the Constitution and laws of the United States; and to rebut this supposed claim, the gentleman from Virginia (Mr. Rives) has gravely quoted the Constitution, to prove that the Constitution, and the laws made in pursuance thereof, are the supreme laws of the land—as if the State claimed the right to act contrary to this provision of the Constitution. Nothing can be more erroneous: her object is not to resist laws made in pursuance of the Constitution, but those made without its authority, and which encroached on her reserved powers. She claims not even the right of judging of the delegated powers; but of those that are reserved, and to resist the former, when they encroach upon the latter. . . .

Having made these remarks, the great question is now presented, Has Congress the right to pass this bill? which I will next proceed to consider. The decision of this question involves the inquiry into the provisions of the bill. What are they? It puts at the disposal of the President the army and navy, and the entire militia of the country; it enables him, at his pleasure, to subject every man in the United States, not exempt from militia duty, to martial law; to call him from his ordinary occupation to the field, and under the penalty of fine and imprisonment, inflicted by a court martial, to imbrue his hand in his brother's blood. There is no limitation on the power of the sword, and that over the purse is equally without restraint; for among the extraordinary features of the bill, it contains no appropriation, which, under existing circumstances, is tantamount to an unlimited appropriation. The President may, under its authority, incur any expenditure, and pledge the national faith to meet it. He may create a new national debt, at the very moment of the termination of the former—a debt of millions, to be paid out of the proceeds of the labor of that section of the country whose dearest constitutional rights this bill prostrates! Thus exhibiting the extraordinary spectacle, that the very section of the country which is urging this measure, and carrying the sword of devastation against us, are, at the same time, incurring a new debt, to be paid by those whose rights are violated; while those who violate them are to receive the benefits, in the shape of bounties and expenditures. And for what purpose is the unlimited control of the purse and of the sword thus placed at the disposition of the executive? To make war against one of the free and sovereign members of this confederation, which the bill proposes to deal with, not as a State, but as a collection of banditti or outlaws. Thus exhibiting the impious spectacle of this government, the creature of the States, making war against the power to which it owes its existence. The bill violates the Constitution, plainly and palpably, in many of its provisions, by authorizing the President, at his pleasure, to place the different ports of this Union on an unequal footing, contrary to that provision of the Constitution which declares that no preference shall be given to one port over another. It also violates the Constitution by authorizing him, at his discretion, to impose cash duties on one port, while credit is allowed in others; by enabling the President to regulate commerce, a power vested in Congress alone; and by drawing within the jurisdiction of the United States courts powers never intended to be conferred on them. As great as these objections are, they become insignificant in the provisions of a bill which, by a single blow—by treating the States as a mere lawless mass of individuals—prostrates all the barriers of the Constitution. I will pass over the minor considerations, and proceed directly to the great point. This bill proceeds on the ground that the entire sovereignty of this country belong to the American people, as forming one great community, and regards the States as mere fractions or counties, and not as an integral part of the Union: having no more right to resist the encroachments of the government than a county has to resist the authority of a State; and treating such resistance as the lawless acts of so many individuals, without possessing sovereignty or political rights. It has been said that the bill declares war against South Carolina. No. It decrees a massacre of her citizens! War has something ennobling about it, and, with all its horrors, brings into action the highest qualities, intellectual and moral. It was, perhaps, in the order of Providence that it should be permitted for that very purpose. But this bill declares no war, except, indeed, it be that which savages wage—a war, not against the community, but the citizens of whom that community is composed. But I regard it as worse than *savage* warfare—as an attempt to take away life under the color of law, without the trial by jury, or any other safeguard which the Constitution has thrown around the life of the citizen! It authorizes the President, or even his deputies, when they may suppose the law to be violated, without the intervention of a court or jury, to kill without mercy or discrimination!

It has been said by the Senator from Tennessee (Mr. Grundy) to be a measure of peace! Yes, such peace as the wolf gives to the lamb—the kite to the dove! Such peace as Russia gives to Poland, or death to its victim! A peace, by extinguishing the political existence of the State, by awing her into an abandonment of the exercise of every power which constitutes her a sovereign community. It is to South Carolina a question of self-preservation; and I proclaim it, that, should this bill pass, and an attempt be made to enforce it, it will be resisted, at every hazard—even that of death itself. Death is not the greatest calamity: there are others still more terrible to the free and brave, and among them may be placed the loss of liberty and honor. There are thousands of her brave sons who, if need be, are prepared cheerfully to lay down their lives in defence of the State, and the great principles of constitutional liberty for which she is contending. God forbid that this should become necessary! It never can be, unless this government is resolved to bring the question to extremity, when her gallant sons will stand prepared to perform the last duty—to die nobly.

I go on the ground that this Constitution was made by the States; that it is a federal union of the States, in which the several States still retain their sovereignty. If these views be correct, I have not characterized the bill too strongly, which presents the question whether they be or be not. . . .

But to return to the point immediately under consideration. I know that it is not only the opinion of a large majority of our country, but it may be said to be the opinion of the age, that the very beau ideal of a perfect government is the government of a majority, acting through a representative body, without check or limitation on its power; yet, if we may test this theory by experience and reason, we shall find that, so far from being perfect, the necessary tendency of all governments, based upon the will of an absolute majority, without constitutional check or limitation of power, is to faction, corruption, anarchy, and despotism; and this, whether the will of the majority be expressed directly through an assembly of the people themselves, or by their representatives. I know that, in venturing this assertion, I utter what is unpopular both within and without these walls; but where truth and liberty are concerned, such considerations should not be regarded. I will place the decision of this point on the fact that no government of the kind, among the many attempts which have been made, has ever endured for a single generation, but, on the contrary has invariably experienced the fate which I have assigned to it. Let a single instance be pointed out, and I will surrender my opinion. But, if we had not the aid of experience to direct our judgment, reason itself would be a certain guide. The view which considers the community as an unit, and all its parts as having a similar interest, is radically erroneous. However small the community may be, and however homogeneous its interests, the moment that government is put into operation, as soon as it begins to collect taxes and to make appropriations, the different portions of the community must, of necessity, bear different and opposing relations in reference to the action of the government. There must inevitably spring up two interests—a direction and a stock-holder interest—an interest profiting by the action of the government, and interested in increasing its powers and action; and another, at whose expense the political machine is kept in motion. . . .

If we turn our attention from these supposed cases, and direct it to our government and its actual operation, we shall find a practical confirmation of the truth of what has been stated, not only of the oppressive operation of the system of an absolute majority, but also a striking and beautiful illustration, in the formation of our system, of the principle of the concurring majority, as distinct from the absolute, which I have asserted to be the only means of efficiently checking the abuse of power, and, of course, the only solid foundation of constitutional liberty. That our government, for many years, has been gradually verging to consolidation; that the Constitution has gradually become a dead letter; and that all restrictions upon the power of government have been virtually removed, so as practically to convert the General Government into a government of an absolute majority, without check or limitation, cannot be denied by any one who has impartially observed its operation.

It is not necessary to trace the commencement and gradual progress of the causes which have produced this change in our system; it is sufficient to state that the change has taken place within the last few years. What has been the result? Precisely that which might have been anticipated: the growth of faction, corruption, anarchy, and, if not despotism itself, its near approach, as witness in the provision of this bill. And from what have these consequences sprung? We have been involved in no war. We have been at peace with all the world. We have been visited with no national calamity. Our people have been advancing in general intelligence, and, I will add, as great and alarming as has been the advance of political corruption among the mercenary corps who look to government for support, the morals and virtue of the community at large have been advancing in improvement. What, I will again repeat, is the cause? No other can be assigned but a departure from the fundamental principles of the Constitution, which has converted the Government into the will of an absolute and irresponsible majority, and which, by the laws that must inevitably govern in all such majorities, has placed in conflict the great interests of the country: by a system of hostile legislation, by an oppressive and unequal imposition of taxes, by unequal and profuse appropriations, and by rendering the entire labor and capital of the weaker interest subordinate to the stronger.

This is the cause, and these the fruits, which have converted the government into a mere instrument of taking money from one portion of the community to be given to another, and which has rallied around it a great, a powerful, and mercenary corps of office-holders, office-seekers, and expectants, destitute of principle and patriotism, and who have no standard of morals or politics but the will of the executive—the will of him who has the distribution of the loaves and the fishes. I hold it impossible for any one to look at the theoretical illustration of the principle of the absolute majority in the cases which I have supposed, and not be struck by the practical illustration in the actual operation of our government. Under every circumstance, the absolute majority will ever have its American system (I mean nothing offensive to any senator); but the real meaning of the American system is, that system of plunder which the strongest interest has ever waged, and will ever wage, against the weaker, where the latter is not armed with some efficient and constitutional check to arrest its action. Nothing but such check on the part of the weaker interest can arrest it; mere constitutional limitations are wholly insufficient. Whatever interest obtains possession of the government will, from the nature of things, be in favor of the powers, and against the limitations imposed by the Constitution, and will resort to every device that can be imagined to remove those restraints. On the contrary, the opposite interest, that which I have designated as the stockholding interest, the tax-payers, those on whom the system operates, will resist the abuse of powers, and contend for the limitations. And it is on this point, then, that the contest between the delegated and the reserved powers will be waged; but in this contest, as the interests in possession of the government are organized and armed by all its powers and patronage, the opposite interest, if not in like manner organized and possessed of a power to protect themselves under the provisions of the Constitution, will be as inevitably crushed as would be a band of unorganized militia when opposed by a veteran and trained corps of regulars. Let it never be forgotten that power can only be opposed by power, organization by organization; and on this theory stands our beautiful federal system of government. No free system was ever farther removed from the principle that the absolute majority, without check or limitation, ought to govern. To understand what our government is, we must look to the Constitution, which is the basis of the system. I do not intend to enter into any minute examination of the origin and the source of its powers: it is sufficient for my purpose to state, what I do fearlessly, that it derived its power from the people of the separate States, each ratifying by itself, each binding itself by its own separate majority, through its separate convention, the concurrence of the majorities of the several States forming the Constitution, thus taking the sense of the whole by that of the several parts, representing the various interests of the entire community. It was this concurring and perfect majority which formed the Constitution, and not that majority which would consider the American people as a single community, and which, instead of representing fairly and fully the interests of the whole, would but represent the interests of the stronger section. No candid man can dispute that I have given a correct description of the constitution-making power: that power which created and organized the government, which delegated to it, as a common agent, certain powers, in trust for the common good of all the States, and which imposed strict limitations and checks against abuses and usurpations. In administering the delegated powers, the Constitution provides, very properly, in order to give promptitude and efficiency, that the government shall be organized upon the principle of the absolute majority, or, rather, of two absolute majorities combined: a majority of the States considered as bodies politic, which prevails in this body; and a majority of the people of the States, estimated in federal numbers, in the other house of Congress. A combination of the two prevails in the choice of the President, and, of course, in the appointment of judges, they being nominated by the President and confirmed by the Senate. It is thus that the concurring and the absolute majorities are combined in one complex system: the one in forming the Constitution, and the other in making and executing the laws; thus beautifully blending the moderation, justice, and equity of the former, and more perfect majority, with the promptness and energy of the latter, but less perfect.

To maintain the ascendancy of the Constitution over the law-making majority is the great and essential point, on which the success of the system must depend: unless that ascendancy can be preserved, the necessary consequence must be, that the laws will supersede the Constitution, and, finally, the will of the executive, by the influence of his patronage, will supersede the laws, indications of which are already perceptible. This ascendancy can only be preserved through the action of the States as organized bodies, having their own separate governments, and possessed of the right, under the structure of our system, of judging of the extent of their separate powers, and of interposing their authority to arrest the enactments of the General Government within their respective limits. It will not enter at this time into the discussion of this important point, as it has been ably and fully presented by the senator from Kentucky (Mr. [George M.] Bibb), and others who preceded him in this debate on the same side, whose arguments not only remain unanswered, but are unanswerable. It is only by this power of interposition that the reserved rights of the States can be peacefully and efficiently protected against the encroachments of the General Government, that the limitations imposed upon its authority will be enforced, and its movements confined to the orbit allotted to it by the Constitution. . . .

Against the view of our system which I have presented, and the right of the State to interpose, it is objected that it would lead to anarchy and dissolution. I consider the objection as without the slightest foundation; and that, so far from tending to weakness or Disunion, it is the source of the highest power and of the strongest cement. Nor is its tendency in this respect difficult of explanation. The government of an absolute majority, unchecked by efficient constitutional restraint, though apparently strong, is, in reality, an exceedingly feeble government. That tendency to conflict between the parts, which I have shown to be inevitable in such governments, wastes the powers of the state in the hostile action of contending factions, which leaves very little more power than the excess of the strength of the majority over the minority. But a government based upon the principle of the concurring majority, where each great interest possesses within itself the means of self-protection, which ultimately requires the mutual consent of all the parts, necessarily causes that unanimity in council, and ardent attachment of all the parts to the whole, which give an irresistible energy to a government so constituted. . . .

But, to return to the General Government, we have now sufficient experience to ascertain that the tendency to conflict in its action is between the southern and other sections. The latter having a decided majority, must habitually be possessed of the powers so natural to the human breast, they must become the advocates of the power of government, and in the same degree opposed to the limitations; while the other and weaker section is as necessarily thrown on the side of the limitations. One section is the natural guardian of the delegated powers, and the other of the reserved; and the struggle on the side of the former will be to enlarge the powers, while that on the opposite side will be to restrain them within their constitutional limits. The contest will, in fact, be a contest between power and liberty, and such I consider the present—a contest in which the weaker section, with its peculiar labor, productions, and institutions, has at stake all that can be dear to freemen. Should we be able to maintain in their full vigor our reserved rights, liberty and prosperity will be our portion; but if we yield, and permit the stronger interest to concentrate within itself all the powers of the government, then will our fate be more wretched than that of the aborigines whom we have expelled. In this great struggle between the delegated and reserved powers, so far from repining that my lot, and that of those whom I represent, is cast on the side of the latter, I rejoice that such is the fact; for, though we participate in but few of the advantages of the government, we are compensated, and more than compensated, in not being so much exposed to its corruptions. Nor do I repine that the duty, so difficult to be discharged, as the defence of the reserved powers against apparently such fearful odds, has been assigned to us. To discharge successfully this high duty requires the highest qualities, moral and intellectual; and should we perform it with a zeal and ability proportioned to its magnitude, instead of being mere planters, our section will become distinguished for its patriots and statesmen. But, on the other hand, if we prove unworthy of this high destiny—if we yield to the steady encroachment of power, the severest calamity and most debasing corruption will overspread the land. Every Southern man, true to the interests of his section, and faithful to the duties which Providence has allotted him, will be for ever excluded from the honors and emoluments of this government, which will be reserved for those only who have qualified themselves, by political prostitution, for admission into the Magdalene Asylum.

NOTES

1. *Annals of America*, vol. 4 (Chicago: Encyclopaedia Britannica, 1968), 428.
2. "Ordinance of Nullification," in *The Nullification Era: A Documentary Record*, William H. Freehling, ed. (New York: Harper and Row, 1967), 151.

3. Letter Samuel C. Jackson to William Truc, in Freehling, *The Nullification Era*, 165.
4. Richard E. Ellis, *The Union at Risk: Jacksonian Democracy, States' Rights, and the Nullification Crisis* (New York: Oxford University Press, 1987), 179.
5. Carl Kell, "A Rhetorical History of James Hamilton, Jr.: The Nullification Era in South Carolina, 1816–1834," Ph.D. diss., University of Kansas, 1971, 148.
6. Ralph T. Eubanks, "The Rhetoric of the Nullifiers," in *Oratory in the Old South*, Waldo W. Braden, ed. (Baton Rouge: Louisiana State University Press, 1970), 39.
7. Most of this biographical material is from Dumas Malone, *Dictionary of American Biography*, vol. VIII (New York: Charles Scribner's Sons, 1932), 187–188; and Kell, "A Rhetorical History of James Hamilton, Jr."
8. Delivered October 21, 1828. Text from Kell, "A Rhetorical History of James Hamilton, Jr.," 137–205.
9. Most of this biographical material on Calhoun is taken from the sketches by Richard N. Current in *The Encyclopedia of Southern History*, David C. Roller and Robert W. Twyman, eds. (Baton Rouge: Louisiana State University Press), 171 and by Emory Thomas in *Encyclopedia of Southern Culture*, Charles Reagan Wilson and William Ferris, eds. (Chapel Hill: The University of North Carolina Press, 1989), 1183–1184.
10. Delivered in the U.S. Senate, February 15 and 16, 1833. Text in *The Papers of John C. Calhoun*, vol. XII, 1833–1835, Clyde N. Wilson, ed. (Columbia: University of South Carolina Press, 1979), 45–94. Wilson editorialized about this version of the speech: "The version of this well-known speech selected for reproduction is that prepared by Calhoun himself for the 1843 edition of his *Speeches*."

FOR FURTHER READING

Ericson, David F. "The Nullification Crisis, American Republicanism, and the Force Bill Debate." *Journal of Southern History* 61 (1995), 249–270.
Freehling, William W. *Prelude to Civil War, the Nullification Controversy in South Carolina, 1816–1836*. New York: Harper and Row, 1965.
Maier, Pauline. "The Road Not Taken: Nullification, John C. Calhoun, and the Revolutionary Tradition in South Carolina." *South Carolina Historical Magazine* 82 (1981), 1–19.
Peterson, Merrill D. *Olive Branch and Sword—The Compromise of 1833*. Baton Rouge: Louisiana State University Press, 1982.

John C. Calhoun

Bartlett, Irving H. *John C. Calhoun: A Biography*. New York: Norton, 1994.
Coit, Margaret L. *John C. Calhoun, American Portrait*. Boston: Houghton Mifflin, 1950.
Curry, Herbert L. "John C. Calhoun." In *A History and Criticism of American Public Address*, vol. II, William Norwood Brigance, ed. New York: McGraw-Hill, 1943.
Niven, John. *John C. Calhoun and the Price of Union: A Biography*. Baton Rouge: Louisiana State University Press. 1988.
Wiltse, Charles M. *John C. Calhoun, Nationalist: 1782–1828, John C. Calhoun, Nullifier: 1829–1839*, and *John C. Calhoun, Sectionalist: 1840–1850*. Indianapolis: Bobbs-Merrill, 1944, 1949, 1951.

CHAPTER 4

Envisioning the Perfect Society: The Defense of Slavery and the South

Slavery of the black African was the rock which nearly shattered the American nation. For four decades, North and South debated, argued, skirmished, preached, and finally fought over this issue. During the process, southerners became increasingly paranoid and defensive about their peculiar institution, until, at the end, they believed their only recourse was secession, and ultimately, if need be, civil war. When the war was over, however, and slavery was overcome, few in the South regretted its demise. There was no attempt to reinstitute it (although some of the state Black Codes came close in the years immediately after the war). It was almost as if the South collectively breathed a sigh of relief and was generally pleased to see the institution destroyed. But from 1820 to 1865, southern leadership did everything possible politically, rhetorically, and militarily to preserve and defend human bondage.

Significantly, it was recognized and acknowledged by many that slavery made a difference within the new American nation. James Madison, the "Father of the Constitution," was a Virginia planter and slave owner who remarked that it was "pretty well understood that the real difference of interests lay, not between the large & small but between North & South'n States. The institution of slavery & its consequences formed the line of discrimination."[1]

Even though sentiment for abolition did not gain wide support until the nineteenth century, there were always some Americans who opposed slavery. In New Jersey, New York, Pennsylvania, and New England slavery was declared illegal in the 1770–1790 period, due primarily to the Quakers in that area who applied pressure to the institution. Not only was there Quaker influence in this Northern area, there were also few slaves with which to deal. In 1790 less than six percent of American slaves lived in the North, by 1820 less than one percent, and during the 1820s it had dwindled to less than one-tenth of one percent.[2] One of the important legislative acts of the early nation was the Northwest Ordinance of 1787, which laid out the parameters for governing the area which later became Michigan, Ohio, Indiana, Illinois, and Wisconsin. That document outlawed slavery in the region, and it might have seemed that bondage was headed for extinction. During that same period, however, the debates over the United States Constitution firmly entrenched the practice of slavery in the supreme law of the land.

The debates in Congress over the admission of Missouri marked the first significant round in the debate that continued for the next forty years. In some Missouri Compromise Congressional speeches, several southerners spoke against slavery, among them John Randolph, John Tyler, and George Tucker, all of Virginia. In this debate, however, other southern orators fired the first volley in their long struggle to preserve the institution.[3]

During the decade of the 1820s several newspapers were established in the North to attack slavery; leading that effort was Benjamin Lundy's *Genius of Universal Emancipation*, published in Baltimore on the border between the sections. Militant abolition began in 1831 with the founding in Boston of William Lloyd Garrison's *Liberator*; the paper and its editor took an absolutely uncompromising stand on the issue. Garrison believed that emancipation should be immediately imposed by the national government, with no compensation for the slave-owners and no resettlement in Africa. Forced abolition, if necessary, was acceptable for Garrison and his militant followers. Their tactics rapidly hardened the issue to the point that ultimately, neither the South nor the North could compromise further.

By the 1820s there were 130 anti-slavery societies in the United States; amazingly, 106 were in the southern states. That early southern liberalism soon ended as the Garrison faction of the abolition movement grew in strength. In 1832, Virginians debated slavery in their constitutional convention. Many delegates to the convention argued against the practice, but it was finally protected by the new state constitution. This debate demonstrated the strong anti-slavery sentiment in the region (though Virginia is admittedly an upper-South state), but it also was the last time any significant discussion was held in the South in which slavery drew any opposition. The South coalesced around its peculiar institution and southerners no longer allowed dissent south of the Mason-Dixon Line.

Why was the South so defensive and protective of slavery? There were a host of reasons, but perhaps four were more important than the others: economic issues, cultural factors, the concept of states' rights, and the South's self image. In the first place, slavery produced an overwhelming amount of the region's agricultural products, as slaves grew virtually all of the sugar, rice, and cotton. Almost all other crops such as tobacco, wheat, and hemp used substantial slave labor. Therefore, the economic factors were strong influences on the southern mind. In fact, in James Hammond's speech included in this chapter, we see the ultimate expression of this point of view when the South Carolina Senator admonishes the North that "King Cotton" would bring the rest of the world to the southern side, should war be the final outcome.

A second reason the South became so adamant about slavery was that it saw the institution as the best means of social control. By 1860, there were some 4,000,000 black slaves in the southern states, with the black population of the six deep South states standing at 49 percent of those states' total. Somehow, the white South thought, those millions had to be kept under the watchful and paternalistic eye of the white man. Several events led southerners to perceive a need for an effective and permanent means for controlling this large black population, which they saw as only a step removed from barbarism and the primitive society of Africa. In 1791, a slave in Saint-Dominique, Toussaint Louverture, led a successful slave revolt on that Caribbean island which created the nation of Haiti. In 1800, Gabriel Prosser led 1000 slaves in a Richmond, Virginia, revolt that was crushed. Twenty-two years latter, Denmark Vesey, a black preacher, promoted a rebellion in Charleston, South Carolina, the very heart of the slavery empire. Less than a decade later, the followers of Nat Turner in Virginia murdered some 60 whites and several hundred blacks were subsequently killed. Although none of the southern slave uprisings were ultimately successful, the specter of what could happen lurked in the shadows around every slave cabin and infiltrated into every slave-owner's house. A wave of repression swept the South in the 1840s and 1850s. Anti-slavery tracts, books, and newspapers were prohibited anywhere in the South and any would-be critic of slavery or the southern way of life was silenced, banned, exiled from the section, or in extreme cases, lynched.[4]

A major factor in the debate was the idea that the states had the right to determine their own domestic institutions. Much of John C. Calhoun's work as a political thinker was intended to devise ways to protect the southern minority against the northern majority and to defend the rights of states in their relationship to the Federal government. Virtually all white southerners agreed on this point and believed that the South must be allowed to deal with the matter in its own time and in its own way.[5] Many Northerners, including Abraham Lincoln, agreed with them.

A final factor was the South's perception and image of itself. By the late 1840s, the South was being left behind politically, economically, and demographically. The North was booming, cities were growing, the railroads were expanding, and population was mushrooming. The southern region of the country, however, was little different from what it had been a few decades earlier. Still rural and agricultural, the South depended on water ways, not the iron horse, for transportation and commerce. In politics, the South had become a minority within the nation, and its people were sensitive and pessimistic about their future. The attacks on slavery came at the same time that the region began to realize it was not keeping up with the rest of the nation.

In a defensive posture, the leadership of the South increasingly defended slavery, and by extension, all of southern society and culture. What Charles Snydor called "the vision of the perfect South,"[6] became so strong, it ultimately led to the Civil War, and to the creation of the Old South and Lost Cause myths, which underpinned white supremacy, the Jim Crow years, and the massive resistance to civil rights for all Americans in the mid-part of the twentieth century.

By the late 1830s, the South stood almost alone in the world in defending slavery. England had abolished human bondage throughout the British Empire and Latin American nations (except for Cuba and Brazil) quickly followed suit. Defend it the South did, however, to the bitter end of the bloody Civil War.

A result of the South's defense of an indefensible institution was the foundation of the region's strong and still continuing conservative tendencies. Clement Eaton sums it up well:

> [There was] a deep sense of insecurity in the mind of the Southerner as he looked into the future and realized that the South was becoming more and more a minority section . . . Southerners sought desperately to preserve the landmarks of the past. It was during the antebellum period that the Southern mind acquired the habit of conservatism, a staunch, ingrown feeling, that was to extend far into the future.[7]

Traces of this conservatism are evident even more than a century later, and are clearly seen in the companion volume I have written on twentieth century southern public communication.[8]

ROBERT A. TOOMBS

Robert Toombs was born in Georgia in 1810, and before he died in 1885 he served his state, the South, and the Confederacy in various posts, including United States congressman and senator and Confederate secretary of state. During his years in Congress, he was a strong Unionist, supported the Compromise of 1850, and helped Georgia accept it as well. Throughout his Senate career, he attempted to preserve the Union, but the election of Lincoln in 1860 convinced Toombs that further support of the Union was useless. He left his Senate seat and helped lead Georgia out of the Union and into the Confederacy. After a short period as secretary of state under Jefferson Davis, he resigned from the cabinet and was commissioned a general in the Confederate Army. Wounded at the battle of Antietam, he left the military and went home to Georgia.

The rest of his life was unhappy and unpleasant, as Toombs remained a strongly unreconstructed rebel. After returning to Georgia from Europe where he had fled after the Civil War, Toombs refused to take the oath of allegiance to the United States, and he did not apply for a pardon for his Confederate activities. Having never regained his citizenship, his days of service to his state were limited to a stint as legal counsel to Georgia and as a member of the state constitutional convention in 1877. Toombs even strongly opposed the New South initiatives of his fellow Georgians, and as a result of his bitter outlook, he lost most of his influence in the state.

The following speech on slavery, one of the most complete statements ever made of the southern point of view, was one of several in a series presented on the topics of slavery and abolition to the people of Boston, the heartland of abolition fervor. Toombs spoke from a prepared text and according to the New York *Express*, he appeared to be "much calmer, and cooler than in his excited harangues in Congress, or on the Georgia stump."[9]

BOSTON LECTURE ON SLAVERY[10]

Slavery—Its Constitutional Status—Its Influences on The African Race and Society

I propose to submit to you this evening some considerations and reflections upon two points.

1st. The constitutional powers and duties of the Federal Government in relation to Domestic Slavery.

2nd. The influence of Slavery as it exists in the United States upon the Slave and Society.

Under the first head I shall endeavor to show that Congress has no power to limit, restrain, or in any manner to impair slavery; but, on the contrary, it is bound to protect and maintain it in the States where it exists, and wherever its flag floats, and its jurisdiction is paramount.

On the second point, I maintain that so long as the African and Caucasian races co-exist in the same society, that the subordination of the African is its normal, necessary and proper condition, and that such subordination is the condition best calculated to promote the highest interest and the greatest happiness of both races, and consequently of the whole society: and that the abolition of slavery, under these conditions, is not a remedy for any of the evils of the system. I admit that the truth of these propositions, stated under the second point, is essentially necessary to the existence and permanence of the system. They rest on the truth that the white is the superior race, and the black the inferior, and that subordination, with or without law, will be the status of the African in this mixed society, and, therefore, it is the interest of both, and especially of the black race, and of the whole society, that this status should be fixed, controlled, and protected by law. The perfect equality of the superior race, and the legal subordination of the inferior, are the foundations on which we have erected our republican systems. Their soundness must be tested by their conformity to the sovereignty of right, the universal law which ought to govern all people in all centuries. This sovereignty of right is *justice*, commonly called natural justice, not the vague uncertain imaginings of men, but natural justice as interpreted by the written oracles, and read by the light of the revelations of natures's God. In this sense I recognize a "higher law," and the duty of all men, by legal and proper means, to bring every society in conformity with it.

I proceed to the consideration of the first point.

The old thirteen States, before the revolution, were dependent colonies of Great Britain—each was a separate and distinct political community, with different laws and each became an independent and sovereign State by the Declaration of Independence. At the time of this declaration slavery was a *fact*, and a fact recognized by law in each of them, and the slave trade was lawful commerce by the laws of nations and the practice of mankind. This declaration was drafted by a slaveholder, adopted by the representatives of slaveholders, and did not emancipate a single African slave; but, on the contrary, one of the charges which it submitted to the civilized world against King George was, that he had attempted to excite "domestic insurrection among us." At the time of this declaration we had no common government; the articles of confederation were submitted to the representatives of the States eight days afterwards, and were not adopted by all of the States until 1781. These loose and imperfect articles of union sufficed to bring us successfully through the revolution. Common danger was a stronger bond of union than these articles of confederation, after that ceased, they were inadequate to the purposes of peace. They did not emancipate a single slave.

The Constitution was framed by delegates elected by the State legislatures. It was an emanation from the sovereign States as independent, separate, communities. It was ratified by conventions of these separate States, each acting for itself. The members of these conventions represented the sovereignty of each State, but they were not elected by the whole people of either of the States. Minors, women, slaves, Indians, Africans, bond and free, were excluded from participating in this act of sovereignty. Neither were all the white male inhabitants, over twenty-one years old, allowed to participate in it. Some were excluded because they had no land, others for the want of good character, others again because they were nonfreemen, and a large number were excluded for a great variety of still more unimportant reasons. None exercised this high privilege except those upon whom each State, for itself, had adjudged it wise, safe, and prudent to confer it.

By this Constitution these States granted to the Federal Government certain well defined and clearly specified powers in order *"to make a more perfect Union, establish justice, insure domestic tranquility, provide for the common defence and general welfare, and to secure the blessings of liberty to (themselves and their) posterity."* And with great wisdom and forecast this Constitution lay down a plain, certain, and sufficient rule for its own interpretation, by declaring that *"the powers not herein delegated to the United States by the Constitution nor prohibited by it to the States, are reserved to the States respectively, or to the people."* The Federal Government is therefore a limited Government. It is limited expressly to the exercise of the enumerated powers, and of such others only *"which shall be necessary and proper to carry into execution"* these enumerated powers. The declaration of the purposes for which these powers were granted can neither increase or diminish them. If any one or all of them were to fail by reason of the insufficiency of the granted powers to secure them, that would be a good reason for a new grant, but could never enlarge the granted powers. That declaration was itself a limitation instead of an enlargement of the granted powers. If a power expressly granted be used for any other purpose than those declared such use would be a violation of the grant and a fraud on the Constitution, and therefore it follows, that if anti-slavery action by Congress is not warranted by any express power, nor within any of the declared purposes for which any such power was granted, the exercise of even a granted power to effect that action, under any pretence whatever, would fall under the just condemnation of the Constitution.

The history of the times, and the debates in the convention which framed the Constitution, show that this whole subject was much considered by them, and "perplexed them in the extreme"; and these provisions of the Constitution which related to it, were earnestly considered by the State conventions, which adopted it. Incipient legislation, providing for emancipation, had already been adopted by some of the States. Massachusetts had declared that slavery was extinguished in her limits by her bill of rights; the African slave-trade had been legislated against in many of the States, including Virginia and Maryland, and North Carolina. The public mind was unquestionably tending towards emancipation. This feeling displayed itself in the South as well as in the North. Some of the delegates from the present slaveholding States thought that the power to abolish, not only the African slave-trade, but slavery in the States, ought to be given to the Federal Government; and that the Constitution did not take this shape, was made one of the most prominent objections to it by Luther Martin, a distinguished member of the convention from Maryland, and Mr. Mason of Virginia, was not far behind him in his emancipation principles; Mr. Madison sympathized to a great extent, to a much greater extent than some of the representatives from Massachusetts, in this anti-slavery feeling; hence we find that anti-slavery feelings were extensively indulged in by many members of the convention, both from slaveholding and non-slaveholding States. This fact has led to many and grave errors; artful and unscrupulous men have used it much to deceive the northern public. Mere opinions of individual men have been relied upon as authoritative expositions of the Constitution. Our reply to them is simple, direct: they were not the opinions of the collective body of the people, who made, and who had the right to make this government; and, therefore, they found no place in the organic law, and by that alone are we bound; and, therefore, it concerns us rather to know what was the collective will of the whole, as affirmed by the sovereign States, than what were the opinions of individual men in the convention. We wish to know what was done by the whole, not what some of the members thought was best to be done. The result of the struggle was, that not a single clause was inserted in the Constitution giving power to the Federal Government any where, either to abolish, limit, restrain, or in any other manner to impair the system of slavery in the United States: but on the contrary every clause which was inserted in the Constitution on this subject, does in fact, and was intended either to *increase* it, to *strengthen* it, or to *protect* it. To support these positions, I appeal to the Constitution itself, to the contemporaneous and all subsequent authoritative interpretations of it. The Constitution provides for the *increase* of slavery by prohibiting the suppression of the slave-trade for twenty years after its adoption.

Slavery is *strengthened* by the 3d clause, 2d section of 1st article, which fixes the basis of representation according to numbers by providing that the *"numbers shall be determined by adding to the whole number of free persons, including those bound to service for a term of years, and excluding Indians not taken, three-fifths of all persons."* This provision *strengthens* slavery by giving the existing slaveholding States many more representatives in Congress than they would have if slaves were considered only as property; it was much debated, but finally adopted, with the full understanding of its import, by a great majority.

The Constitution protects it, impliedly, by withholding all power to injure it, or limit its duration, but it *protects* it expressly *by the 3d clause of 2d section of the 4th article, by the 4th section of the 4th article, and by the 15th clause of the 1st article*. The 3d clause of the 2d section, 4th article, provides that "no persons held to service or labor in one State by the laws thereof, escaping into another, shall in consequence of any law or regulation therein, be discharged from such service or labor, but shall be delivered up on claim of the party to whom such service or labor may be due." The 4th section of the 4th article provides that Congress shall protect each State "on application of the legislature (or of the executive when the legislature cannot be convened) against domestic violence." The 15th clause of the 8th section of the 1st article, makes it the duty of Congress "to provide for calling forth the militia to execute the laws of the Union, *suppress insurrections*, and repel invasions." The first of these three clauses last referred to protects slavery by following the escaping slave into non-slaveholding States and returning him to bondage, the other clauses place the whole military power of the Republic in the hands of the Federal Government to repress "domestic violence" and "insurrections." Under this Constitution, if he flies to other lands, the supreme law follows, captures, and returns him; if he resists the law by which he is held in bondage, the same Constitution brings its military power to his subjugation. . . .

In inviting your calm consideration of the second point in my lecture, I am fully persuaded that even if I should succeed in convincing your reason and judgement of its truth, I shall have no aid from your sympathies in this work; yet, if the principles upon which our social system is founded are sound, the system itself is humane and just as well as necessary. Its permanence is based upon the idea of the superiority by nature of the white race over the African; that this superiority is not transient and artificial, but permanent and natural; that the same power which made his skin unchangeably black, made him inferior, intellectually, to the white race, and incapable of an equal struggle with him in the career of progress and civilization; that it is necessary for his preservation in this struggle, and for his own interest as well as that of the society of which he is a member, that he should be a servant and not a freeman in the commonwealth.

I have already stated that African slavery existed in all of the colonies at the commencement of the American revolution. The paramount authority of the Crown, with or without the consent of the colonies, had introduced it, and it was inextricably interwoven with the frame-work of society, especially in the southern States. The question was not presented for our decision whether it was just or beneficial to the African, to tear him away by force or fraud from bondage in his own country and place him in a like condition in ours. England and the Christian world had long before settled that question for us. At the final overthrow of British authority in these States our ancestors found seven hundred thousand Africans among them, already in bondage, and concentrated from our climate and productions chiefly in the present slaveholding States. It became their duty to establish governments for themselves, and these people, and they brought wisdom, experience, learning, and patriotism to the great work. They sought that system of government which would secure the greatest and most enduring happiness to the whole society. . . .

The slaveholding States, acting upon these principles, finding the African race among them in slavery, unfit to be trusted with political power, incapable as freemen of securing their own happiness, or promoting the public prosperity, recognized their condition as slaves, and subjected it to legal control. There are abundant means of obtaining evidence of the effects of this policy on the slave and society, accessible to all who seek the truth. We say its wisdom is vindicated by its results, and that under it, the African in the slave-holding States is found in a better position than he has ever attained in any other age or country, whether in bondage or freedom. In support of this point, I propose to trace him rapidly from his earliest history to the present time. The monuments of the ancient Egyptians carry him back to the morning of time—older than the pyramids—they furnish the evidence, both of his national identity and his social degradation before history began. We first behold him a slave in foreign lands, we then find the great body of his race slaves in their native land, and after thirty centuries, illuminated by both ancient and modern civilization, have passed over him, we still find him a slave of savage masters, as incapable as himself of even attempting a single step in civilization—we find him there still, without government or laws or protection, without letters or arts or industry, without religion, or even the aspirations which would raise him to the rank of an idolater, and in his lowest type, his almost only mark of humanity is, that he walks erect in the image of the Creator. Annihilate his race to day and you will find no trace of his existence within half a score of years, and he would not leave behind him a single discovery, invention, or thought worthy of remembrance by the human family. . . .

The southern States, acting upon the same admitted facts, treat them differently. They keep them in the subordinate condition in which they found them, protect them against themselves, and compel them to contribute to their own and the public interests and welfare; and under this system, we appeal to facts, open to all men, to prove that the African race has attained a higher degree of comfort and happiness than his race has ever before attained in any other age or country. Our political system gives the slave great and valuable rights. His life is equally protected with that of his master: his person is secure from assault against all others except his master, and his master's power in this respect is placed under salutary legal restraints. He is entitled by law, to a home, to ample food and clothing, and exempted from "excessive" labor; and when no longer capable of labor, in old age and disease, he is a legal charge upon his master. His family, old and young, whether capable of labor or not, from the cradle to the grave, have the same legal rights; and in these legal provisions, they enjoy as large a proportion of the products of their labor as any class of unskilled hired laborers in the world. We know that these rights are, in the main, faithfully secured to them; but I rely not on our knowledge, but submit our institutions to the same tests by which we try those of all other countries. These are supplied by our public statistics. They show that our slaves are larger consumers of animal food than any population in Europe, and larger than any other laboring population in the United States; and that their natural increase is equal to that of any other people; these are true and undisputable tests that their physical comforts are amply secured. . . .

But it is objected that religious instruction is denied the slave—while it is true that religious instruction and privileges are not enjoyed by law in all of the States, the number of slaves who are in connection with the different churches abundantly proves the universality of their enjoyment of those privileges. And a much larger number of the race in slavery enjoy the consolations of religion than the efforts of the combined Christian world have been able to convert to Christianity out of all the millions of their countrymen who remained in their native land. . . .

It is also objected that our slaves are debarred the benefits of education. This objection is also well taken, and is not without force. And for this evil the slaves are greatly indebted to the abolitionists—formerly in none of the slaveholding States was it forbidden to teach slaves to read and write, but the character of the literature sought to be furnished them by the abolitionists caused these States to take counsel rather of their passions than their reason, and to lay the axe at the root of the evil; better counsels will in time prevail, and this will be remedied. It is true that the slave, from his protected position, has less need of education than the free laborer who has to struggle for himself in the warfare of society; yet, it is both useful to him, his master, and society. . . .

The next aspect in which I propose to examine this question is, its effects upon the material interests of the slave-holding States. Thirty years ago slavery was assailed, mainly on the ground that it was a dear, wasteful, unprofitable labor, and we were urged to emancipate the blacks, in order to make them more useful and productive members of society. The result of the experiment in the West India Islands, to which I have before referred, not only disproved, but utterly annihilated this theory. The theory was true as to the white race, and was not true as to the black, and this single fact made thoughtful men pause and ponder, before advancing further with this folly of abolition. An inquiry into the wealth and productions of the slave-holding States of this Union demonstrates that slave labor can be economically and profitably employed, at least in agriculture, and leaves the question in great doubt, whether it cannot be thus employed in the South more advantageously than any other description of labor. The same truth will be made manifest by a comparison of the production of Cuba and Brazil, not only with Haiti and Jamaica, but with the free races, in similar latitudes, engaged in the same or similar productions in any part of the world. The slave-holding States, with one-half of the white population and between three and four millions of slaves, furnish above three-fifths of the annual exports of the Republic, containing twenty-three millions of people, and their entire products including every branch of industry greatly exceed *per capita* those of the more populous northern States. . . .

The opponents of slavery, passing by the question of material interests, insist that its effects on the society where it exists is to demoralize and enervate it, and render it incapable of advancement and a high civilization; and upon the citizen to debase him morally and intellectually. Such is not the lesson taught by history, either sacred or profane, nor the experience of the past or the present.

To the Hebrew race were committed the oracles of the most High, slaveholding priests administered at his altar, and slaveholding prophets and patriarchs received his revelations and taught them to their own and transmitted them to all future generations of men. The highest forms of ancient civilization, and the noblest development of the individual man, are to be found in ancient slave-holding commonwealths of Greece and Rome. In eloquence, in rhetoric, in poetry and painting, in architecture and sculpture, you must still go and search amid the wreck and ruins of their genius for the "pride of every model and the perfection of every master," and the language and literature of both, stamped with immortality, passes on to mingle itself with the thought and speech of all lands and all centuries. Time will not allow me to multiply illustrations. That domestic slavery neither enfeebles or deteriorates our race; that it is not inconsistent with the highest advancement of man and society, is the lesson taught by all ancient and confirmed by all modern history. Its effect in strengthening the attachment of the dominant race to liberty, was eloquently expressed by Mr. Burke, the most accomplished and philosophical statesman England ever produced. In his speech on conciliation with America, he uses the following strong language; "Where this is the case those who are free are by far the most proud and jealous of their freedom. I cannot alter the nature of man. The fact is so, and these people of the southern colonies are much more strongly, and with a higher and more stubborn spirit attached to liberty than those to the northward. Such were all the ancient commonwealths, such were our Gothic ancestors, and such in our day were the Poles, such will be all masters of slaves who are not slaves themselves. In such a people the haughtiness of domination combines itself with the spirit of freedom, fortifies it and renders it invincible."

No stronger evidence of what progress society may make with domestic slavery can be desired, than that which the present condition of the slave-holding States present. For near twenty years, foreign and domestic enemies of their institutions, have labored by pen and speech, to excite discontent among the white race, and insurrections among the black; these efforts have shaken the National Government to its foundations, and bursted the bonds of Christian unity among the churches of the land, yet the objects of their attacks—these States—have scarcely felt the shock. In surveying the whole civilized world the eye rests not on a single spot where all classes of society are so well content with their social system, or have greater reason to be so, than in the slaveholding States of this Union. Stability, progress, order, peace, content, prosperity, reign throughout our borders. Not a single soldier is to be found in our widely extended domain to overawe or protect society. The desire for organic change nowhere manifests itself. Within less than seventy years, out of five feeble colonies, with less than one and a half millions of inhabitants, have emerged fourteen Republican States, containing nearly ten millions of inhabitants, rich, powerful, educated, moral, refined, prosperous and happy; each with Republican governments adequate to the protection of public liberty and private rights, which are cheerfully obeyed, supported and upheld by all classes of society. With a noble system of internal improvements penetrating almost every neighborhood, stimulating and rewarding the industry of our people; with moral and intellectual surpassing physical improvements; with churches, schoolhouses and colleges daily multiplying throughout the land, bringing education and religious instruction to the homes of all the people, they may safely challenge the admiration of the civilized world. None of this great improvement and progress have been even aided by the Federal Government; we have neither sought from it, protection for our private pursuits, nor appropriations for our public improvements. They have been effected by the unaided individual efforts of an enlightened, moral, energetic and religious people. Such is our social system, and such our condition under it. Its political wisdom is vindicated in its effects on society; its morality by the practices of the patriarchs and the teachings of the apostles; we submit it to the judgment of mankind, with the firm conviction that the adoption of no other system under our circumstances would have exhibited the individual man, bond or free, in a higher development or society in a happier civilization.

JAMES HENRY HAMMOND

James Henry Hammond was a strong spokesman for southern nationalism and one of those who could be considered a "father" of the Confederacy.[11] A leader in the South Carolina nullification crisis in support of Calhoun and the nullifiers, he later advocated secession as the only true solution to the South's woes. He always was opposed to secession by only one state, however, constantly urging that several states must join together in any walkout from the Union.

Hammond at various times was a newspaper editor, a United States congressman, a two-term governor, United States senator, and a very successful and prosperous planter who strongly advocated scientific methods of farming. His election to the Senate occurred in 1857, and he served there until Lincoln's election in 1860, at which time he resigned and returned to South Carolina. Hammond did not have an official role in the Confederate government, but he supported it until his death in 1864.

The speech included here was probably Hammond's most important public address. In it he speaks of the importance of "King Cotton" to the South and to the world at large. He also clearly describes the southern defense of slavery with his narrative about the necessary "mud-sill" of the perfect southern society which was provided by slavery. His biographer said that Hammond "achieved national prominence with his provocative speech."[12] The Boston *Traveller* paints a clear picture of Hammond on the day of this speech. The newspaper reporter wrote that the orator was "Tall, long-limbed, bald-headed, spectacled, clothed in black."[13] Hammond himself confided in his diary that the speech "fixed me as the Peer of any of the Senators. That was glorious to me—but it finished me—prostrated me physically."[14] Twenty-five thousand copies were printed and Hammond was praised throughout the South for his portrayal of the issues.

ON THE ADMISSION OF KANSAS[15]

[*Editor's note*: After a long and tedious discussion of the Kansas issue and popular sovereignty, Hammond moves into the genuine concern of his southern constituents: slavery and the defense of the South.]

If we never acquire another foot of territory for the South look at her. Eight hundred and fifty thousand square miles. As large as Great Britain, France, Austria, Prussia, and Spain. Is not that territory enough to make an empire that shall rule the world? With the finest soil, the most delightful climate, whose staple productions none of those great countries can grow, we have three thousand miles of continental shoreline, so indented with bays and crowded with islands, that when their shore lines are added, we have twelve thousand miles. Through the heart of our country runs the great Mississippi, the father of waters, into whose bosom are poured thirty-six thousand miles of tributary streams; and beyond we have the desert prairie wastes, to protect us in our rear. Can you hem in such a territory as that? You talk of putting up a wall of fire around eight hundred and fifty thousand square miles so situated! How absurd.

But, in this territory lies the great valley of the Mississippi, now the real, and soon to be the acknowledged seat of the empire of the world. The sway of that valley will be as great as ever the Nile knew in the earlier ages of mankind. We own the most of it. The most valuable part of it belongs to us now; and although those who have settled above us are now opposed to us, another generation will tell a different tale. They are ours by all the laws of nature; slave-labor will go over every foot of this great valley where it will be found profitable to use it, and some of those who may not use it are soon to be united with us by such ties as will make us one and inseparable. The iron horse will soon be clattering over the sunny plains of the South to bear the products of its upper tributaries to our Atlantic ports, as it now does through the ice-bound North. There is the great Mississippi, a bond of union made by Nature herself. She will maintain it forever.

On this fine territory we have a population four times as large as that with which these colonies separated from the mother country, and a hundred, I might say a thousand fold as strong. Our population is now sixty per cent greater than that of the whole United States when we entered into the second war of independence. It is as large as the whole population of the United States was ten years after the conclusion of that war, and our exports are three times as great as those of the whole United States then. Upon our muster rolls we have a million of men. In a defensive war, upon any emergency, every one of them would be available. At any time, the South can raise, equip, and maintain in the field, a larger army than any Power of the earth can send against her, and an army of soldiers—men brought up on horseback, with guns in their hands.

If we take the North, even when the two large States of Kansas and Minnesota shall be admitted, her territory will be one hundred thousand square miles less than ours. I do not speak of California and Oregon; there is no antagonism between the South and those countries, and never will be. The population of the North is fifty per cent greater than ours. I have nothing to say in disparagement either of the soil of the North, or the people of the North, who are a brave, and energetic race, full of intellect. But they produce no great staple that the South does not produce; while we produce two or three, and those the very greatest, that she can never produce. As to her men, I may be allowed to say, they have never proved themselves to be superior to those of the South, either in the field or in the Senate.

But the strength of a nation depends in a great measure upon its wealth, and the wealth of a nation, like that of a man, is to be estimated by its surplus production. You may go to your trashy census books, full of falsehood and nonsense—they tell you, for example, that in the State of Tennessee, the whole number of house-servants is not equal to one-half of those in my own house, and such things as that. You may estimate what is made throughout the country from these census books, but it is no matter how much is made if it is all consumed. If a man is worth millions of dollars and consumes his income, is he rich? Is he competent to embark on any new enterprise? Can he build ships or railroads? And could a people in that condition build ships and roads or go to war? All the enterprises of peace and war depend upon the surplus productions of a people. They may be happy, they may be comfortable, they may enjoy themselves in consuming what they make; but they are not rich, they are not strong. It appears, by going to the reports of the Secretary of the Treasury, which are authentic, that last year the United States exported in round numbers $279,000,000 worth of domestic produce, excluding gold and foreign merchandise re-exported. Of this amount $158,000,000 worth is the clear produce of the South; articles that are not and cannot be made at the North. There are then $80,000,000 worth of exports of products of the forest, provisions, and breadstuffs. If we assume that the South made but one-third of these, and I think that is a low calculation, our exports were $185,000,000, leaving to the North less than $95,000,000.

In addition to this, we sent to the North $30,000,000 worth of cotton, which is not counted in the exports. We sent to her $7 or $8,000,000 worth of tobacco, which is not counted in the exports. We sent naval stores, lumber, rice, and many other minor articles. There is no doubt that we sent to the North $40,000,000 in addition; but suppose the amount to be $35,000,000, it will give us a surplus production of $220,000,000. But the *recorded* exports of the South now are greater than the whole exports of the United States in any year before 1856. They are greater than the whole average exports of the United States for the last twelve years including the two extraordinary years of 1856 and 1857. They are nearly double the amount of the average exports of the twelve preceding years. If I am right in my calculations as to $220,000,000 of surplus produce, there is not a nation on the face of the earth, with any numerous population, that can compete with us in produce *per capita*. It amounts to $16.66 per head, supposing that we have twelve million people. England with all her accumulated wealth, with her concentrated and educated energy, makes but sixteen-and-a-half dollars of surplus production per head. I have not made a calculation as to the North, with her $95,000,000 surplus; admitting that she exports as much as we do, with her eighteen millions of population it would be but little over twelve dollars a head. But she cannot export to us and abroad exceeding ten dollars a head against our sixteen dollars. I know well enough that the North sends to the South a vast amount of the productions of her industry. I take it for granted that she, at least, pays us in that way for the thirty or forty million dollars worth of cotton and other articles we send her. I am willing to admit that she sends us considerably more; but to bring her up to our amount of surplus production, to bring her up to $220,000,000 a year, the South must take from her $125,000,000; and this, in addition to our share of the consumption of the $333,000,000 worth introduced into the country from abroad, and paid for chiefly by our own exports. The thing is absurd; it is impossible; it can never appear anywhere but in a book of statistics.

With an export of $220,000,000 under the present tariff, the South organized separately would have $40,000,000 of revenue. With one-fourth the present tariff she would have a revenue adequate to all her wants, for the South would never go to war; she would never need an army or a navy, beyond a few garrisons on the frontiers and a few revenue cutters. It is commerce that breeds war. It is manufactures that require to be hawked about the world, that give rise to navies and commerce. But we have nothing to do but to take off restrictions on foreign merchandise and open our ports, and the whole world will come to us to trade. They will be glad to bring and carry for us, and we never shall dream of a war. Why the South has never yet had a just cause of war. Every time she had drawn her sword it has been on the point of honor, and that point of honor has been mainly loyalty to her sister colonies and sister States, who have ever since plundered and calumniated her.

But if there were no other reason why we should never have war, would any sane nation make war on cotton? Without firing a gun, without drawing a sword, should they make war on us we could bring the whole world to our feet. The South is perfectly competent to go on, one, two, or three years without planting a seed of cotton. I believe that if she was to plant but half her cotton, for three years to come, it would be an immense advantage to her. I am not so sure but that after three total years' abstinence she would come out stronger than ever she was before, and better prepared to enter afresh upon her great career of enterprise. What would happen if no cotton was furnished for three years? I will not stop to depict what every one can imagine, but this is certain: England would topple headlong and carry the whole civilized world with her, save the South. No, you dare not make war on cotton. No power on earth dares to make war upon it. Cotton *is* king. Until lately the Bank of England was king, but she tried to put her screws as usual, the fall before last, upon the cotton crop, and was utterly vanquished. The last power has been conquered. Who can doubt that has looked at recent events that cotton was supreme? When the abuse of credit had destroyed credit and annihilated confidence, when thousands of the strongest commercial houses in the world were coming down, and hundreds of millions of dollars of supposed property evaporating in thin air, when you came to a dead lock, and revolutions were threatened, what brought you up? Fortunately for you it was the commencement of the cotton season and we have poured it upon you one million six hundred thousand bales of cotton just at the crisis to save you from destruction. That cotton, but for the bursting of your speculative bubbles in the North, which produced the whole of this convulsion, would have brought us $1,000,000,000. We have sold it for $65,000,000, and saved you. Thirty-five million dollars we, the slaveholders of the South, have put into the charity box for your magnificent financiers, your "cotton lords," your "merchant princes."

But sir, the greatest strength of the South arises from the harmony of her political and social institutions. This harmony gives her a frame of society, the best in the world, and an extent of political freedom, combined with entire security, such as no other people ever enjoyed upon the face of the earth. Society precedes government; creates it, and ought to control it; but as far as we can look back in historic times we find the case different; for government is no sooner created than it becomes too strong for society, and shapes and molds, as well as controls it. In later centuries the progress of civilization and of intelligence has made the divergence so great as to produce civil wars and revolutions; and it is nothing now but the want of harmony between governments and societies which occasions all the uneasiness and trouble and terror that we see abroad. It was this that brought on the American Revolution. We threw off a Government not adapted to our social system, and made one for ourselves. The question is how far have we succeeded! The South so far as that is concerned, is satisfied, harmonious, and prosperous.

In all social systems there must be a class to do the menial duties, to perform the drudgery of life. That is, a class requiring but a low order of intellect and but little skill. Its requisites are vigor, docility, fidelity. Such a class you must have, or you would not have that other class which leads progress, civilization, and refinement. It constitutes the very mud-sill of society and of political government; and you might as well attempt to build a house in the air, as to build either the one or the other, except on this mud-sill. Fortunately for the South, she found a race adapted to that purpose to her hand. A race inferior to her own, but eminently qualified in temper, in vigor, in docility, in capacity to stand the climate, to answer all her purposes. We use them for our purpose, and call them slaves. We found them slaves by the "common consent of mankind," which, according to Cicero, "*lex naturæ est.*" The highest proof of what is Nature's law. We are old-fashioned at the South yet; it is a word discarded now by "ears polite;" I will not characterize that class at the North with that term; but you have it; it is there; it is everywhere; it is eternal.

The Senator from New York said yesterday that the whole world had abolished slavery. Aye, the *name*, but not the *thing*; all the powers of the earth cannot abolish that. God only can so it when he repeals the *fiat*, "the poor ye always have with you;" for the man who lives by daily labor, and scarcely lives at that, and who has put out his labor in the market, and take the best he can get for it; in short, your whole class of manual laborers and "opera-tives," as you call them, are essentially slaves. The difference between us is, that our slaves are hired for life and well compensated; there is no starva-tion, no begging, no want of employment among our people, and not too much employment either. Yours are hired by the day, not cared for, and scantily compensated, which may be proved in the most painful manner, at any hour in any street in any of your large towns. Why, you meet more beg-gars in one day, in any single street of the city of New York, than you would meet in a lifetime in the whole South. We do not think that whites should be slaves either by law or necessity. Our slaves are black, of another and infe-rior race. The *status* in which we have placed them is an elevation. They are elevated from the condition in which God first created them, by being made our slaves. None of that race on the whole face of the globe can be compared with the slaves of the South. They are happy, content, unaspiring, and ut-terly incapable, from intellectual weakness, ever to give us any trouble by their aspirations. Yours are white, of your own race; you are brothers of one blood. They are your equals in natural endowment of intellect, and they feel galled by their degradation. Our slaves do not vote. We give them no politi-cal power. Yours do vote, and being the majority, they are the depositaries of all your political power. If they knew the tremendous secret, that the ballot-box is stronger than "an army with banners," and could combine, where would you be! Your society would be reconstructed, your government over-thrown, your property divided, not as they have mistakenly attempted to initiate such proceedings by meeting in parks with arms in their hands, but by the quiet process of the ballot-box. You have been making war upon us to our very hearthstones. How could you like for us to send lecturers and agi-tators North, to teach these people this, to aid in combining, and to lead them!

MR. WILSON and others. Send them along.

MR. HAMMOND. You say send them along. There is no need of that. Your people are waking. They are coming here. They are thundering at our doors for homesteads, one hundred and sixty acres of land for nothing, and Southern Senators are supporting them. Nay, they are assembling, as I have said, with arms in their hands, and demanding work at $1,000 a year for six hours a day. Have you heard that the ghosts of Mendoza and Torquemada are stalking in the streets of your great cities? That the inquisition is at hand? There is afloat a fearful rumor that there have been consultations for Vigi-lance Committees. You know what that means.

Transient and temporary causes have thus far been your preservation. The great West has been open to your surplus population, and your hordes of semi-barbarian immigrants, who are crowding in year by year. They make a great movement, and you call it progress. Whither? It is progress; but it is progress towards Vigilance Committees. The South have [*sic*] sus-tained you in a great measure. You are our factors. You bring and carry for us. One hundred and fifty million dollars of our money passes annually through your hands. Much of it sticks; all of it assists to keep your machinery together and in motion. Suppose we were to discharge you; suppose we were to take our business out of your hands; we should consign you to anarchy and poverty. You complain of the rule of the South: that has been another cause that has preserved you. We have kept the Government conservative to the great purposes of Government. We have placed her, and kept her, upon the Constitution; and that has been the cause of your peace and prosperity. The Senator from New York says that that is about to be at an end; that you intend to take the Government from us; that it will pass from our hands. Perhaps what he says is true; it may be; but do not forget—it can never be forgotten—it is written on the brightest page of human history—that we, the slaveholders of the South, took our country in her infancy, and, after ruling her for sixty out of the seventy years of her existence, we shall surrender her to you without a stain upon her honor, boundless in prosperity, incalculable in her strength, the wonder and the admiration of the world. Time will show what you will make of her; but no time can ever diminish our glory or your responsibility.

NOTES

1. Bruce Levine, *Half Slave and Half Free: The Roots of Civil War* (New York: Hill and Wang, 1992), 13.

2. Levine, *Half Slave*, 48.

3. Carl Degler, *Place over Time: The Continuity of Southern Distinctiveness* (Baton Rouge: Louisiana State University Press, 1977), 36.

4. Levine, *Half Slave*, 166. See also, Clement Eaton, *The Mind of the Old South*, rev. ed. (Baton Rouge: Louisiana State University Press, 1967), 304–305; and William Freehling, *The Road to Disunion*, vol. I, *Secessionists at Bay: 1776–1854* (New York: Oxford University Press, 1990), 98–118.

5. William W. Freehling, *The Road to Disunion*, 36.

6. Charles Sydnor, *The Development of Southern Sectionalism, 1819–1848* (Baton Rouge: Louisiana State University Press, 1948), 339.

7. Eaton, *Mind of the Old South*, 312.

8. W. Stuart Towns, ed., *Public Address in the Twentieth-Century South: The Evolution of a Region* (Westport, CT: Praeger Publishing Co., 1998).

9. Quoted in William Y. Thompson, *Robert Toombs of Georgia* (Baton Rouge: Louisiana State University Press, 1966), 104. This brief biographical sketch is based on Thompson's book, the only major biography of Toombs since U. B. Phillips' *The Life of Robert Toombs*, written in 1913.

10. Robert Toombs, "A Lecture Delivered in the Tremont Temple, Boston, Massachusetts, on the 24th January, 1856." Pamphlet, n.p., n.d, copy in the Library of Congress.

11. The major source of this biographical sketch is "James Henry Hammond," in *Dictionary of American Biography*, vol. VIII, Dumas Malone, ed. (New York: Charles Scribner's Sons, 1932), 207–208.

12. Drew Gilpin Faust, *James Henry Hammond and the Old South: A Design for Mastery* (Baton Rouge: Louisiana State University Press, 1982), 347.

13. Quoted in Faust, *James Henry Hammond*, 345.

14. Eaton, *Mind of the Old South*, 58.

15. Delivered in the U.S. Senate, March 4, 1858 (Washington, D.C.: Lemuel Towers, 1858). The speech is also found in *Congressional Globe*, 35th Cong., 1st Sess., Appendix, 69–70.

FOR FURTHER READING

Franklin, John Hope. *From Slavery to Freedom: A History of Negro Americans*. 3rd ed. New York: Alfred M. Knopf, 1967.

Genovese, Eugene. *Roll, Jordan, Roll: The World the Slaves Made*. New York: Pantheon Books, 1974.

Harding, Vincent. *There Is a River: The Black Struggle for Freedom in America*. New York: Harcourt Brace Jovanovich, 1981.

Jordan, W. D. *White over Black: American Attitudes Toward the Negro, 1550–1812*. Chapel Hill: University of North Carolina Press, 1968.

Miller, William Lee. *Arguing About Slavery: The Great Battle in the United States Congress*. New York: Alfred A. Knopf, 1996.

Stampp, Kenneth M. *The Peculiar Institution: Slavery in the Ante-Bellum South*. New York: Vintage Books, 1956.

Robert A. Toombs

Leathers, Dale G. "Robert A. Toombs." In *American Orators before 1900: Critical Studies and Sources*, Bernard K. Duffy and Halford R. Ryan, eds. New York: Greenwood Press, 1987, 377–384.

James Henry Hammond

Bleser, Carol K., ed. *The Hammonds of Redcliffe*. New York: Oxford University Press, 1981.

Stegmaier, Mark J. "Intensifying the Sectional Conflict: William Seward Versus James Hammond in the Lecompton Debate of 1858." *Civil War History* 31 (Spring 1985), 197–221.

CHAPTER 5

Disrupting the Union:
The House Divided

What can be said about the most traumatic event in United States history? Abraham Lincoln asserted that a house divided against itself could not stand; his election to the presidency in November 1860 was the catalyst that proved he was right. Almost immediately after the results of the election were announced, the South, led by fire-eaters in South Carolina, made definitive plans for secession, which four decades of debate and compromise had only postponed, not prevented.

South Carolina was the first state to secede from the Union on December 20; South Carolina's declaration of secession ended with this paragraph:

> We, therefore, the people of South Carolina, by our delegates in convention assembled, appealing to the Supreme Judge of the world for the rectitude of our intentions, have solemnly declared that the Union heretofore existing between this state and the other states of North America is dissolved; and that the state of South Carolina has resumed her position among the nations of the world, as [a] separate and independent state, with full power to levy war, conclude peace, contract alliances, establish commerce, and to do all other acts and things which independent states may of right do.[1]

Very quickly, Mississippi, Florida, Alabama, Georgia, Louisiana, and Texas followed suit, in that order, and delegates met in February in Montgomery, Alabama, to form a Confederate government. In a matter of days, they adopted a provisional Constitution and elected a provisional president and vice president (Jefferson Davis of Mississippi and Alexander Stephens from Georgia).

Writing a new Constitution was not difficult for the delegates. For decades, Southerners had been arguing in strong support of the United States Constitution, in fact, contending that all the South really wanted was to live under the precise terms of that document. They claimed the Northern states, and the abolitionists especially, would not allow the South to live in peace under the Constitution and that their opposition was stifling the rights of citizens to own the property in slaves that was clearly recognized and protected under the Supreme Law of the Land. The Confederate convention simply adopted the original Constitution, strengthening those parts that stood specifically for their point of view. They made certain that property in slaves was obviously protected, and they insured clearly the sovereignty of the states within the new confederation. In addition, they prohibited use of government funding for internal improvements, limited the term of office for the president and vice-president to one six-year period, but gave the president line-item veto power. Finally, in a effort to attract the Upper South and Border states into the Confederacy, the Constitution abolished the importation of slaves.

Even though the Deep South states moved quickly and apparently decisively to establish the new government, secession was hardly a unified feeling across the entire South. In fact, one of the reasons South Carolina and her sister states moved so rapidly was that they did not want the emotion that Lincoln's election had created to wane before action was taken. Even the leadership in these six states, where disunion sentiment was by far the strongest, refused to hold referenda on the issue of secession.[2]

There was not a unified front in the South early in the new year of 1861, but in April, President Davis decided to force the issue and ordered General P.G.T. Beauregard to take the United States fort in the Charleston harbor. On April 12, Confederate forces fired on Fort Sumter and three days later the garrison surrendered. Quickly, the four hesitant states of the Upper South decided to cast their lot with the Confederacy. Virginia, Arkansas, North Carolina, and Tennessee joined forces with the lower South. Over the next few months, a southern "government in exile," was formed from groups of Kentuckians and Missourians, demonstrating the small, but vocal support for the Confederacy in those border states. These governments in exile, recognized by the Confederacy, became the twelfth and thirteenth states of the Confederate government, but they had little impact on the war effort.

By 1861, southern leadership in general believed that the North was never going to back down from its demands that the South give up its institution of slavery and renounce its political values of state rights and sovereignty. For the South, the only answer was secession and a confederacy of like-minded states. If war came—so be it—they believed God was on their side.

WILLIAM LOWNDES YANCEY

Yancey was often characterized in his own time, and by later historians, as the chief of the "fire-eaters," those southerners for whom secession was the only answer.[3] Yancey was born in Georgia in 1814, but spent more than a decade in the North, where his family moved while he was still a youngster. In 1833 he returned to his father's home state of South Carolina, where he edited a newspaper in Greenville in which he denounced the nullifiers and fought the imposition of a loyalty oath for state employees. It is likely that Yancey's stand was influenced by his Greenville readership, located as it was in the Piedmont area of South Carolina, far from the slave-holding, nullifier hotbed of Charleston.

Soon after marrying in 1833, Yancey and his new bride moved to Alabama where he became a planter. Wiped out by a succession of problems, including his own mismanagement and three months of jail after killing his wife's uncle, Yancey turned to law and journalism, both of which eventually led to politics. He served in the Alabama legislature and state senate in the early 1840s, where he advocated liberal ideas such as free public education and the right of married women to control their property. In 1844 Yancey was elected to Congress, but he resigned in 1846. By 1850, he was advocating secession and spreading his gospel throughout the South in countless political rallies and various ceremonial events. Yancey also took his cause into the heartland of the opposition. In the fall of 1860, he spoke in support of presidential candidate John Breckenridge in New York, Albany, Boston, Washington, and Cincinnati. Like his speaking in his home region, Yancey was unwilling to compromise, and while his listeners were potentially hostile, he spoke to large audiences which greeted him with cheers and applause.[4]

Yancey was appointed a Confederate commissioner to Great Britain, but he resigned after a year and returned to Alabama. His district elected him to the Confederate Senate, but he died before the War's end after months of directing strong opposition to President Jefferson Davis.

In this Washington speech, given in the middle of the 1860 presidential campaign, Yancey's main contention is the long-held southern view that the Constitution is the supreme law of the land—William Seward's "higher law" notwithstanding—and that all the South wants is for the Constitution to be followed. If it is adhered to, Yancey asserts, the minority region will be protected in its rights of property (slavery) and in the rights of states within the Union. If not—disunion must be the answer, although he claims that most southerners do not want to come to that end.

EQUAL RIGHTS IN A COMMON GOVERNMENT[5]

Fellow-citizens, I am no party man, and I do not address you as a party man to-night. Strange as it may seem to you, after what you have heard from some quarters, I come before you this evening as the friend of the Constitution and the Union under the Constitution, and as the enemy of any other Union, coming from what source it may.

My friends, there is one issue before you, and to all sensible men but one issue, and but two sides to that issue. The slavery question is but one of the symbols of that issue; the commercial question is but one of the symbols of that issue; the Union question is but one of those symbols; the only issue before this country in the canvass is the integrity and safety of the Constitution. He is a true Union man who intends to stand by that Constitution with all its checks and balances. He is a disunion man who means to destroy one single letter of that sacred instrument. It has been said that the South asks you to trespass upon the constitutional rights of the other States; it is said that the South seeks to aggrandize itself at the expense of other sections; that we want this Government to carry slavery and force it upon a people who do not desire it. With all proper respect for those who say this, I, as a Southern man say that in every iota of its utterances it is false. The South has aggressed upon no section. She asks no section to yield anything that is for her safety or for her protection. All that the South has ever asked of the Government is to keep its hands off us and let the Constitution work its own way. The South has been aggressed upon; the South has been trenched upon; four-fifths of her territory, in which she has equal rights, has been torn from her; and by the acts of Government she has been excluded from it. Revenues have been raised at the rate of two or three dollars in the South to one from any other section for the support of this great Government, but the South makes no complaint of mere dollars and cents. Touch not the honor of my section of the country, and she will not complain of almost anything else you may do; but touch her honor and equality and she will stand up in their defence, if necessary in arms.

All, then, that the South asks in this contest is that you shall observe the constitutional checks and balances with reference to her. She is not willing that her rights shall be submitted to the will of mere numerical majorities. For our fathers, our ancestors, and the great patriots of the North agreed that it should be otherwise. It was the written compact of our fathers that the minority should receive protection from the Constitution against the mere selfish and avaricious will of a preponderant majority. Parties divided themselves originally in this country upon that great principle. One desired that the majority should rule in all things, while the other—the State Rights party of the Country—desired it should be different. This latter party carried the day in the formation of the Constitution and placed checks upon the advancement of the majority. And this written Constitution was the compact by which majorities should restrain themselves with reference to the rights of minorities. Majorities need no protection save their own power. Hence it is easy for the North to cry out for the Union at all hazards and under all circumstances. It is easy for the North, with its majorities of millions, to say they are for this Union anyhow. No matter who may be elected, no matter what may be done, still they will stand to the Union as the great cause of their prosperity. Why? Because, with no constitution at all, the North can protect themselves with the predominant vote in the country. But how is it with the South? How is it with the minority of the country—the minority States of the Government? If they leave it to the mere will of preponderant majorities in Congress, the North, as in all other cases, will seek its advancement of power, will seek its own selfish aggrandizement, and will distribute the money of the Government among themselves, raise as much as they please, and do all for their own advancement at the expense of minorities. Minorities, gentlemen, are the true friends of our Constitution, because that Constitution is their shield and their protector against the unchecked and unlicensed will of the majority.

Hence it is that my section of the South stands by that Constitution. You do not hear so much said there with such flippant tongues about the Constitution as you do at the North; but you hear much said there about the Constitution, about its strict construction—about the rigid enforcement of its checks and its balances in favor of these minorities, because to them it is a thing of life and death. Within this Government that Constitution must prevail, or the minority will be placed as a "lamb that is led to the slaughter." But let that Constitution be preserved, and the South is content to abide its fate under the workings of that instrument. The North may well cry out Union! Union! Union! at all hazards and to the last extremity. And the North, even now, I understand, at midnight, is arming itself and training its midnight bands for the purpose of enforcing the Union of a mere majority upon the South. I understand these are "Wide Awakes," as they call themselves—that is, they think themselves very "wide awake," but they will find some men in the Southern States, gentlemen, sufficiently "wide awake" to meet them. A brave people and true people, gentlemen, will fear no "Wide Awakes."

No man is more wide awake than he who loves his own fireside, his own wife, and his own child, and aggresses on nobody, but determines as far as God gives him power, that nobody shall aggress on him. And there are no men who hear me to-night who would flinch like cowards if they found that others were merely bent upon aggressing upon their people when they could do so! As a distinguished friend of mine said to me the other day, the battles of the Revolution were fought with shotguns. Our people were not furnished with the great armament of modern warfare then, but being armed with the right, they were enabled to meet the powerful array of the then greatest nation of the earth, and wipe out the British lion from the country.

Now, I desire simply to say to you to-night that the South, standing on nothing but the Constitution, fears no aggression, fears no section, and that Constitution the South intends to stand by. If, in the progress of party division and party elections, that Constitution shall be trampled under foot; if a Government shall be instituted here which shall be a usurpation of the Government of Washington and our fathers; if this temple of liberty, based upon that Constitution, shall be subverted, and, instead of a Constitutional Government a "higher-law" Government shall be established, you will find, gentlemen, that the Constitution will have friends, even in that hour; and if driven from all other sections of the country, and there is no spot where the ark of the covenant of our safety can rest and be protected, it will be on Southern soil, where the friends of the Constitution live.

We do not desire, at the South, disunion; I know of but few advocates at the South of this measure. I can point to hundreds of distinguished Northern men who are far in advance of any men at the South upon the question of disunion. I know, in the Northern States, men who want a "higher-law," who want a different Constitution, who want another Bible—aye, and who, in religion, even call for another Jesus Christ. Disunion, *per se*, exists in that union. I know of no disunion, *per se*, at the South. The humble individual who addresses you to-night has probably been more denounced as a dis unionist than almost any other man in the Union. I tell you, gentlemen, my disunion consists in this: I stand by the Constitution. I intend that the provisions of the Constitution, which I look upon as the shield of the South in this Union, shall be carried out and enforced. If that Constitution is taken away from the South in this Union, and the South is then to remain in the Union, I consider that we would then have no rights, for we would then be placed at the feet of a dominant, sectional, abolition majority. I say then, that the South stands by the Constitution, as a shield in this Union. When this shield shall be taken from their breasts by a dominant sectional majority, who seek to reduce this Government to the will of a mere majority, for its own sectional purposes, who intend to make us hewers of wood and drawers of water—we intend to take that Constitution with us; and gentlemen, imitating the great example of George Washington, if there is no other place where we can erect and keep this Constitution, we will take the banner of liberty and plant it on the mountains, and there we will entrench ourselves as a body of freemen.

But, as I said to you, we hope that day is far distant from us, and that none of us may live to see its dawn. I, so help me God, will consider that to be an evil hour, when this Government shall be so rent by factions that the charter of our liberties shall be trodden under foot, and the compact of our fathers disregarded by their degenerate sons. It would indeed be an evil hour, but we are compelled to look it in the face. A large party, numbering in itself now, it is said, a plurality, if not a majority, of the people in this country is banded together with a discipline such as no other party has, having hopes which no other party has, led by men of eminent ability, with Abraham Lincoln its candidate, with Seward as its chief statesman and chief advocate, who from Maine to the furthest frontier of civilization, proclaims war, an "irrepressible war," upon the institutions of one half of this union; who proclaims, gentlemen, that the manner in which he interprets the constitution is that it shall give freedom to everything in human shape upon the face of the earth; who proclaims, gentlemen, therefore, that this Constitution which is based upon a recognition of negroes as an inferior race, that is based upon its recognition of property in slaves, that is based upon the recognition of slavery as a State institution, based upon its recognition as property which requires that property to be delivered up by the hostile states into which it may become fugitive—that this Constitution is to be utterly disregarded by him, and only his wild, insane, revolutionary and incendiary notions are the interpretations to be placed upon the constitution by this new government, if elevated to power.

Suppose that party gets into power; suppose another John Brown raid takes place in a frontier state; suppose "Sharp's rifles" and pikes and bowie knives, and all the implements of warfare are brought to bear upon an inoffensive, peaceful and unfortunate people, and that Lincoln or Seward is in the Presidential chair, where will then be a force of United States Marines to check that band? Suppose this is the case—that the frontiers of the country will be lighted up by the flames of midnight arson, as it is in Texas; that towns are burned; that the peace of our families is disturbed; that poison is found secreted throughout the whole country in immense quantities; that men are found prowling about in our land distributing that poison in order that it may be placed in our springs and our wells; with arms and ammunitions placed in the hands of this semi-barbarous people, what will be our fate? Where will be the United States Marshals to interfere? Where will be the dread of this General Government that exists under this present administration? Where will be the fear of Federal officers of a United States army to intimidate or prevent such movements? Why, gentlemen, if Texas is now inflamed, and the peace of Virginia is invaded now under this administration, and under the present aspect of affairs, tell me what will be when a "higher-law" government reigns in the city of Washington? Where then will be our peace, where will be our safety, when these people are instigated to insurrection; when men are prowling about throughout this whole country, knowing that they are protected by an administration which says that by the Constitution freedom is guaranteed to every individual on the face of the earth? Can you expect any people of spirit or courage, true to themselves, true to their firesides, true to their own families—can you expect such a people, I say, to give up all regard for the Constitution, permit it to be trampled under foot, to acknowledge this "higher-law" government, to give to their assent—can you expect, I say, any brave and heroic people thus to be untrue to their families and their firesides, and to the great principles of eternal freedom and self-preservation?

We will preserve those rights, and those who would fail to rise in their defence are deserving of the execration and contempt, not of all mankind only, but of every republican who would place this government over us. We would deserve to be pitched out of this land into the sea, and drowned in the surf that breaks upon its shores. We would deserve that there should be no further propagation of such a race of cowards. We will remember that Washington, the greatest rebel the world ever produced, led the way in defence of the great principle of freedom—in defence of those institutions upon which our Government is based, and under which it has so long prospered as a nation.

I say to you, then, though we deprecate disunion, we will have the union of our fathers. It has been said that the South has aggressed upon the North. When and where has my people ever aggressed upon the people of any other section? When and where has any Southern statesman proposed a wrong to be done to the West, the North-west, the East, or the North-east?

Never. History will Proclaim it. This age proclaims it. Our enemies will proclaim it by their silence when we defy them to answer the question.

Ours, then, is a position of defence within the limits of the Constitution. We uphold its banner. We intend to defend its principles. We ask only equal rights in our common government. Nothing more, and, so help me God, we will submit to nothing less.

BENJAMIN MORGAN PALMER

Benjamin Morgan Palmer enjoyed a long and illustrious career as one of the leading Presbyterian ministers in the South.[6] He was born in Charleston, South Carolina, on June 25, 1818; attended college at Amherst, received an undergraduate degree from the University of Georgia and a divinity degree from Columbia Seminary in South Carolina. After finishing his higher education, Palmer served a short time as a minister in Savannah, Georgia, then was called to a prestigious pulpit in Columbia, South Carolina. Ten years later, he returned to his graduate school alma mater and taught for two years. Then Palmer accepted a pastorate at the First Presbyterian Church in New Orleans, where he preached until his death on May 25, 1902.

Throughout his long and fruitful career, Palmer played a major role in southern religious circles. He not only supported and defended slavery as we see in this sermon, he strongly supported secession. During the Civil War Palmer served as a roaming chaplin, preaching often to Confederate soldiers and others on the home front. He served as the first moderator of the Southern Presbyterian Church formed in Augusta, Georgia, in 1861. After the war, Palmer continually defended the southern branch of the denomination and opposed all attempts to reunite the northern and southern wings of Presbyterianism.

This sermon, delivered on Thanksgiving Day shortly after the election of Abraham Lincoln to the presidency, clearly sums up the southern point of view on slavery and secession. Palmer unreservedly supports both. He declares that the purpose of the southern people is "to conserve and to perpetuate the institution of domestic slavery as now existing." He rejoices in the move of the South toward secession and urges southerners to "reclaim the powers they have delegated." Palmer's words echoed around the South. In New Orleans, and other southern cities such as Mobile, thousands of copies of the sermon were printed and distributed. William O. Rogers, who was in the congregation on Thanksgiving Day, wrote later that, "perhaps no other public utterance during that trying period of anxiety and hesitancy did so much to bring New Orleans city and the entire State of Louisiana squarely and fully to the side of secession and the Confederacy."[7]

THANKSGIVING SERMON[8]

The voice of the Chief Magistrate has summoned us to-day to the house of prayer. This call, in its annual repetition, may be too often only a solemn state-form; nevertheless it covers a mighty and a double truth. . . .

In obedience to this great law of religious feeling, not less than in obedience to the civil ruler who represents this commonwealth in its unity, we are now assembled. Hitherto, on similar occasions, our language has been the language of gratitude and song. "The voice of rejoicing and salvation was in the tabernacles of the righteous." Together we praised the Lord "that our garners were full, affording all manner of store; that our sheep brought forth thousands and ten thousands in our streets; that our oxen were strong to labor, and there was no breaking in nor going out, and no complaining was in our streets." As we together surveyed the blessings of Providence, the joyful chorus swelled from millions of people, "Peace be within thy walls and prosperity within thy palaces." But, to-day, burdened hearts all over this land are brought to the sanctuary of God. We "see the tents of Cushan in affliction, and the curtains of the land of Midian do tremble." We have fallen upon times when there are "signs in the sun, and in the moon, and in the stars; upon the earth distress of nations, with perplexity; the sea and the waves roaring; men's hearts failing them for fear and for looking after those things which are coming" in the near yet gloomy future. Since the words of this proclamation were penned by which we are convened, that which all men dreaded, but against which all men hoped, has been realized; and in the triumph of a sectional majority we are compelled to read the probable doom of our once happy and united confederacy. It is not to be concealed that we are in the most fearful and perilous crisis which has occurred in our history as a nation. The cords which, during four-fifths of a century, have bound together this growing republic are now strained to their utmost tension: they just need the touch of fire to part asunder forever. Like a ship laboring in the storm and suddenly grounded upon some treacherous shoal—every timber of this vast confederacy strains and groans under the pressure. Sectional divisions, the jealousy of rival interests, the lust of political power, a bastard ambition which looks to personal aggrandizement rather than to the public weal, a reckless radicalism which seeks for the subversion of all that is ancient and stable, and a furious fanaticism which drives on its ill-considered conclusions with utter disregard of the evil it engenders—all these combine to create a portentous crisis, the like of which we have never known before, and which puts to a crucifying test the virtue, the patriotism and the piety of the country. . . .

During the heated canvass which has just been brought to so disastrous a close, the seal of a rigid and religious silence has not been broken. I deplored the divisions amongst us as being, to a large extent, impertinent in the solemn crisis which was too evidently impending. Most clearly did it appear to me that but one issue was before us; an issue soon to be presented in a form which would compel the attention. That crisis might make it imperative upon me as a Christian and a divine to speak in language admitting no misconstruction. Until then, aside from the din and strife of parties, I could only mature, with solitary and prayerful thought, the destined utterance. That hour has come. At a juncture so solemn as the present, with the destiny of a great people waiting upon the decision of an hour, it is not lawful to be still. Whoever may have influence to shape public opinion, at such a time must lend it, or prove faithless to a trust as solemn as any to be accounted for at the bar of God.

Is it immodest in me to assume that I may represent a class whose opinions in such a controversy are of cardinal importance? The class which seeks to ascertain its duty in the light simply of conscience and religion; and which turns to the moralist and the Christian for support and guidance. The question, too, which now places us upon the brink of revolution, was in its origin a question of morals and religion. It was debated in ecclesiastical councils before it entered legislative halls. It has riven asunder the two largest religious communions in the land: and the right determination of this primary question will go far toward fixing the attitude we must assume in the coming struggle. I sincerely pray God that I may be forgiven if I have misapprehended the duty incumbent upon me to-day; for I have ascended this pulpit under the agitation of feeling natural to one who is about to deviate from the settled policy of his public life. It is my purpose—not as your organ, compromitting you, whose opinions are for the most part unbeknown to me, but on my sole responsibility—to speak upon the one question of the day; and to state the duty which, as I believe, patriotism and religion alike require of us all. I shall aim to speak with a moderation of tone and feeling almost judicial, well befitting the sanctities of the place and the solemnities of the judgment day.

In determining our duty in this emergency it is necessary that we should first ascertain the nature of trust providentially committed to us. A nation often has a character as well defined and intense as that of the individual. This depends, of course upon a variety of causes operating through a long period of time. It is due largely to the original traits which distinguish the stock from which it springs, and to the providential training which has formed its education. But, however derived, this individuality of character alone makes any people truly historic, competent to work out its specific mission, and to become a factor in the world's progress. The particular trust assigned to such a people becomes the pledge of the divine protection; and their fidelity to it determines the fate by which it is finally overtaken. What that trust is must be ascertained from the necessities of their position, the institutions which are the outgrowth of their principles and the conflicts through which they preserve their identity and independence. If then the South is such a people, what, at this juncture, is their providential trust? I answer, that it is *to conserve and to perpetuate the institution of domestic slavery as now existing*. It is not necessary here to inquire whether this is precisely the best relation in which the hewer of wood and drawer of water can stand to his employer; although this proposition may perhaps be successfully sustained by those who chose to defend it. Still less are we required, dogmatically, to affirm that it will subsist through all time. Baffled as our wisdom may now be, in finding a solution of this intricate social problem, it would nevertheless be the height of arrogance to pronounce what changes may or may not occur in the distant future. In the grand march of events Providence may work out a solution undiscoverable by us. What modifications of soil and climate may hereafter be produced, what consequent changes in the products on which we depend, what political revolutions may occur among the races which are now enacting the great drama of history: all such inquiries are totally irrelevant because no prophetic vision can pierce the darkness of that future. If this question should ever arise, the generation to whom it is remitted will doubtless have the wisdom to meet it, and Providence will furnish the lights in which it is to be resolved. All that we claim for them and for ourselves is liberty to work out this problem guided by nature and God, without obtrusive interference from abroad. These great questions of providence and history must have free scope for their solution; and the race whose fortunes are distinctly implicated in the same is alone authorized, as it is alone competent, to determine them. It is just this impertinence of human legislation, setting bounds to what God only can regulate, that the South is called this day to resent and resist. The country is convulsed simply because "the throne of iniquity frameth mischief by a law." Without, therefore, determining the question of duty for future generations, I simply say, that for us, as now situated, the duty is plain of conserving and transmitting the system of slavery, with the freest scope for its natural development and extension. Let us, my brethren, look our duty in the face. With this institution assigned to our keeping, what reply shall we make to those who say that its days are numbered? My own conviction is, that we should at once lift ourselves, intelligently, to the highest moral ground and proclaim to all the world that we hold this trust from God, and in its occupancy we are prepared to stand or fall as God may appoint. If the critical moment has arrived at which the great issue is joined, let us say that, in the sight of all perils, we will stand by our trust; and God be with the right!

The argument which enforces the solemnity of this providential trust is simple and condensed. It is bound upon us, then, by the *principle of self-preservation*, that "first law" which is continually asserting its supremacy over all others. Need I pause to show how this system of servitude underlies and supports our material interests? That our wealth consists in our lands and in the serfs who till them? That from the nature of our products they can only be cultivated by labor which must be controlled in order to be certain? That any other than a tropical race must faint and wither beneath a tropical sun? Need I pause to show how this system is interwoven with our entire social fabric? That these slaves form parts of our households, even as our children; and that, too, through a relationship recognized and sanctioned in the scriptures of God even as the other? Must I pause to show how it has fashioned our modes of life, and determined all our habits of thought and feeling, and moulded the very type of our civilization? How then can the hand of violence be laid upon it without involving our existence? The so-called free states of its country are working out the social problem under conditions peculiar to themselves. These conditions are sufficiently hard, and their success is too uncertain, to excite in us the least jealousy of their lot. With a teeming population, which the soil cannot support—with their wealth depending upon arts, created by artificial wants—with an eternal friction between the grades of their society—with their labor and their capital grinding against each other like the upper and nether millstones—with labor cheapened and displaced by new mechanical inventions, bursting more asunder the bonds of brotherhood; amid these intricate perils we have given them our sympathy and our prayers, and have never sought to weaken the foundations of their social order. God grant them complete success in the solution of all their perplexities! We, too, have our responsibilities and trials; but they are all bound up in this one institution, which has been the object of such unrighteous assault through five and twenty years. If we are true to ourselves we shall, as this critical juncture, stand by it and work out our destiny.

This duty is bound upon us again *as the constituted guardians of the slaves themselves.* Our lot is not more implicated in theirs, than is their lot in ours; in our mutual relations we survive or perish together. The worst foes of the black race are those who have intermeddled on their behalf. We know better than others that every attribute of their character fits them for dependence and servitude. By nature the most affectionate and loyal of all races beneath the sun, they are also the most helpless: and no calamity can befall them greater than the loss of that protection they enjoy under this patriarchal system. Indeed the experiment has been grandly tried of precipitating them upon freedom which they know not how to enjoy; and the dismal results are before us in statistics that astonish the world. With the fairest portions of the earth in their possession and with the advantage of a long discipline as cultivators of the soil, their constitutional indolence has converted the most beautiful islands of the sea into a howling waste. It is not too much to say that if the South should, at this moment, surrender every slave, the wisdom of the entire world, united in solemn council, could not solve the question of their disposal. Their transportation to Africa, even if it were feasible, would be but the most refined cruelty; they must perish with starvation before they could have time to relapse into their primitive barbarism. Their residence here, in the presence of the vigorous Saxon race, would be but the signal for their rapid extermination before they had time to waste away through listlessness, filth, and vice. Freedom would be their doom; and equally from both they call upon us, their providential guardians, to be protected. I know this argument will be scoffed abroad as the hypocritical cover thrown over our own cupidity and selfishness; but every southern master knows its truth and feels its power. My servant, whether born in my house or bought with my money, stands to me in the relation of a child. Though providentially owing me service, which, providentially, I am bound to exact, he is, nevertheless, my brother and my friend; and I am to him a guardian and a father. He leans upon me for protection, for counsel, and for blessing; and so long as the relation continues no power, but the power of almighty God shall come between him and me. Were there no argument but this, it binds upon us the providential duty of preserving the relation that we may save him from a doom worse than death.

It is a duty which we owe, further, *to the civilized world*. It is a remarkable fact that during these thirty years of unceasing warfare against slavery, and while a lying spirit has inflamed the world against us, that world has grown more and more dependent upon it for sustenance and wealth. Every tyro knows that all branches of industry fall back upon the soil. We must come, every one of us, to the bosom of this great mother for nourishment. In the happy partnership which has grown up in providence between the tribes of this confederacy, our industry has been concentrated upon agriculture. To the North we have cheerfully resigned all the profits arising from manufacture and commerce. Those profits they have, for the most part, fairly earned, and we have never begrudged them. We have sent them our sugar and bought it back when refined; we have sent them our cotton and bought it back when spun into thread or woven into cloth. Almost every article we use, from the shoe-lachet to the most elaborate and costly article of luxury, they have made and we have bought; and both sections have thriven by the partnership, as no people ever thrived before since the first shining of the sun. So literally true are the words of the text, addressed by Obadiah to Edom, "All the men of our confederacy, the men that were at peace with us, have eaten our bread at the very time they have deceived and laid a wound under us." Even beyond—this the enriching commerce, which has built the splendid cities and marble palaces, of England as well as America, has been largely established upon the products of our soil; and the blooms upon southern fields gathered by black hands, have fed the spindles and looms of Manchester and Birmingham not less than of Lawrence and Lowell. Strike now a blow at this system of labor and the world itself totters at the stroke. Shall we permit that blow to fall? Do we not owe it to civilized man to stand in the breach and stay the uplifted arm? If the blind Samson lays hold of the pillars which support the arch of the world's industry, how many more will be buried beneath its ruins than the lords of the Philistines? "Who knoweth whether we are not come to the kingdom for such a time as this?"

Last of all, in this great struggle, *we defend the cause of God and Religion*. The abolition spirit is undeniably atheistic. The demon which erected its throne upon the guillotine in the days of Robespierre and Marat, which abolished the Sabbath and worshiped reason in the person of a harlot, yet survives to work other horrors, of which those of the French revolution are but the type. Among a people so generally religious as the American, a disguise must be worn; but it is the same old threadbare disguise of the advocacy of human rights. From a thousand Jacobin clubs here, as in France, the decree has gone forth which strikes at God by striking at all subordination and law. Availing itself of the morbid and misdirected sympathies of men, it has entrapped weak consciences in the meshes of its treachery; and now, at last, has seated its high priest upon the throne, clad in the black garments of discord and schism, so symbolic of its ends. Under this specious cry of reform, it demands that every evil shall be corrected, or society become a wreck—the sun must be stricken from the heavens, if a spot is found upon his disc. The Most High, knowing his own power which is infinite, and his own wisdom which is unfathomable, can afford to be patient. But these self-constituted reformers must quicken the activity of Jehovah or compel his abdication. In their furious haste, they trample upon obligations sacred as any which can bind the conscience. It is time to reproduce the obsolete idea that Providence must govern man, and not that man should control Providence. In the imperfect state of human society, it pleases God to allow evils which check others that are greater. As in the physical world, objects are moved forward, not by a single force, but by the composition of forces; so in his moral administration, there are checks and balances whose intimate relations are comprehended only by himself. But what reck they of this—these fierce zealots who undertake to drive the chariot of the sun? working out the single and false idea which rides them like a nightmare, they dash athwart the spheres, utterly disregarding the delicate mechanism of Providence; which moves on, wheels within wheels, with pivots and balances and springs, which the great designer alone can control. This spirit of atheism, which knows no God who tolerates no evil, no Bible which sanctions law, and no conscience that can be bound by oaths and covenants, has selected us for its victims, and slavery for its issue. Its banner-cry rings out already upon the air—"liberty, equality, fraternity," which simply interpreted mean bondage, confiscation and massacre. With its tricolor waving in the breeze—it waits to inaugurate its reign of terror. To the South the high position is assigned of defending, before all nations, the cause of all religion and of all truth. In this trust, we are resisting the power which wars against constitutions and laws and compacts, against Sabbaths and sanctuaries, against the family, the state, and the church; which blasphemously invades the prerogatives of God, and rebukes the Most High for the errors of his Administration; which, if it cannot snatch the reins of empire from his grasp, will lay the universe in ruins at his feet. Is it possible that we shall decline the onset?

This argument, then, which sweeps over the entire circle of our relations, touches the four cardinal points of duty *to ourselves, to our slaves, to the world, and to almighty God*. It establishes the nature and solemnity of our present trust, to *preserve and transmit our existing system of domestic servitude, with the right, unchallenged by man, to go and root itself wherever Providence and nature may carry it*. This trust we will discharge in the face of the worst possible peril. Though war be the aggregation of all evils, yet, should the madness of the hour appeal to the arbitration of the sword, we will not shrink even from the baptism of fire. If modern crusaders stand in serried ranks upon some plain of Esdraelon, there shall we be in defense of our trust. Not till the last man has fallen behind the last rampart, shall it drop from our hands; and then only in surrender to the God who gave it.

Against this institution a system of aggression has been pursued through the last thirty years. Initiated by a few fanatics, who were at first despised, it has gathered strength from opposition until it has assumed its present gigantic proportions. No man has thoughtfully watched the progress of this controversy without being convinced that the crisis must at length come. Some few, perhaps, have hoped against hope, that the gathering imposthume might be dispersed, and the poison be eliminated from the body politic by healthful remedies. But the delusion has scarcely been cherished by those who have studied the history of fanaticism in its path of blood and fire through the ages of the past. The moment must arrive when the conflict must be joined, and victory decide for one or the other. As it has been a war of legislative tactics, and not of physical force, both parties have been maneuvering for a position; and the embarrassment has been, whilst dodging amidst constitutional forms, to make an issue that should be clear, simple, and tangible. Such an issue is at length presented in the result of the recent Presidential election. Be it observed, too, that it is an issue made by the North not by the South; upon whom, therefore, must rest the entire guilt of the present disturbance. With a choice between three national candidates, who have more or less divided the votes of the South, the North, with unexampled unanimity, have cast their ballot for a candidate who is sectional, who represents a party that is sectional, and the ground of that sectionalism, prejudice against the established and constitutional rights and immunities and institutions of the South. What does this declare—what can it declare, but that from henceforth this is to be a government of section over section; a government using constitutional forms only to embarrass and divide the section ruled, and as fortresses through whose embrasures the cannon of legislation is to be employed in demolishing the guaranteed institutions of the South? What issue is more direct, concrete, intelligible than this? I thank God that, since the conflict must be joined, the responsibility of this issue rests not with us, who have ever acted upon the defensive; and that it is so disembarrassed and simple that the feeblest mind can understand it.

The question with the South to-day is not what issue shall *she* make, but how shall she meet that which is prepared for her? Is it possible that we can hesitate longer than a moment? In our natural recoil from the perils of revolution, and with our clinging fondness for the memories of the past, we may perhaps look around for something to soften the asperity of this issue, for some ground on which we may defer the day of evil, for some hope that the gathering clouds may not burst in fury upon the land. . . .

What say you to this, to whom this great providential trust of conserving slavery is assigned? "Shall the throne of inequity have fellowship with thee, which frameth mischief by a law?" It is this that makes the crisis. Whether we will or not, this is the historic moment when the fate of this institution hangs suspended in the balance. Decide either way, it is the moment of our destiny—the only thing affected by the decision is the complexion of that destiny. If the South bows before this throne, she accepts the decree of restriction and ultimate extinction, which is made the condition of her homage.

As it appears to me, the course to be pursued in this emergency is that which has already been inaugurated. Let the people in all the Southern states, in solemn council assembled, reclaim the powers they have delegated. Let those conventions be composed of men whose fidelity has been approved—men who bring the wisdom, experience and firmness of age to support and announce principles which have long been matured. Let these conventions decide firmly and solemnly what they will do with this great trust committed to their hands. Let them pledge each other in sacred covenant, to uphold and perpetuate what they cannot resign without dishonor and palpable ruin. Let them further, take all the necessary steps looking to separate and independent existence; and initiate measures for framing a new and homogeneous confederacy. Thus, prepared for every contingency, let the crisis come. Paradoxical as it may seem, if there be any way to save, or rather to re-construct, the union of our forefathers, it is this. Perhaps, at the last moment, the conservative portions of the North may awake to see the abyss into which they are about to plunge. Perchance they may arise and crush out forever, the abolition hydra, and cast it into the grave from which there shall never be a resurrection.

Thus, with restored confidence, we may be rejoined a united and happy people. But, before God, I believe that nothing will effect this but the line of policy which the South has been compelled in self-preservation to adopt. I confess frankly, I am not sanguine that such an auspicious result will be reached. Partly, because I do not see how new guarantees are to be grafted upon the Constitution, nor how, if grafted, they can be more binding than those which have already been trampled underfoot; but chiefly, because I do not see how such guarantees can be elicited from the people at the North. It can be disguised, that almost to a man, they are anti-slavery where they are not abolition. A whole generation has been educated to look upon the system with abhorrence as a national blot. They hope, and look, and pray for its extinction within a reasonable time, and cannot be satisfied unless things are seen drawing to that conclusion. We, on the contrary, as its constituted guardians, can demand nothing less than that it should be left open to expansion, subject to no limitations save those imposed by God and nature. I fear the antagonism is too great, and the conscience of both parties too deeply implicated to allow such a composition of the strife. Nevertheless since it is within the range of possibility in the Providence of God, I would not shut out the alternative.

Should it fail, what remains but that we say to each other, calmly and kindly, what Abraham said to Lot: "Let there be no strife, I pray thee, between me and thee, and between my herdmen and thy herdmen, for we be brethren; Is not the whole land before thee? Separate thyself I pray thee, from me—if thou will take the left hand, then I will go to the right, or if thou depart to the right hand, then I will go to the left." Thus, if we cannot save the Union, we may save the inestimable blessings it enshrines; if we cannot preserve the vase, we will preserve the precious liquor it contains.

In all this, I speak for the North no less than for the South; for upon our united and determined resistance at this moment, depends the salvation of the whole country—in saving ourselves we shall save the North from the ruin she is madly drawing down upon her own head.

The position of the South is at this moment sublime. If she has grace given to her to know her hour she will save herself, the country, and the world. It will involve, indeed, temporary prostration and distress; the dikes of Holland must be cut to save her from the troops of Philip. But I warn my countrymen the historic moment once passed, never returns. If she will arise in her majesty, and speak now as with the voice of one man, she will roll back for all time, the curse that is upon her. If she succumbs now, she transmits that curse as an heirloom to posterity. We may, for a generation, enjoy comparative ease, gather up our feet in our beds, and die in peace; but our children will go forth beggared from the homes of their fathers. Fishermen will cast their nets where your proud commercial navy now rides at anchor, and dry them upon the shore now covered with your bales of merchandise. Sapped, circumvented, undermined, the institutions of your soil will be overthrown; and within five and twenty years, the history of St. Domingo will be the record of Louisiana. If dead men's bones can tremble, ours will move under the muttered curses of sons and daughters, denouncing the blindness and love of ease which have left them an inheritance of woe.

I have done my duty under as deep a sense of responsibility to God and man, as I have ever felt. Under a full conviction that the salvation of the whole country is depending upon the action of the South, I am impelled to deepen the sentiment of resistance in the Southern mind, and to strengthen the current now flowing towards a union of the South, in defense of her chartered rights. It is a duty which I shall not be called to repeat, for such awful junctures do not occur twice in a century. Bright and happy days are yet before us; and before another political earthquake shall shake the continent, I hope to be "where the wicked cease from troubling and where the weary are at rest."

It only remains to say, that whatever be the fortunes of the South, I accept them for my own. Born upon her soil, of a father thus born before me—from an ancestry that occupied it while yet it was a part of England's possessions—she in every sense, my mother. I shall die upon her bosom—she shall know no peril, but it is my peril—no conflict, but it is my conflict—and no abyss of ruin, into which I shall not share her fall. May the Lord God cover her head in this her day of battle!

JEFFERSON DAVIS

Jefferson Davis, the first and only president of the Confederate States of America, was born in Kentucky, but his family moved to Mississippi when Jefferson was young. He graduated from West Point in 1828 and served in the Army until 1835, when he resigned and returned to live as a planter in his home state. Serving in the House of Representatives for part of a term in 1845–1846, he commanded a Mississippi regiment in the Mexican War. Because of his background and interests in the military, he expected and wanted a command in the Confederate Army, but his compatriots elected him president instead.

Davis drew considerable criticism from throughout the South for his heavy-handed running of the Confederate government. Much of what he had to do in order for the fledgling nation to have any attempt at succcess, flew counter to the whole theory underlying the Confederacy: state rights. There is little doubt that Davis was not suited for executive leadership, as he became too immersed in details of the different departments, was too unyielding and inflexible, and could not overcome his distant and aloof personality in order to become a popular leader and inspirer of his people. While probably no one could have led the Confederate States to a military victory, Davis devoted himself to the impossible task.

After the War, Davis was arrested by the Union army and held in jail for two years. While he never went to court, he never applied for a pardon, and was, therefore, for the rest of his life, a man without a country. During the last quarter century of his life, he remained mostly in Mississippi, speaking occasionally at veterans' reunions and writing his apologia. He died at Beauvoir, his home on the Mississippi Gulf Coast, in 1889.

The speech included here was given in Montgomery, Alabama, on February 18, 1861, when Davis was inaugurated as the Provisional President of the Confederacy. In this inaugural, Davis addresses three audiences: the Confederates, whom he tried to reassure that the Confederacy was strong and would endure; the Union, especially the border states which he hoped to attract to the Confederate banner; and the world, especially those nations that depended upon Southern cotton.

INAUGURAL ADDRESS OF THE PRESIDENT OF THE PROVISIONAL GOVERNMENT [9]

Gentlemen of the Congress of the Confederate States of America, Friends, and Fellow-citizens: Called to the difficult and responsible station of Chief Magistrate of the Provisional Government which you have instituted, I approach the discharge of the duties assigned to me with humble distrust of my abilities, but with a sustaining confidence in the wisdom of those who are to guide and aid me in the administration of public affairs, and an abiding faith in the virtue and patriotism of the people. Looking forward to the speedy establishment of a permanent government to take the place of this, which by its greater moral and physical power will be better able to combat with many difficulties that arise from the conflicting interests of separate nations, I enter upon the duties of the office to which I have been chosen with the hope that the beginning of our career, as a Confederacy, may not be obstructed by hostile opposition to our enjoyment of the separate existence and independence we have asserted, and which, with the blessing of Providence, we intend to maintain.

Our present political position has been achieved in a manner unprecedented in the history of nations. It illustrates the American idea that governments rest on the consent of the governed, and that it is the right of the people to alter or abolish them at will whenever they become destructive of the ends for which they were established. The declared purpose of the compact of the Union from which we have withdrawn was to "establish justice, insure domestic tranquility, provide for the common defense, promote the general welfare, and secure the blessings of liberty to ourselves and our posterity;" and when, in the judgment of the sovereign States composing this Confederacy, it has been perverted from the purposes for which it was ordained, and ceased to answer the ends for which it was established, a peaceful appeal to the ballot box declared that, so far as they are concerned, the Government created by the compact should cease to exist. In this they merely asserted the right which the Declaration of Independence of July 4, 1776, defined to be "inalienable." Of the time and occasion of its exercise they as sovereigns were the final judges, each for itself. The impartial and enlightened verdict of mankind will vindicate the rectitude of our conduct; and He who knows the hearts of men will judge of the sincerity with which we have labored to preserve the Government of our fathers in its spirit.

The right solemnly proclaimed at the birth of the United States, and which has been solemnly affirmed and reaffirmed in the Bill of Rights of the States subsequently admitted into the Union of 1789, undeniably recognizes in the people the power to resume the authority delegated for the purposes of government. Thus the sovereign States here represented have proceeded to form this Confederacy; and it is by abuse of language that their act has been denominated a revolution. They formed a new alliance, but within each State its government has remained; so that the rights of person and property have not been disturbed. The agent through which they communicated with foreign nations is changed, but this does not necessarily interrupt their international relations. Sustained by the consciousness that the transition from the former Union to the present Confederacy has not proceeded from a disregard on our part of just obligations, or any failure to perform every constitutional duty, moved by no interest or passion to invade the rights of others, anxious to cultivate peace and commerce with all nations, if we may not hope to avoid war, we may at least expect that posterity will acquit us of having needlessly engaged in it. Doubly justified by the absence of wrong on our part, and by wanton aggression on the part of others, there can be no cause to doubt that the courage and patriotism of the people of the Confederate States will be found equal to any measure of defense which their honor and security may require.

An agricultural people, whose chief interest is the export of commodities required in every manufacturing country, our true policy is peace, and the freest trade which our necessities will permit. It is alike our interest and that of all those to whom we would sell, and from whom we would buy, that there should be the fewest practicable restrictions upon the interchange of these commodities. There can, however, be but little rivalry between ours and any manufacturing or navigating community, such as the Northeastern States of the American Union. It must follow, therefore, that mutual interest will invite to good will and kind offices on both parts. If, however, passion or lust of dominion should cloud the judgment or inflame the ambition of those States, we must prepare to meet the emergency and maintain, by the final arbitrament of the sword, the position which we have assumed among the nations of the earth.

We have entered upon the career of independence, and it must be inflexibly pursued. Through many years of controversy with our late associates of the Northern States, we have vainly endeavored to secure tranquility and obtain respect for the rights to which we were entitled. As a necessity, not a choice, we have resorted to the remedy of separation, and henceforth our energies must be directed to the conduct of our own affairs, and the perpetuity of the Confederacy which we have formed. If a just perception of mutual interest shall permit us peaceably to pursue our separate political career, my most earnest desire will have been fulfilled. But if this be denied to us, and the integrity of our territory and jurisdiction be assailed, it will but remain for us with firm resolve to appeal to arms and invoke the blessing of Providence on a just cause.

As a consequence of our new condition and relations, and with a view to meet anticipated wants, it will be necessary to provide for the speedy and efficient organization of branches of the Executive department having special charge of foreign intercourse, finance, military affairs, and the postal service. For purposes of defense, the Confederate States may, under ordinary circumstances, rely mainly upon the militia; but it is deemed advisable, in the present condition of affairs, that there should be a well-instructed and disciplined army, more numerous than would usually be required on a peace establishment. I also suggest that, for the protection of our harbors and commerce on the high seas, a navy adapted to those objects will be required. But this, as well as other subjects appropriate to our necessities, have doubtless engaged the attention of Congress.

With a Constitution differing only from that of our fathers in so far as it is explanatory of their well-known intent, freed from sectional conflicts, which have interfered with the pursuit of the general welfare, it is not unreasonable to expect that States from which we have recently parted may seek to unite their fortunes to ours under the Government which we have instituted. For this your Constitution makes adequate provision; but beyond this, if I mistake not the judgment and will of the people, a reunion with the States from which we have separated is neither practicable nor desirable. To increase the power, develop the resources, and promote the happiness of the Confederacy, it is requisite that there should be so much of homogeneity that the welfare of every portion shall be the aim of the whole. When this does not exist, antagonisms are endangered which must and should result in separation.

Actuated solely by the desire to preserve our own rights, and promote our own welfare, the separation by the Confederate States has been marked by no aggression upon others, and followed by no domestic convulsion. Our industrial pursuits have received no check, the cultivation of our fields had progressed as heretofore, and, even should we be involved in war, there would be no considerable diminution in the production of the staples which have constituted our exports, and in which the commercial world has an interest scarcely less than our own. This common interest of the producer and consumer can only be interrupted by exterior force which would obstruct the transmission of our staples to foreign markets—a course of conduct which would be as unjust, as it would be detrimental, to manufacturing and commercial interests abroad.

Should reason guide the action of the Government from which we have separated, a policy so detrimental to the civilized world, the Northern States included, could not be dictated by even the strongest desire to inflict injury upon us; but, if the contrary should prove true, a terrible responsibility will rest upon it, and the suffering of millions will bear testimony to the folly and wickedness of our aggressors. In the meantime there will remain to us, besides the ordinary means before suggested, the well-known resources for retaliation upon the commerce of an enemy.

Experience in public stations, of subordinate grade to this which your kindness was conferred, has taught me that toil and care and disappointment are the price of official elevation. You will see many errors to forgive, many deficiencies to tolerate; but you shall not find in me either want of zeal or fidelity to the cause that is to me the highest in hope, and the most enduring affection. Your generosity has bestowed upon me an undeserved distinction, one which I neither sought nor desired. Upon the continuance of that sentiment, and upon your wisdom and patriotism, I rely to direct and support me in the performance of the duties required at my hands.

We have changed the constituent parts, but not the system of government. The Constitution framed by our fathers is that of these Confederate

States. In their exposition of it, and in the judicial construction it has received, we have a light which reveals its true meaning.

Thus instructed as to the true meaning and just interpretation of that instrument, and ever remembering that all offices are but trusts held for the people, and that powers delegated are to be strictly construed, I will hope by due diligence in the performance of my duties, though I may disappoint your expectations, yet to retain, when retiring, something of the good will and confidence which welcome my entrance into office.

It is joyous in the midst of perilous times to look around upon a people united in heart, where one purpose of high resolve animates and actuates the whole; where the sacrifices to be made are not weighted in the balance against honor and right and liberty and equality. Obstacles may retard, but they cannot long prevent, the progress of a movement sanctified by its justice and sustained by a virtuous people. Reverently let us invoke the God of our fathers to guide and protect us in our efforts to perpetuate the principles which by his blessing they were able to vindicate, establish, and transmit to their posterity. With the continuance of his favor ever gratefully acknowledged, we may hopefully look forward to success, to peace, and to prosperity.

NOTES

1. "South Carolina Declaration of Secession," _The Annals of America_, vol. 9, 1858–1865 (Chicago: Encyclopaedia Britannica, Inc.), 209.

2. Carl Degler, _Place over Time: The Continuity of Southern Distinctiveness_ (Baton Rouge: Louisiana State University Press, 1977), 96–97. See also, James C. Cobb, _The Most Southern Place on Earth: The Mississippi Delta and the Roots of Regional Identity_ (New York: Oxford University Press, 1992), 31, where he argues that many planters in the overwhelmingly black Mississippi delta had misgivings about leaving the Union and would have preferred to gain the Constitutional guarantees they sought within the Union.

3. Clement Eaton calls Yancey the "outstanding fire eater of the South" in _A History of the Old South_ (New York: Macmillan, 1949), 534. Robert T. Oliver in _History of Public Speaking in America_ (Boston: Allyn and Bacon, 1965), 203, described Yancey as the "apostle of Disunion."

4. Hal W. Fulmer, "William Lowndes Yancey," in _American Orators before 1900, Critical Studies and Sources_, Bernard K. Duffy and Halford R. Ryan, eds. (New York: Greenwood Press, 1987), 400–401.

5. Delivered in Washington, D.C., September 21, 1860. Text in _Library of Southern Literature_, vol. 13, Edwin A. Alderman and Joel Chandler Harris, eds. (New Orleans: The Martin & Hoyt Company, 1910), 6033–6039.

6. Biographical studies of Palmer are few and brief; most of this biographical sketch is from two sources: "Benjamin Morgan Palmer," in _Dictionary of American Religious Biography_, 2nd ed., Henry Warner Bowden, ed. (Westport, CT: Greenwood Press, 1993), 413–414; and Charles F. Arrowood, "Benjamin Morgan Palmer," in _Dictionary of American Biography_, vol. XIV, Dumas Malone, ed. (New York: Charles Scribner's Sons, 1924), 175–176.

7. Quoted in Thomas Cary Johnson, *The Life and Letters of Benjamin Morgan Palmer* (Richmond, VA: Presbyterian Committee of Publication, 1906), 219.

8. Delivered in the First Presbyterian Church, New Orleans, Louisiana, Thursday, November 29, 1860 (New Orleans: True Witness and Sentinel, 1860).

9. The ceremonies connected with the first inauguration of President Davis were held in front of the Capitol at Montgomery, Alabama. The speech text is found in *Jefferson Davis, Constitutionalist; His Letters, Papers and Speeches*, vol. V, Dunbar Roland, ed. (Jackson: Mississippi Department of Archives and History, 1923), 49–53.

FOR FURTHER READING

Freehling, William W. *The Road to Disunion: Secessionists at Bay, 1776–1854.* New York: Oxford University Press, 1990.

McPherson, James M. *Battle Cry of Freedom: The Civil War Era.* New York: Oxford University Press, 1988.

Rable, George C. *The Confederate Republic: A Revolution Against Politics.* Chapel Hill: The University of North Carolina Press, 1994.

Roland, Charles P. *An American Iliad: The Story of the Civil War.* Lexington: University Press of Kentucky, 1991.

William Lowndes Yancey

Mitchell, Rexford S. "William L. Yancey." In *A History and Criticism of American Public Address*, vol. 2, William N. Brigance, ed. New York: McGraw-Hill, 1943.

Perritt, H. Hardy. "The Fire-Eaters." In *Oratory in the Old South, 1828–1860*, Waldo W. Braden, ed. Baton Rouge: Louisiana State University Press, 1970, 234–257.

Walther, Eric H. "We Shall Fire the Southern Heart: William Lowndes Yancey." In *The Fire Eaters*. Baton Rouge: Louisiana State University Press, 1992, 48–82.

Benjamin Morgan Palmer

Eubank, Wayne C., "Benjamin Morgan Palmer's Thanksgiving Sermon, 1860." In *Antislavery and Disunion, 1858–1861: Studies in the Rhetoric of Compromise and Conflict*, J. Jeffery Auer, ed. New York: Harper and Row, 1963, 291–309.

Johnson, Thomas Cary, "Benjamin Morgan Palmer." In *Library of Southern Literature*, vol. IX, Edwin A. Alderman and Joel Chandler Harris, eds. New Orleans: The Martin & Hoyt Company, 1908, 3907–3913.

Jefferson Davis

Davis, William C. *Jefferson Davis: The Man and His Hour.* New York: HarperCollins, 1991.

Dorgan, Howard. "Jefferson Davis." In *American Orators before 1900, Critical Studies and Sources*, Bernard K. Duffy and Halford R. Ryan, eds. New York: Greenwood Press, 1987, 113–119.

Towns, Stuart. " 'To Preserve the Traditions of Our Fathers': The Post-War Speaking Career of Jefferson Davis." *The Journal of Mississippi History* 52 (May 1990), 111–124.

William Pinkney. Courtesy of Library of Congress Prints and Photographs Division. LC-USZ 62-10446

William Smith. Courtesy of Library of Congress Prints and Photographs Division. LC 7277A1 My 7 42

John C. Calhoun. Courtesy of Library of Congress Prints and
Photographs Division. LC BH 82-5144

Robert A. Toombs. Courtesy of Library of Congress Prints and Photographs Division. LC-BH 826-1478

Jefferson Davis. Courtesy of Library of Congress Prints and Photographs Division. LC USZ 62-4852

Alfred Moore Waddell. Courtesy of Library of Congress Prints and Photographs Division. LC BH 832-416

Benjamin Harvey Hill. Courtesy of Library of Congress Prints and Photographs Division. LC BH 826-3691

Lucius Quintus Cincinnatus Lamar. Courtesy of Library of Congress Prints and Photographs Division. LC-USZ62-9441

Henry Woodfin Grady. Courtesy of Library of Congress Prints and Photographs Division. LC USZ 62-93574

John Brown Gordon. Courtesy of Library of Congress Prints and Photographs Division.
LC B 813-1986

Zebulon Baird Vance. Courtesy of Library of Congress Prints and Photographs Division. LC BH 826-32492

Atticus Greene Haygood. Courtesy of Atticus G. Haygood Papers, Special Collections, Robert W. Woodruff Library, Emory University.

CHAPTER 6

Reconstruction: The Bitterness Continues

The bitterness of the previous four decades of North-South hostility hardly ended at Appomattox Court House in April 1865. For the next dozen years, white southerners chaffed under the hardships of Reconstruction: military occupation; Negro, Carpetbag, Scalawag rule; and the slow recovery of the southern economy. Further, these real and perceived ills formed the basis for the next generation's—even the next century's—white southern perception of and attitude toward the North, the Republican Party, and the national government. It is impossible to understand the bitter and vociferous opposition to the 1960s Civil Rights movement, for example, without an understanding of the South's experience of Reconstruction and Redemption.

The region was devastated after the war. In a vivid summary of the economic and human losses, James McPherson writes:

> The war not only killed one-quarter of the Confederacy's white men of military age. It also killed two-fifths of southern livestock, wrecked half of the farm machinery, ruined thousands of miles of railroad, left scores of thousands of farms and plantations in weeds and disrepair, and destroyed the principal labor system on which southern productivity had been based. Two-thirds of assessed southern wealth vanished in the war. The wreckage of the southern economy caused the 1860s to become the decade of least economic growth in American history before the 1930s. It also produced a wrenching redistribution of wealth and income between North and South. As measured by the census, southern agricultural and manufacturing capital declined by 46 percent between 1860 and 1870, while northern capital increased by 50 percent. In 1860 the southern states had contained 30 percent of the national wealth; in 1870, only 12 percent. Per capita commodity output (including agriculture) was almost equal in North and South in 1860; by 1870 the North's per capita output was 56 percent greater.[1]

Not only did the South have to deal with this economic and social disaster brought about by the war, they had to endure Reconstruction. This twelve-year period during which the southern states were brought back into the Union under terms imposed by Congress, under the control of the Republican Party, was difficult for the defeated region. White southerners for years remembered vividly the desolation left by Sherman's March to the Sea through Georgia and South Carolina, the post-war treatment of Jefferson Davis as a prisoner, the presence of Negro troops in the region after the war, and the whites who came south to teach and otherwise upgrade the lives of the freed Negro and to fill the political vacuum left by the former Confederate governments.[2]

Feelings ran high in the South long after Appomattox. Eliza Frances Andrews of Washington, Georgia, wrote of a typical emotional response toward the North: "Since the Yankees have treated us so abominably, burning and plundering our country and bringing a gang of Negro soldiers here to insult us, I don't see how anybody can tolerate the sight of their odious old flag again."[3]

It must be understood, however, that this era, while devastating to the southern political and cultural spirit, was not altogether the unmitigated horror of the Reconstruction myth, as constructed by a generation of white southerners, and nourished and believed by another half-century of whites.

The legends that grew up about Reconstruction had whites, North and South, believing that after the Reconstruction Act of 1867, which created five military districts under the control of Union generals and their troops, the South was dominated by state governments run by uneducated blacks, unscrupulous Carpetbaggers (northerners who came South after the War), and disloyal Scalawags (primarily men who had been southern Unionists before and during the War). These governments, according to the legend, bankrupted their states, enriched their leaders' pockets with illegal gain, and drove a wedge between southern whites and their former slaves.

As most legends go, there were elements of truth in this one as well. Military rule ended, however, in most of the southern states in 1868 and in all states by 1870. Troops were not fully withdrawn from Florida, Louisiana, and South Carolina until the compromises of 1877, but the military did not control those three states after 1870. Blacks served in state governments, but only in South Carolina and Louisiana were they in the majority in the state legislature and most served only at the local level. Only a handful went to Congress, two to the Senate, and none served as a governor.

Congress, especially the Radical Republicans, feared that the gains made for the southern blacks were about to be wiped out by the white southerner's insistence on establishing and maintaining at all costs a sharp dividing line between the races. State after state across the region in 1865–1866 enacted harsh "black codes" which almost had the effect of re-enslaving Negroes. Southern blacks were prevented from testifying against whites, holding political office, or voting, and subjected to a form of peonage which tied them in many places back to the plantation or locality where they had been slaves.

In reaction to these harsh laws, Congress enacted the Fourteenth Amendment which guaranteed equal protection of the laws to all Americans and created military districts under Northern generals and troops—some black—to administer the states prior to their readmission to the Union. For a state to be readmitted, there had to be a government in place that would ratify the Fourteenth Amendment. All southern states capitulated and their reconstruction governments were in operation by 1868. These governments wrote more democratic state constitutions, established public schools, began to rebuild the crushed economy, and expanded social services for the newly freed Negro and the poorer whites.[4]

In reaction to this Republican rule, especially allowing the Negro to vote, the white South retaliated with a wave of violence in the late 1860s and early 1870s. Led by the Ku Klux Klan, violence and the threat of violence swept the region as whites attempted to intimidate blacks and keep them "in their place." Congress responded with a series of Enforcement Acts in 1870 and 1871. These acts gave the federal government jurisdiction over election supervisors appointed by federal courts.

It was not many years, however, before the Republicans tired of their crusade to uplift and protect the southern Negro, and it was not long before conservative white leadership filled that vacuum. These new administrations were called "Redeemer" governments and their leaders "Redeemers," as they supposedly "redeemed" the South from black rule and northern domination and returned the region to honest and responsible government. There was considerable religious meaning in this word, as southerners certainly saw the change of governments in terms of being able to start anew with southern whites back in control and in their rightful place of political leadership. The South had, in effect, been "born again."

In truth, corruption and fraud did not end with the accession of redeemers, and certainly the lot of the Negro was made much worse over the next few decades. Tennessee, North Carolina, and Virginia underwent redemption in 1870, followed by Georgia the next year. Alabama, Arkansas, and Texas were redeemed in 1874. Mississippi was redeemed over a two year period in 1875–1876, and the final three states, Florida, Louisiana, and South Carolina were redeemed in 1877.

ALFRED MOORE WADDELL

Alfred M. Waddell was one of the first of the redeemers seated in Congress. North Carolina, his home state, rejoined the Union in 1870, and Waddell was elected to the House of Representatives soon thereafter. His constituents reelected him in 1872, 1874, and 1876.

Born in Hillsboro, North Carolina, on September 16, 1834, Waddell graduated from the University of North Carolina in 1853 and began practicing law in Wilmington in 1855. Prior to the war, he developed strong Unionist feelings, opposed secession, and even edited a unionist newspaper. With the onset of war, he served in the Confederate Army as a lieutenant colonel in the North Carolina cavalry. After the war, Waddell supported limited negro suffrage, a position that eventually cost him his Congressional seat in 1878. Throughout his career, he was a popular ceremonial speaker, and many organizations called on him for speaking appearances over a wide-ranging territory. After a bloody race riot in Wilmington in 1898, he was elected mayor and helped return the city to peace and quiet. He served as mayor until 1905. Waddell died in Wilmington on March 17, 1912.[5]

In this speech to Congress, Waddell opposes the bill, passed three weeks later, called the Ku Klux Act. This bill makes it a federal crime to conspire or wear a disguise for the purpose of depriving anyone of the legal protection of the law. Federal troops were later sent to South Carolina and President Grant took the extraordinary step of suspending the writ of habeas corpus in several South Carolina counties due to the violence there. Waddell's major theme is that this act unnecessarily give dangerous power to the president. In support of this claim, the North Carolinian paints the classic verbal picture of the South's perceptions about reconstruction and its impact on the region and his state.

ENFORCEMENT OF THE FOURTEENTH AMENDMENT[6]

Mr. Speaker, it ought not to operate to the prejudice of the State most deeply interested in the legislation contemplated here that her Representatives have deferred to others and have yielded to them all the earlier hours of this debate. Such a course was consonant with our feelings, and I think somewhat characteristic. It is impossible, even in the hour allowed by the rule, for any opponent of this bill to do justice either to the subject or to himself. I shall not discuss it in its constitutional aspects, but I ask the indulgence of the House for a few moments while I comment upon the alleged causes which are supposed to justify it, particularly as touching my own State. In its effects the bill is ostensibly to be of universal application, but the debate has developed the fact, if it was not already known, that it is merely a party scheme, the operation of which is intended to be confused to that portion of the country which gentlemen take particular pleasure in designating as "the insurrectionary States." It is an indictment against them, founded upon voluminous hearsay testimony, and the prosecutors have, unfortunately, I think, for the peace of the country, presented their arguments to the House, not in the calm spirit which should characterize the discussion of a subject so vast and far-reaching, but rather in the temper of the heated partisan.

Now, sir, I shall not follow this example. I am not of that political temperament and never was, and it is gratifying to me to feel that there are gentlemen on the other side who know the fact. My friend, the honorable gentleman from Pennsylvania to whose manly and generous conduct I am chiefly indebted to for my prompt admission to the seat I occupy, a friendly service for which I wish to make this public acknowledgement, knows that ever since the termination of the late war my efforts have been directed to the promotion of peace, justice, and good order in my native State; he knows that as early as the summer of 1865, before the Government had taken any step toward the enfranchisement of the race of which he is the eloquent champion, and when the majority of those who are now his political associates were afraid to advocate that measure I, alone and in the face of a public opinion of which even he had scarcely a just appreciation, made a public speech in its favor. For this reason I have hoped that what I might say in regard to the condition of affairs in North Carolina would be accepted by him and others as at least free from misrepresentation and undue prejudice....

I have voted, Mr. Speaker, on every occasion for an investigation into these alleged outrages in my State, not because I believed in the necessity or in the power of Congress to send out such an itinerant grand jury, but because I was unwilling to give the slightest ground for the suspicion that either I or my constituents were averse to the most rigid investigation which could be instituted into the terrible crimes which are laid at our doors; and after I was appointed on the committee of thirteen, I tried, on three different occasions, to get the floor in order that I might ask to be excused from serving, because I desired to see that committee composed exclusively of gentlemen from the northern States. I was willing for an investigation, because I am satisfied that, when the whole truth is known, the people of the North will begin to understand some of the grievous burdens which the people of North Carolina have been compelled to bear, and which they have borne in a manner that justifies me in saying that if inexhaustible patience be an attribute of God, they have exhibited at least one Divine quality.

I do not deny that crimes have been committed in North Carolina. I do not deny that in a small portion of the State bands of disguised men have violated the criminal laws of the State. Although without personal knowledge on the subject, the published testimony satisfies me that such has been the case, just as I am satisfied that similar outrages have occurred, and are daily occurring, in the States of the North and Northwest—the only difference being that the Ku Klux Klan of the South wore disguises, which prevented recognition and consequent punishment, while those of the North commit their crimes undisguised and in open day. . . .

But while I admit that crimes have been committed and that from various causes the perpetrators of them have escaped punishment, I do most emphatically deny that the people, or any considerable portion of them, countenance or encourage the wrong-doers. I deny that there has been or is now any resistance to the execution of the laws, State or Federal. I deny that the property or lives of loyal men (which too often means licensed thieves) are not safe down there; and I assert that the humblest officer in the State, even though he be a negro constable, so black that charcoal would make a white mark on him, can go in safety, alone, and at midnight, and arrest the best citizen of the State.

Admitting all that can justify and truthfully be said against her people, I assert that in no State of this Union is there now or has there been less crime of any kind than in the State of North Carolina. I assert that a more quiet, peaceable, and law-abiding people than her citizens do not live on earth, not even excepting that favored land which was blessed by the nativity and now rejoices in the existence of the gentleman from Massachusetts. Still they have been pilloried before the world as a decivilized community, in which social chaos prevailed; the State has been represented as one in which the genius of murder held high carnival, as an accursed land of outlaws and assassins, in which there was no protection for life, liberty, or property, and upon which the iron hand of military power must be laid to reduce it to order and peace!

We, her Representatives on this floor, have sat quietly and listened to the denunciations of our people by gentlemen who have no other acquaintance with them than such as they have gathered from their slanderers and traducers, until we would have been lost in amazement except for the fact that no style of argument other than that of generosity can surprise us. We have no bitter words to say to gentlemen on the other side while defending our State and our people. They have worn the collar six long, weary years in silence and sorrow, and if they had not been sustained by the deathless spirit of true heroism and love of liberty they would have utterly succumbed to their fate. They must still submit to whatever legislation is provided for them; but, although reduced to a condition of political degradation heretofore unknown in this country, although smitten by poverty, plundered and oppressed, they still struggle manfully on, clinging to the hope that their countrymen will yet do them justice, and restore to them their rights.

I will describe to you in a few words the true condition of the people of North Carolina after the war, and their experience during the past five years of Republican rule, while under the absolute control of "the party of progress and great moral ideas," and I will say that at the outset that no party in the history of this country ever had such an opportunity to perpetuate its power by intrenching itself behind impregnable lines, and no party ever so utterly wasted its opportunities and so covered itself with disgrace. Coming out of the great struggle like a strong man exhausted by fever, the State lay prostrate and helpless. I shall not insult the intelligence of the House by dwelling on the evils attending the annihilation of the entire labor system of a country at a single blow, nor shall I harrow my own feelings by a recital of the sufferings and humiliation to which our people were subjected. Suffice it to say that they presented a condition which demanded, if not the experiment of active charity, at least the privilege of exemption from further molestation. They had complied with all that was required of them by the Government, and only desired to rebuild, as best they might, their waste places. The public debt of the State, principal and interest, was about seventeen million dollars, an immense sum to people so impoverished as they were.

Well sir, without going further into details, this was our condition when "the party of great moral ideas" took possession. They proclaimed their intention to be, while elevating the colored race, to inaugurate a new era of reform in all other respects—an enterprise, for his participation in which, one of the new legislators declared that his name would descend to "de arkives of grabity," a region which the plummet of philology has, I believe, never yet explored.

They took charge of all the departments of the State government, and after multiplying officers *ad infinitum* under a constitution entirely new to the people; after wiping out the judicial system which had become venerable, and to which the people were attached, even descending in a spirit of petty revenge to the business of changing the names of localities offensively; after destroying the State University without substituting anything in its stead, and after many similar preliminaries, they increased the State debt at a single bound to the comfortable figure of $35,000,000 for the purpose of building railroads and developing resources generally—a legislative feat which was accomplished by the judicious expenditure of $200,000 by a loyal gentleman in the establishment of a free bar-room in the capitol, with peanuts thrown in. Ten millions of this debt having been declared unconstitutional by the supreme court, there was still left and now stands a debt of $25,000,000. No railroad has been built, and the money was used by a loyal gentleman named Littlefield, from Pennsylvania, and an enterprising native named Swepson, partly I believe in buying out the State of Florida from a gentleman from Wisconsin.

Loyal Leagues had been organized throughout the State, in which the colored population were welded together in solid mass under oath in opposition to the native whites, and the practical teaching of these organizations was that the latter must be kept down. The crop thus sowed began to come up in crimes, the perpetrators of which sometimes escaped detection, and sometimes were convicted only to be pardoned and turned loose on society again.

I said a few moments ago that I had no personal knowledge of any of these outrages, but I will qualify that expression. In the practice of my profession I was present in court once when a very bad case was testified to. The prosecuting witness, who was the victim, was a poor colored man, who exhibited his scars and told the pitiful story of how, while sitting by his humble hearth, in the twilight of an autumn evening, he had been seized, conducted from his house to the bushes, and there cruelly flogged by three of his neighbors. *They were colored neighbors*, and in answer to his demand why he was so outraged, they told him that he had stayed at home on the day of election, instead of going and voting the Republican ticket. They admitted, as I was informed, before the committing magistrate that they had done the deed under instructions from the chief of the Loyal League for that county. Those men were tried by a white jury, sentenced by a Democratic judge to the penitentiary, and duly pardoned out by the Republican Governor, Mr. Holden.

Similar occurrences took place in other parts of the State, except that generally it was a white man's property burned up or his wife or daughter insulted; and, as might have been expected, retaliation sometimes occurred, and then it was that these deplorable crimes were committed, crimes which I denounce as severely as any man in the United States; crimes which I am happy to know no longer take place in North Carolina, and which have never been countenanced, so far as I know, by any decent man in the State.

I have not told the hundredth part of the story. I have said nothing about the imbecile, drunken, and (in at least one case) corrupt judges who have been foisted on those people, and who now grease the bench, and soil the ermine once wore by a pure and learned judiciary. I have not even mentioned the acts of Governor Holden in importing a band of cutthroats, under Kirk and Bergen, into the State, and the tortures inflicted upon the aged, distinguished, and unoffending citizens, for which he has been impeached, convicted, and removed from office. I will not dwell on these things, for I wish to avoid the utterance of any intemperate language, or to give expression even to the righteous indignation which their remembrance excites.

I will allude to one matter, and in doing so I hope I shall carefully regard the proprieties of this occasion. It has been asserted that the perpetrators of these cowardly crimes were confederate soldiers, who might be tried by drum-head court-martial for violation of their parole and shot. Mr. Speaker, the only evidence of that fact is the statement of a self-confessed perjurer, that he "supposed" it was so, because almost every man in the country had been in the army. Sir, this is the most cruel slander which has yet been hurled against a gallant people. Whatever the opinion entertained in regard to the criminality of the southern people in waging war by those who received a different political education, I spit upon and the world will laugh to scorn the allegation that the soldiers who fought four years against overwhelming odds and so brilliantly illustrated the martial qualities of the American people are a set of skulking and cowardly assassins. No, sir, whatever else you may say about them, you cannot utter that libel without making yourself ridiculous, and no one of the thousands of gallant Federal soldiers who met them when this continent shook beneath the thunder of artillery and the tread of armies will ever so disgrace himself and dishonor his own comrades as to speak that slanderous word. They were crushed, sir, and returned with bleeding hearts and tattered garments to desolated homes, but, thank God, sir, they kept their plighted faith, and their honor is unstained.

Now, Mr. Speaker, to return to the bill under consideration, I wish to utter my solemn protest against its passage, not merely because it will affect the people whom I represent, but as an American citizen, who, regardless of your incredulity, still loves his country and earnestly desires to promote her glory and prosperity.

If the people of the South were inspired by a sentiment of revenge toward their countrymen, and if, like Samson of old, they wished to involve the whole American people with themselves in a common ruin, I know no way in which that sentiment could be more swiftly and surely gratified than by the passage of this bill. Pass it and you tear down the last column on which rests the still fair but disfigured temple of American liberty. Pass it, and by congressional enactment you will have established an absolute despotism, not over the South alone, but over the whole country. Pass it, and the whole power of this Government will be in the hands of one, whose hands never relax their grasp on anything that is put to them. And then you will see that of which you have now but a glimpse; then you will indeed see him "instruct his princes after his will and teach his Senators"—not to oppose his schemes of aggrandizement.

If gentlemen will not listen to the protest of the people of the southern States against this rank usurpation, because they are accustomed to disregard appeals from that quarter, let them at least, for their own sake and that of their children, whose rights and liberties are imperiled, cease this violent, unconstitutional, and revolutionary legislation, which can bring only evil upon the country, the whole country; for the man must be a stark fool who cannot see that, however strong the disposition to limit the operation of this bill to the southern States, it will inevitably and inexorably extend its deadly influence over the whole land.

I feel, Mr. Speaker, the extraordinary circumstances by which I and my southern colleagues find ourselves surrounded on this occasion. I feel that I stand here to-day a messenger, sent back by those who have passed through the bitter waters of a Dead sea, to warn their more fortunate brethren who have not yet reached its shores of what awaits them in its passage, and to arrest their footsteps. It will be well with them if they heed the warning. But if they do not, if they will persist in their blind march into the region of political darkness and death, *we* will at least have the satisfaction of knowing that the calamities which surely await them are in no wise chargeable to us.

I do not doubt that some gentlemen on the other side really believe all the horrible stories which have been told them in regard to the condition of affairs in North Carolina and throughout the South, and are sincerely concerned about it. It is, perhaps, natural for those who have been taught from childhood to regard the people of that portion of the country as semi-barbarians, if not absolutely *hostes humani generis*, to lend a willing ear to any discreditable report concerning them. It is not, perhaps, extravagant to say that, unconsciously it may be, they are just the least bit prejudiced on this subject. But I accord to them, notwithstanding this, a willingness, if not a desire, to do justice even to us.

Do those gentlemen ever study the situation of our people by the light of history and the experience of other nations? With *their* estimate of southern character, ought they not to have expected even worse things during the past six years than their own credulity has been able to realize? When general demoralization accompanied victory and unlimited prosperity for them, did they expect defeat, humiliation, and bankruptcy to bring an elysium of peace, order, and contentment to us? With capital all gone, labor completely disorganized, and the whole land in tears, did they expect unbroken quiet to reign and the shattered wheels of local government to turn smoothly, though in the hands of ignorance and vice?

And yet, sir, had not the recuperative energy of those people been the wonder of our day? Is not the rapidity of their progress toward prosperity, in spite of the paralyzing legislation to which they have been subjected, and the numberless evils with which they have been afflicted, unparalleled in the history of the world? Is not the single fact that the cotton crop of this past year is the largest but one which was ever raised, and the additional fact that there has been an equal development of the other industries of the country, an overwhelming argument to disprove the existence of such a state of things as had been represented here? Ay, sir; no amount of hearsay testimony given by interested witnesses as to the prevalence of general disorder throughout the South can stand a moment against such facts as these. They are the most unerring witnesses that can be found, and they are *unimpeached*.

Now, Mr. Speaker, I shall bring my remarks to a close, and in doing so I desire to address myself to gentlemen who contemplate voting for this measure. The people of those States which gentlemen seem to take the pleasure in designating as "the States lately in rebellion," people whom gentlemen still continue to denominate "rebels" in this sixth year of peace, are quite accustomed to military rule, the suspense of the writ of *habeas corpus*, and the like. It is no new thing to them. Bad and disgraceful as it is to American civilization, it is better than some of the so-called civil governments which have existed in those States. If your eagerness to secure the blessings of that kind of government is so great that you cannot be happy until it is established everywhere throughout the country, perhaps, those of us who have experienced those blessings ought not to be so selfish as to oppose your equal participation in them. It is barely possible, after all, that under the influence of a catholic spirit the southern people may rejoice with you in the accomplishment of your purpose. But I serve notice on you now and here, before the American people, that when your purpose is accomplished, when by a reckless violation of the Constitution of your country, in order to carry elections and to maintain a party in power, you shall have delivered over your constituents, bound hand and foot, to the mercy of a military despot, you cannot turn your frightened gaze toward those upon whom you have so long been accustomed to lay your burdens, and pile upon their bowed heads this last load of crime and folly.

BENJAMIN HARVEY HILL

Ben Hill, another southerner who opposed secession, was born in Jasper County, Georgia, on September 14, 1823. He graduated with honors from the University of Georgia, and after studying law he was admitted to the bar in 1845. He went through the ranks of lawyer, state representative (1851–1852), and state senator (1859–1860), before serving as a Unionist delegate to the state secession convention in 1861. Later a member of the Provisional Confederate Congress, Hill continued serving in the Confederate Congress and Senate throughout the War. Immediately following the War, Union forces imprisoned him briefly during May and June 1865. After his release, he returned to the practice of law, and was vocal and active in Georgia politics after 1867. Georgia voters sent Hill to the U.S. House of Representatives in 1875, and to the Senate in 1877 where he served until he died of cancer in 1882.[7]

Speaking to a political rally in Atlanta, Hill's speech sounds a tone of reconciliation to the North, but at the same time, defends the South and its perception of the nature of the Constitution and the Union. He places the blame for the problems the South perceives squarely on the political figures who seek to hold their power in Washington: the Radical Republicans who control Congress.

SPEECH DELIVERED IN ATLANTA[8]

Ladies, Friends, and Fellow-citizens: It would be utterly vain for me to attempt to find language to express my appreciation of this greeting, and I shall not make the effort. I am very far, however, from appropriating it as only a compliment to myself. I accept the demonstration as evidence of the interest which the people are very naturally feeling in the great issues which are soon to break, in all their force, upon the country. . . .

The theory that "the conqueror has a right to prescribe terms to the conquered" has no application whatever to the Federal Government and the States composing it. It is a provision only of the laws of nations, and even there has only a limited application. If the United States conquered Mexico, the conqueror could prescribe certain terms to the conquered. But the United States have no right, authority, or power under the Constitution, to conquer one of their own States. That would be to conquer part of themselves. If they conquer one State, they can conquer all the States; that is, conquer themselves, and thus destroy their own existence as well as authority. If the government can use force on a State at all, it can only do so to enforce its Constitutional authority and no more. The late war was not waged to conquer States. It was waged to preserve the Constitutional authority of the

Union, and the result cannot legitimately exceed both the authority and the purpose. It is to this great heresy—the conqueror can prescribe terms for the conquered—we owe all the troubles of the past ten years. It has cursed the country more than did secession and war. It has been the fountain of unlimited powers in the Federal Government and of immeasurable wrongs upon the people. The assertion and denial of this heresy constitutes the great fundamental issue between the Radical and Democratic parties, and the final determination of that issue must settle the question whether we shall have a central government of unlimited or limited powers....

Passing, then, from the mere party and personal views that the canvass has suggested, I beg to submit to you calmly and dispassionately, in a conversational style, a few thoughts as to the future. The one great work of statesmanship in this generation, in this country, is to make peace between the Northern and Southern people. Without that, nothing else valuable can be accomplished. With that, everything that is good will follow. How is that peace to be made? Mark my language, to make peace between the peoples of the respective sections. He is a stupid visionary who supposes he can ever make peace between the politicians of the two sections. These politicians have been the disturbers of the peace for twenty years. They have acquired power by reason of their success in keeping the peace disturbed, and their only hope of continuing in power is to continue to be disturbers of that peace. The people must be reached, the people of the North and of the South, and they must be reached in such a manner as to show them that they have a common interest and ought to have a common feeling.

Well, it is a very puzzling question at first view, but, my friends, it is like most every other great problem, it is at last solved by a very simple process, very simple. What must be the basis of peace? There can be but one basis of permanent peace between the North and the South. What is it? It is simple. Simply, only a return by the North and by the South, by the East and by the West, by States and by individuals to the common Constitution. The great trouble in the past has been that some of our Southern friends have attempted to save the Constitution by destroying the Union. The great trouble with the Northern people is that they have attempted to save the Union by destroying the Constitution. The remedy for both grievances is simply for the North and the South to return to the Constitution and the Union as the only guarantee of liberty, and the only hope of peace, while they are one and inseparable. I do not hesitate, therefore, to say to you, that when, upon taking my seat in Congress, I shall take the oath to support the Constitution of the country, I shall take that oath without mental reservation, and I shall keep it without partiality or prejudice. I shall concede to Massachusetts everything that I claim for Georgia, and I shall claim for Georgia everything I concede to Massachusetts. The man who spins cotton in New England, will be as much my fellow-citizen as the man who grows cotton in Georgia. The man who cuts ice in Massachusetts will be as much entitled to my protection as the man who gathers oranges in Florida. I shall realize the great fact that Massachusetts and Georgia are parties to the same Union, under the same Constitution, with exactly the same rights and bound exactly by the same obligations. And I shall feel, and I shall delight to feel, that this whole country, from sea to sea and from the Lakes to the Gulf, is *my* country, and there is not a foot of its soil I would desecrate nor a being in it whose rights I would impair. . . .

Secession, coercion, Reconstruction, are all over; the records are made up! Who was right and who was wrong, we will remit to posterity, as the only impartial judge, to determine. Of course, in my judgment, when that great trial shall come, the South will have nothing to fear. I believe that when the future historian, reviewing the terrible scenes of the last fifteen years, shall come to write his impartial judgment, he will say that, while there is much in the misfortunes of the South to regret, there is nothing in her history of which to be ashamed.

Why is it that we cannot make peace? Why is it that the intelligence of the people North and South is not equal to the task of saying we let by-gones be by-gones? Why can we not let the past go, and unite our hands and our hearts for the purpose of repairing the wrongs done, and make him the greatest hero who shall do most to repair them? I repeat, these wrongs must stop, or peace is impossible. Of that there can be no doubt. Thieves must cease to be tax-gatherers. Usurpers must cease to be rulers. Louisiana must be unchained. Sunlight must be let in on the shadowed face of South Carolina. Arkansas must be free as Massachusetts. Georgia must be the political equal of New York. There must be no handcuffed sovereignty at the celebration of Liberty's Centennial! The heart can never be glad, save in hypocrisy; the lips can never cheer, save in mockery, while the limbs are fettered!

Fellow-citizens, what is in the way? Why is it that ten years after actual war has ceased the spirit of war still continues? There must be a cause—there must be a reason. Have we not sufficient intelligence to find that reason? Have we not sufficient patriotism to cure it when we find it? Fellow-citizens, the reason is plain. It is no use to struggle hard to find it. It is a reason founded in an unfortunate law of human nature, confirmed by every chapter of human experience. You may be astonished at its simplicity when I announce it. Why is it, I repeat, that the people of the North and the South, ten years after the war has ceased in fact, have kept up this war in spirit? The reason is simply this: The greed of power has absorbed and destroyed the love of country with those who administer the government. The men who, for the most part, have held high positions in the administration of the government acquired that power by virtue of the war—the passions of the war. Is it not natural, does not all history confirm it, that those who acquire what they desire by certain means are willing to continue those means that they may continue the result? And is it not true that almost everybody in power in the United States now, acquires that power by virtue of the passions of the war? Will anybody doubt that? Can anybody doubt it?

Can you expect men who owe all their greatness to strife, to passion, to mad war, to make peace? Can they cease to feed on that which alone gives them power? Does any intelligent man in America believe that the disfranchisement of white men, disabilities upon educated men, the robberies, oppressions, usurpations, and insults by the rule of carpet-bagism over a prostrate people were ever authorized and permitted by those in power at Washington, as measures of peace? Were they not all born of that passion which gave their authors power; and were they not adopted to keep up passion and to keep their authors in power? Who will say that measures which shame the civilization of the age were adopted as measures of peace?

Now, what is the remedy? It is plain. The people of the North must be made to see that all these harsh measures which have been adopted toward the South, under pretense that they were necessary to keep down rebels, were really adopted to keep up office-holders. And they must be made also to see that if these measures of passion and hate shall continue, they will, sooner or later, overthrow our common free institutions, as has always been the case in every free country where men have acquired power by virtue of the passions of civil wars.

Now, what I say is this, that we must, somehow or other, by some means get away from these politicians who are in power, acquired by the passions of the war, and seek to retain that power by continuing those passions. We must get at the minds of the Northern people, that they may apply the remedy. I believe they will do it. I have a faith that I have never yet abandoned, that, notwithstanding all the wrongs we have witnessed for the past fifteen years, the masses of the Northern people love liberty as well as we do. I believe, if we can ever get to the minds of the Northern people, you will find that they will exhaust every effort to preserve the Constitutional character of this government. I believe they have acquiesced in, rather than approved Reconstruction. I believe that they submitted to, rather than justified, all those harsh measures against the South, because we have been powerless to reach their minds. Their leaders have had success in making the great masses of the Northern people believe that these measures were necessary to keep down another rebellion; and I believe it is true that while the Northern people love liberty, and love the Constitution of the country, and desire to preserve both, they would destroy the Constitution and everything else to keep down another rebellion! Now, then, the Northern mind must be reached, and that Northern mind must be convinced that we of the South sincerely and truly desire to live in the Union according to the Constitution, and we can fearlessly say, the South never was unwilling to live in the Union according to the Constitution.

Without reopening the causes of our secession, I will say that history will abundantly justify the proposition that the South left the Union with regret, and only because she was made to believe the North would not adhere to the Constitution. I believe that every intelligent man will be compelled to sustain the proposition which I fearlessly proclaim, that the South never was an enemy to the Constitution! She was goaded and provoked into secession by what she believed were infidelities to the Constitution. But there is not a line, there is not a record in existence to justify the charge that any Southern State was ever faithless to the Union of our fathers under the Constitution. Now, the trouble North has been this: that they have lost sight of the Union as a principle. The real difference between the North and South I will express to you in a few words. The North, having full confidence in her physical power, has sought to preserve the Union as a fact, I expressed it on a former occasion. She has deified the Union as a fact. It never has occurred to the masses of the Northern people yet, that while they are deifying the Union as a fact, they may utterly destroy it as a principle. The Union as a principle may be a very different thing from the Union as a fact. The Union as a fact may be an empire; it may be a despotism; it may be a monarchy. While the Union as a principle is a Union under the Constitution and can only be republican in form. You see the difference. The North, confident in her physical power, and impassioned by the appeals of her politicians who sought to acquire power, have lost sight of the Union as a principle and have lost sight of the great danger that, in preserving the Union in form, they may convert what is a free republic into a consolidated empire. On the other hand, the Southern people not being physically strong, have studied the Union as a Union of principle, and looking to the principle of union as their safety, they came to regard the Union as desirable only because of the principles upon which it organized. Thus it has happened that, while the South has endeavored to preserve the principle at the expense of the fact, the North has been expecting to preserve the fact at the expense of the principle. The remedy is for patriots everywhere to unite the fact and the principle and keep them forever together. In that event we shall not only have union but also free government. We shall have a Constitutional government and a Constitutional Union. And this much I say: If the North will covenant that the Union shall be Constitutional, the South will covenant that the Union shall be eternal.

Now does it not occur to you that such plain propositions as these, so well fortified by the unfortunate history of the country, leave a door open for reconciliation, for peace, permanent peace? It does occur to me; I feel it. At the same time such have been the passions of the respective sections that there is but one way to get at the intelligence of the North upon this subject and remove the prejudices that have been created and the errors that have been fixed upon their minds. You cannot do it by such speeches as I am making here to-night, because they would not hear them. Their ears are closed to all *ex parte* speeches. You orators cannot do it by making speeches at the North, for the same reason.

It is chiefly through debates in Congress that the minds of the people must be reached. There all sides are heard, and the people will listen, and truths will sparkle from the conflict like fire from the collision of flint and steel. Errors will be corrected, prejudices allayed, suspicions quieted and measures of healing will be provided. The consuming flames of sectional passion will be quenched, and those who keep these passions alive by abusing the high trusts of power in order to keep themselves in place, will be rebuked by the patriotic people of all sections of the country.

It is because of the fearful responsibilities attaching to a seat in Congress that I have not been willing to seek the position. It is because I am unwilling to shrink from duty that I have been unwilling to refuse to accept the position if tendered by the people. In my opinion it is criminal to rush upon such responsibilities, and it is unpatriotic to avoid them.

What work is to be performed by the statesmen of this generation! In glory if successful, in shame if unsuccessful, there is no era in the history of free governments which can approach it in magnitude. A revolution, whose animating principle has been hate, must be arrested. States which have been belligerent, must be made accordant; sections which have been alienated must be reunited; people who have shed fraternal blood must be made friends, and a Union which has been maintained by force must be made again a Union of consent. If this great work can succeed; if a sincere peace, honorable to all parties, can be made, if the spirit of patriotism can be revived and made to animate all of our living as it animated all of our ancestors to mutual glory and common weal, then the history of the human race can furnish no parallel to the wealth, and power, and grandeur which awaits the American people of the dawning century. But if this work shall fail; if this strife of section and spirit of hate shall continue; if those in power shall fan the flames of passion to keep themselves in place; if national statesmen shall still find pleasure in devising sectional wrongs, and the Federal Government shall still furnish troops to foment and sustain usurpations over States, then no pen can describe the horrors that await us. Free government will perish; disunion will come; disintegration will multiply; Punic and Peloponesian wars will rage; factions will rend; empires will divide up all sections and reduce to final slavery all the races of our country.

The Southern extremists dreamed they could destroy the Union without war. Alas, what a dream! And yet far more visionary are those Northern extremists who dream that the Constitution can be destroyed without war. The Constitution and the Union! Would that patriots North and South would wake up to the fact that these two are one. The life of the first is the only hope of the last. Together both will live; divided both must die. In their life are peace and freedom and glories, ever increasing and without end. In their death are strife and war and despotism, ever enslaving and without hope.

Fellow-citizens, I am charged with being ambitious. So I have been ambitious; but for what? To save the South from the abyss of secession; the Union from the horrors of war; liberty from the perils of sectional hate, and my own race from the infamy of self-degradation. I am ambitious; but for what? Simply to hold office? How I pity the poor creature who could think so. I live high above the man who could find a gratification of mere personal vanity in the fact of holding office. I am ambitious once more to see peace! Peace between the sections; peace between the States; peace between the races, and peace—fraternal peace—between those who love the Constitution and those who love the Union. And if, before I die, I can be permitted to see States accordant, sections reconciled, the rights of all our people preserved, with the honor of none tarnished or destroyed, and the rich legacy of free Constitutional government, bequeathed to us by our fathers, transmitted unimpaired to our children, I shall go to my grave with a comfort which the diadems of kings could not confer, and which the wealth and power of emperors could neither buy nor take away.

NOTES

1. James M. McPherson, *Battle Cry of Freedom: The Civil War Era* (New York: Oxford University Press, 1988), 818–819.

2. Clement Eaton, *The Waning of the Old South Civilization 1860s–1880s* (Athens: University of Georgia Press, 1968), 118–121.

3. Quoted in Alan Conway, *The Reconstruction of Georgia* (Minneapolis: University of Minnesota Press, 1966), 26.

4. Howard N. Rabinowitz, *The First New South, 1865–1920* (Arlington Heights, IL: Harlan Davidson, Inc., 1992), 75.

5. There is not a good biography of Alfred Waddell; he deserves a thorough study. The best available sources are a brief sketch in the *Dictionary of American Biography*, vol. XIX, Dumas Malone, ed. (New York: Charles Scribner's Sons, 1936), 300–301, and *The National Cyclopedia of American Biography*, vol. VIII (New York: James T. White and Co, 1924), 124–125.

6. Alfred M. Waddell, *Enforcement of Fourteenth Amendment*. Delivered in the U.S. House of Representatives, April 1, 1871 (Washington, D.C.: F. and J. Rives and Geo. A. Bailey, 1871).

7. Again, there is little good biographical work on Hill. The one full-length treatment is Haywood J. Pearce, *Benjamin H. Hill: Secession and Reconstruction* (Chicago: University of Chicago Press, 1928). A brief eulogistic treatment by Lucian Lamar Knight appears in *Library of Southern Literature*, vol. 6, Edwin A. Alderman and Joel C. Harris, eds. (New Orleans: The Martin & Hoyt Company, 1908), 2389–2394, and an even briefer eulogy in *The National Cyclopedia of American Biography*, vol. X, 194.

8. Delivered on May 12, 1875. Benjamin H. Hill, Jr., *Senator B. H. Hill, of Georgia, His Life, Speeches, and Writings* (Atlanta, GA: T.H.P. Bloodworth, 1893), 432–441.

FOR FURTHER READING

Foner, Eric and Olivia Mahoney. *America's Reconstruction: People and Politics after the Civil War*. New York: HarperCollins Publishers, 1995.

Stampp, Kenneth. *Era of Reconstruction, 1865–1877*. New York: Vintage Books, 1967.

Woodward, C. Vann. *Origins of the New South*. Baton Rouge: Louisiana State University Press, 1951.

———. *Reunion and Reaction: The Compromise of 1877 and the End of Reconstruction*. rev. ed. Garden City, NY: Doubleday Anchor Books, 1956.

CHAPTER 7

A New South Begins to Emerge: Reconciliation and Reunion

For years after the guns had cooled, many white southerners felt no interest nor desire to be reconciled to the victorious North. The decades of bitterness from the 1830s to the end of the War were nourished by the real as well as the perceived wrongs perpetrated upon the South by the Reconstruction governments. Perhaps these feelings are even captured a century-and-a-quarter later by the bumper stickers that can be found along the southern Interstate Highways: "Forgit, Hell No!" uttered by a rough-looking Confederate soldier caricature. A genuine southern hero, General Fitzhugh Lee wrote to a friend in Kentucky: "Don't care a damn to vote—am glad I have sinned beyond forgiveness . . . and in the language of the 'old rebel,' 'am glad I fit agin it, only wish I'd won; and aint gwine to ax no parding for anything I've done'."[1]

The mood in the North toward the "old rebel" was not magnanimous either. Writing from Cambridge, Massachusetts in July 1865, a Confederate veteran, George Daniel Farrar, wrote to his father, "There is no one here who has any feeling but the bitterest hostility towards any one who bears the name of Southerner."[2]

The defeat suffered by the South was total: military, economic, social, and perhaps, most important, spiritual. They had gone to war sure in the belief that right—even God Himself—was on their side. They limped away from the devastation bitter, uncertain, and unreconciled to their conqueror.

There were, however, some southerners who longed for national harmony and an end to the animosity and that number grew with each passing year. As C. Vann Woodward points out, "The South was American a long time before it was Southern in any self-conscious or distinctive way."[3] The Virginian, Patrick Henry, reminded his colleagues in the debates over the ratification of the national constitution, "I am a lover of the American Union. . . . The dissolution of the Union is most abhorrent to my mind."[4]

Three-quarters of a century later, many southerners had opposed the drive toward secession and many were dragged unwillingly to support the Confederacy after the War began. Robert E. Lee's agonizing decision to leave the Union with his native state is, perhaps, the best example. Ten years earlier, Sam Houston, the hero of Texas Independence, remarked in an 1850 Senate speech on the Clay Compromise measures: "What is our country? It is a nation composed of parts, East and West, South and North. It is an entirety. There are no fractions in it. It is a unit, and I trust it will so remain."[5] Houston was governor of Texas in 1861, demonstrating that there were many Texans who shared his Unionist sentiment.

Historian David M. Potter observed that "one of the truly diagnostic, perennial features in the life of the South has been the obsessive impulse of its people" to be both "Southerners and *Americans*." He goes on to say that "Southern loyalties to the Union were never really obliterated but rather were eclipsed by other loyalties with which, for a time, they conflicted."[6] For some of these southerners, it would only be a matter of time before they were able to express again their love of the Union. Two of the more famous expressions were by L.Q.C. Lamar as the Mississippi Congressman eulogized Senator Charles Sumner of Massachusetts and by Atlantan Henry W. Grady in his nationally known address in New York City on the New South.

LUCIUS QUINTUS CINCINNATUS LAMAR

Lucius Quintus Cincinnatus Lamar, a native Georgian, migrated to Mississippi early in his career. He taught at the University of Mississippi for a short while, returned to Georgia, practiced law and was elected to the Georgia State Legislature, before he went back to Mississippi in 1855. Two years later, he was elected to the United States House of Representatives. He remained in the House until Lincoln's election in 1860, when he resigned in order to participate in his state's secession convention in January, 1861. During the War, Lamar served briefly in the Confederate Army, but was soon appointed the Confederacy's Minister to Russia.

After the Civil War, Lamar was a professor and Dean of Law at the University of Mississippi before his election to the House of Representatives in 1872, and to the Senate in 1877. Lamar also served in President Grover Cleveland's cabinet as secretary of the interior. In 1886, Cleveland nominated him for the Supreme Court, and the Senate confirmed him in the following year. Lamar died on January 23, 1893, at Macon, Georgia.

The death of Charles Sumner, a Republican senator from Massachusetts, provided an opportunity for an early reconciliation message. Many southerners perceived Sumner, one of the hated Radical Republicans who had imposed the years of Reconstruction upon the South, as the devil himself. Southern images of Sumner were based not just on his Reconstruction leadership, however, as his career as a thorough-going abolitionist in the prewar years had created the southern perception. In one of the most dramatic scenes in the history of the United States Senate, Congressman Preston Brooks of South Carolina had attacked Sumner and beat him to the point that the Republican had to take an extended sabbatical from the Senate. His death in 1874 was doubtless welcomed by many of his former southern enemies. In writing about Lamar's eulogy on Sumner, Edward Mayes said of Sumner: "To the lot of Mr. Sumner almost beyond any other man it had fallen to antagonize all that the South stood for."[7] In his oration on Sumner, Lamar praises not only his subject, but also the North and northerners, and ends with his magnanimous plea: "My countrymen! *know* one another, and you will *love* one another."

EULOGY ON SUMNER[8]

Mr. Speaker: In rising to second the resolution just offered, I desire to add a few remarks which have occurred to me as appropriate to the occasion. I believe that they express a sentiment which pervades the hearts of all the people whose representatives are here assembled. Strange as, in looking back upon the past, the assertion may seem, impossible as it would have been ten years ago to make it, it is not the less true that to-day Mississippi regrets the death of Charles Sumner, and sincerely unites in paying honors to his memory. Not because of the splendor of his intellect, though in him was extinguished one of the brightest of the lights which have illustrated the councils of the government for nearly a quarter of a century; not because of the high culture, the elegant scholarship, and the varied learning which revealed themselves so clearly in all his public efforts as to justify the application to him of Johnson's felicitous expression, "He touched nothing which he did not adorn"; not this, though these are qualities by no means, it is to be feared, so common in public places as to make their disappearance, in even a single instance, a matter of indifference; but because of those peculiar and strongly marked moral traits of his character which gave the coloring to the whole tenor of his singularly dramatic public career; traits which made him for a long period to a large portion of his countrymen the object of as deep and passionate a hostility as to another he was one of enthusiastic admiration, and which are not the less the cause that now unites all these parties, ever so widely differing, in a common sorrow to-day over his lifeless remains.

It is of these high moral qualities which I wish to speak; for these have been the traits which in after years, as I have considered the successive acts and utterances of this remarkable man, fastened most strongly my attention, and impressed themselves most forcibly upon my imagination, my sensibilities, my heart. I leave to others to speak of his intellectual superiority, of those rare gifts with which nature had so lavishly endowed him, and of the power to use them which he had acquired by education. I say nothing of his vast and varied stores of historical knowledge, or of the wide extent of his reading in the elegant literature of ancient and modern times, or of his wonderful power of retaining what he had read, or of his readiness in drawing upon these fertile resources to illustrate his own arguments. I say nothing of his eloquence as an orator, of his skill as a logician, or of his powers of fascination in the unrestrained freedom of the social circle, which last it was my misfortune not to have experienced. These, indeed, were the qualities which gave him eminence not only in our country, but throughout the world; and which have made the name of Charles Sumner an integral part of our nation's glory. They were the qualities which gave to those moral traits of which I have spoken the power to impress themselves upon the history of the age and of civilization itself; and without which those traits, however intensely developed, would have exerted no influence beyond the personal circle immediately surrounding their possessor. More eloquent tongues than mine will do them justice. Let me speak of the characteristics which brought the illustrious Senator who has just passed away into direct and bitter antagonism for years with my own State and her sister States of the South.

Charles Sumner was born with an instinctive love of freedom, and was educated from his earliest infancy to the belief that freedom is the natural and indefensible right of every intelligent being having the outward form of man. In him, in fact, this creed seems to have been something more than a doctrine imbibed from teachers, or a result of education. To him it was a grand intuitive truth, inscribed in blazing letters upon the tablet of his inner consciousness, to deny which would have been for him to deny that he himself existed. And along with this all-controlling love of freedom he possessed a moral sensibility keenly intense and vivid, a conscientiousness which would never permit him to swerve by the breadth of a hair from what he pictured to himself as the path of duty. Thus were combined in him the characteristics which have in all ages given to religion her martyrs, and to patriotism her self-sacrificing heroes.

To a man thoroughly permeated and imbued with such a creed, and animated and constantly actuated by such a spirit of devotion, to behold a human being or a race of human beings restrained of their natural right to liberty, for no crime by him or them committed, was to feel all the belligerent instincts of his nature roused to combat. The fact was to him a wrong which no logic could justify. It mattered not how humble in the scale of rational existence the subject of this restraint might be, how dark his skin, or how dense his ignorance. Behind all that lay for him the great principle that liberty is the birthright of all humanity, and that every individual of every race who has a soul to save is entitled to the freedom which may enable him to work out his salvation. It mattered not that the slave might be contented with his lot; that his actual condition might be immeasurably more desirable than that from which it had transplanted him; that it gave him physical comfort, mental and moral elevation, and religious culture not possessed by his race in any other condition; that his bonds had not been placed upon his hands by the living generation; that the mixed social system of which he formed an element had been regarded by the fathers of the republic, and by the ablest statesmen who had risen up after them, as too complicated to be broken up without danger to society itself, or even to civilization; or, finally, that the actual state of things had been recognized and explicitly sanctioned by the very organic law of the republic. Weighty as these considerations might be, formidable as were the difficulties in the way of the practical enforcement of his great principle, he held none the less that it sooner or later be enforced, though institutions and constitutions should have to give way alike before it. But here let me do this great man the justice which, amid the excitement of the struggle between the sections—now past—I may have been disposed to deny him. In this fiery zeal, and this earnest warfare against the wrong, as he viewed it, there entered no enduring personal animosity toward the men whose lot it was to be born to the system which he denounced.

It has been the kindness of the sympathy which in these later years he has displayed toward the impoverished and suffering people of the Southern

States that has unveiled to me the generous and tender heart which beat beneath the bosom of the zealot, and has forced me to yield him the tribute of my respect—I might even say of my admiration. Nor in the manifestation of this has there been anything which a proud and sensitive people, smarting under a sense of recent discomfiture and present suffering, might not frankly accept, or which would give them just cause to suspect its sincerity. For though he raised his voice, as soon as he believed the momentous issues of this great military conflict were decided, in behalf of amnesty to the vanquished; and though he stood forward, ready to welcome back as brothers, and to reestablish in their rights as citizens, those whose valor had nearly riven asunder the Union which he loved; yet he always insisted that the most ample protection and the largest safeguards should be thrown around the liberties of the newly enfranchised African race. Though he knew very well that of his conquered fellow-citizens of the South by far the larger portion, even those who most heartily acquiesced in and desired the abolition of slavery, seriously questioned the expediency of investing, in a single day, and without any preliminary tutelage, so vast a body of inexperienced and uninstructed men with the full rights of freemen and voters, he would tolerate no halfway measures upon a point to him so vital.

Indeed, immediately after the war, while other minds were occupying themselves with different theories of reconstruction, he did not hesitate to impress most emphatically upon the administration, not only in public, but in the confidence of private intercourse, his uncompromising resolution to oppose to the last any and every scheme which should fail to provide the surest guarantees for the personal freedom and political rights of the race which he had undertaken to protect. Whether his measures to secure this result showed him to be a practical statesman or a theoretical enthusiast, is a question on which any decision we may pronounce to-day must await the inevitable revision of posterity. The spirit of magnanimity, therefore, which breathes in his utterances and manifests itself in all his acts affecting the South during the last two years of his life, was as evidently honest as it was grateful to the feelings of those toward whom it was displayed.

It was certainly a gracious act toward the South—though unhappily it jarred upon the sensibilities of the people at the other extreme of the Union, and estranged from him the great body of his political friends—to propose to erase from the banners of the national army the mementos of the bloody internecine struggle, which might be regarded as assailing the pride or wounding the sensibilities of the Southern people. That proposal will never be forgotten by that people so long as the name of Charles Sumner lives in the memory of man. But, while it touched the heart of the South, and elicited her profound gratitude, her people would not have asked of the North such an act of self-renunciation.

Conscious that they themselves were animated by devotion to constitutional liberty, and that the brightest pages of history are replete with evidence of the depth and sincerity of that devotion, they cannot but cherish the recollections of sacrifices endured, the battles fought, and the victories won in defense of their hapless cause. And respecting, as all true and brave men must respect, the martial spirit with which the men of the North vindicated the integrity of the Union, and their devotion to the principles of human freedom, they do not ask, they do not wish the North to strike the mementos of her heroism and victory from either records or monuments or battle flags. They would rather that both sections should gather up the glories won by each section: not envious, but proud of each other, and regard them a common heritage of American valor.

Let us hope that future generations, when they remember the deeds of heroism and devotion done on both sides, will speak not of Northern prowess and Southern courage, but of the heroism, fortitude, and courage of Americans in a war of ideas; a war in which each section signalized its consecration to the principles, as each understood them, of American liberty and of the constitution received from their fathers.

It was my misfortune, perhaps my fault, personally never to have known this eminent philanthropist and statesman. The impulse was often strong upon me to go to him and offer him my hand, and my heart with it, and to express to him my thanks for his kind and considerate course toward the people with whom I am identified. If I did not yield to that impulse, it was because the thought occurred that other days were coming in which such a demonstration might be more opportune, and less liable to misconstruction. Suddenly, and without premonition, a day has come at last to which, for such a purpose, there is no to-morrow. My regret is therefore intensified by the thought that I failed to speak to him out of the fullness of my heart while there was yet time.

How often is it that death thus brings unavailingly back to our remembrance opportunities unimproved: in which generous overtures, prompted by the heart, remain unoffered; frank avowals which rose to the lips remain unspoken; and the injustice and wrong of bitter resentments remain unrepaired! Charles Sumner, in life, believed that all occasion for strife and distrust between the North and South had passed away, and that there no longer remained any cause for continued estrangement between these two sections of our country. Are there not many of us who believe the same thing? Is not that the common sentiment—or if it is not, ought it not to be—of the great mass of our people, North and South? Bound to each other by a common constitution, destined to live together under a common government, forming unitedly but a single member of the great family of nations, shall we not now at last endeavor to grow *toward* each other once more in heart, as we are already indissolubly linked to each other in fortunes? Shall we not, over the honored remains of this great champion of human liberty, this feeling sympathizer with human sorrow, this earnest pleader for the exercise of human tenderness and charity, lay aside the concealments which serve only to perpetuate misunderstandings and distrust, and frankly confess that on both sides we most earnestly desire to be one; one not merely in community of language and literature and traditions and country; but more, and better than all that, one also in feeling and in heart? Am I mistaken in this?

Do the concealments of which I speak still cover animosities which neither time nor reflection nor the march of events have yet sufficed to subdue? I cannot believe it. Since I have been here I have watched with anxious scrutiny your sentiments as expressed not merely in public debate, but in the *abandon* of personal confidence. I know well the sentiments of these, my Southern brothers, whose hearts are so infolded that the feeling of each is the feeling of all; and I see on both sides only the seeming of a constraint, which each apparently hesitates to dismiss. The South—prostrate, exhausted, drained of her lifeblood, as well as of her material resources, yet still honorable and true—accepts the bitter award of the bloody arbitrament without reservation, resolutely determined to abide the result with chivalrous fidelity; yet, as if struck dumb by the magnitude of her reverses, she suffers on in silence. The North, exultant in her triumph, and elated by success, still cherishes, as we are assured, a heart full of magnanimous emotions toward her disarmed and discomfited antagonist; and yet, as if mastered by some mysterious spell, silencing her better impulses, her words and acts are the words and acts of suspicion and distrust.

Would that the spirit of the illustrious dead whom we lament to-day could speak from the grave to both parties to this deplorable discord in tones which should reach each and every heart throughout this broad territory: "My countrymen! *know* one another, and you will *love* one another."

HENRY WOODFIN GRADY

Although many southerners glibly used the phrase, "The New South," in speeches and editorials in the last decades of the nineteenth century, Henry W. Grady was the most famous advocate of the New South and its role in the reconciled nation. Grady was born in 1850 in Athens, Georgia, and graduated from his home-town institution, the University of Georgia, in 1868. After a period of further study at the University of Virginia, Grady began a short, but important, career as a journalist. He soon bought a part-interest in the *Atlanta Constitution* and was its editor for over a decade, during which he led the charge for an industrialized and modern South.

It was not only through his editorial pen that Grady was the spokesman for the New South, but his oratory also helped establish his national reputation. The New South speech printed here, given in New York before the New England Society on December 21, 1886, set the tone for several key addresses over the next three years. His most famous speeches were presented before northern audiences: "The New South" at New York in 1886 and a speech at Boston in 1889. "The Solid South" given at the Augusta Georgia Exposition in November 1887, and "The South and Her Problems" presented at the Dallas State Fair in Texas in 1888, were the key statements of Grady's vision for a New South. He defended the South and grossly exaggerated the changes he claimed had come to the region since the end of the War and Reconstruction. Grady's vision was flawed, as he claimed to see the New South as having already arrived, when it in fact had not. His overly optimistic view was accepted as gospel by both North and South, however, and his words helped immeasurably to reunite the sections. More importantly, his rhetoric appealed to northern industrialists who became more willing to invest in the "New South" depicted by Grady; ironically, however, these investments reinforced the region's dependency on northern wealth and industry.

THE NEW SOUTH[9]

"There was a South of slavery and secession—that South is dead. There is a South of union and freedom—that South, thank God, is living, breathing, growing every hour." These words, delivered from the immortal lips of Benjamin H. Hill, at Tammany Hall in 1866, true then, and truer now, I shall make my text to-night.

Mr. President and Gentlemen: Let me express to you my appreciation of the kindness by which I am permitted to address you. I make this abrupt acknowledgement advisedly, for I feel that if, when I raise my provincial voice in this ancient and august presence, I could find courage for no more than the opening sentence, it would be well if, in that sentence, I had met in a rough sense my obligation as a guest, and had perished, so to speak, with courtesy on my lips and grace in my heart. [*Laughter.*] Permitted through your kindness to catch my second wind, let me say that I appreciate the significance of being the first Southerner to speak at this board, which bears the substance, if it surpasses the semblance, of original New England hospitality [*Applause*], and honors a sentiment that in turn honors you, but in which my personality is lost, and the compliment to my people made plain. [*Laughter.*]

I bespeak the utmost stretch of your courtesy to-night. I am not troubled about those from whom I come. You remember the man whose wife sent him to a neighbor with a pitcher of milk, and who, tripping on the top step, fell, with such casual interruptions as the landing afforded, into the basement; and while picking himself up had the pleasure of hearing his wife call out: "John, did you break the pitcher?"

"No, I didn't," said John, "but I be dinged if I don't!" [*Laughter.*]

So while those who call to me from behind may inspire me with energy if not with courage, I ask an indulgent hearing from you. I beg that you will bring your full faith in American fairness and frankness to judgment upon what I shall say. There was an old preacher once who told some boys of the Bible lesson he was going to read in the morning. The boys finding the place, glued together the connecting pages. [*Laughter.*] The next morning he read on the bottom of one page: "When Noah was one hundred and twenty years old he took unto himself a wife, who was"—then turning the page—"one hundred and forty cubits long [*Laughter*], forty cubits wide, built of gopherwood [*Laughter*], and covered with pitch inside and out." [*Loud and continued laughter.*] He was naturally puzzled at this. He read it again, verified it, and then said: "My friends, this is the first time I ever met this in the Bible, but I accept it as an evidence of the assertion that we are fearfully and wonderfully made." [*Immense laughter.*] If I could get you to hold such faith to-night I could proceed cheerfully to the task I otherwise approach with a sense of consecration.

Pardon me one word, Mr. President, spoken for the sole purpose of getting into the volumes that go out annually freighted with the rich eloquence of your speakers—the fact that the Cavalier as well as the Puritan was on the continent in its early days, and that he was "up and able to be about." [*Laughter.*] I have read your books carefully and I find no mention of that fact, which seems to me an important one for preserving a sort of historical equilibrium if for nothing else.

Let me remind you that the Virginia Cavalier first challenged France in this continent—that Cavalier John Smith gave New England its very name, and was so pleased with the job that he has been handing his own name around ever since—and that while Miles Standish was cutting off men's ears for courting a girl without her parent's consent, and forbade men to kiss their wives on Sunday, the Cavalier was courting everything in sight, and that the Almighty had vouchsafed great increase to the Cavalier colonies, the huts in the wilderness being full as the nests in the woods.

But having incorporated the Cavalier as a fact in your charming little books I shall let him work out his own salvation, as he has always done with engaging gallantry, and we will hold no controversy as to his merits. Why should we? Neither Puritan nor Cavalier long survived as such. The virtues and traditions of both happily still live for the inspiration of their sons and the saving of the old fashion. [*Applause.*] But both Puritan and Cavalier were lost in the storm of the first Revolution; and the American citizen, supplanting both and stronger than either, took possession of the Republic bought by their common blood and fashioned to wisdom, and charged himself with teaching men government and establishing the voice of the people as the voice of God. [*Applause.*]

My friend Dr. Talmadge has told you that the typical American has yet to come. Let me tell you that he has already come. [*Applause.*] Great types like valuable plants are slow to flower and fruit. But from the union of these colonist Puritans and Cavaliers, from the straightening of their purposes and the crossing of their blood, slow perfecting through a century, came he who stands as the first typical American, the first who comprehended within himself all the strength and gentleness, all the majesty and grace of this Republic—Abraham Lincoln. [*Loud and continued applause.*] He was the sum of Puritan and Cavalier, for in his ardent nature were fused the virtues of both, and in the depths of his great soul the faults of both were lost. [*Renewed applause.*] He was greater than Puritan, greater than Cavalier, in that he was American [*Renewed applause*] and that in his homely form were first gathered the vast and thrilling forces of his ideal government—charging it with such tremendous meaning and so elevating it above human suffering that martyrdom, though infamously aimed, came as a fitting crown to a life consecrated from the cradle to human liberty. [*Loud and prolonged cheering.*] Let us, each cherishing the traditions and honoring his fathers, build with reverent hands to the type of this simple but sublime life, in which all types are honored; and in our common glory as Americans there will be plenty and to spare for your forefathers and for mine. [*Renewed cheering.*]

In speaking to the toast with which you have honored me, I accept the term, "The New South," as in no sense disparaging to the Old. Dear to me sir, is the home of my childhood and the traditions of my people. I would not, if I could, dim the glory they won in peace and war, or by word or deed take aught from the splendor and grace of their civilization—never equaled and, perhaps, never to be equaled in its chivalric strength and grace. There is a New South, not through protest against the Old, but because of new conditions, new adjustments and, if you please, new ideas and aspirations. It is to this that I address myself, and to the consideration of which I hasten lest it become the Old South before I get to it. Age does not endow all things with strength and virtue, nor are all new things to be despised. The shoemaker who put over his door "John Smith's shop. Founded in 1760," was more than matched by his young rival across the street who hung out his sign: "Bill Jones. Established 1886. No old stock kept in this shop."

Dr. Talmadge has drawn for you, with a master's hand, the picture of your returning armies. He has told you how, in the pomp and circumstance of war, they came back to you, marching with proud and victorious tread, reading their glory in a nation's eyes! Will you bear with me while I tell you of another army that sought its home at the close of the late war—an army that marched home in defeat and not in victory—in pathos and not in splendor, but in glory that equaled yours, and to hearts as loving as ever welcomed heroes home. Let me picture to you the footsore Confederate soldier, as, buttoning up in his faded gray jacket the parole which was to bear testimony to his children of his fidelity and faith, he turned his face southward from Appomattox in April, 1865. Think of him as ragged, half-starved, heavy-hearted, enfeebled by want and wounds; having fought to exhaustion, he surrenders his gun, wrings the hands of his comrades in silence, and lifting his tear-stained and pallid face for the last time to the graves that dot the old Virginia hills, pulls his gray cap over his brow and begins the slow and painful journey. What does he find—let me ask you, who went to your homes eager to find in the welcome you had justly earned, full payment for four years' sacrifice—what does he find when, having followed the battle-stained cross against overwhelming odds, dreading death not half so much as surrender, he reaches the home he left so prosperous and beautiful? He finds his house in ruins, his farm devastated, his slaves free, his stock killed, his barns empty, his trade destroyed, his money worthless; his social system, feudal in its magnificence, swept away; his people without law or legal status, his comrades slain, and the burdens of others heavy on his shoulders. Crushed by defeat, his very traditions are gone; without money, credit, employment, material or training; and besides all this, confronted with the gravest problem that ever met human intelligence—the establishing of a status for the vast body of his liberated slaves.

What does he do—this hero in gray with a heart of gold? Does he sit down in sullenness and despair? Not for a day. Surely God, who had striped him of his prosperity, inspired him in his adversity. As ruin was never before so overwhelming, never was restoration swifter. The soldier stepped from the trenches into the furrow; horses that had charged Federal guns march before the plow, and fields that ran red with human blood in April were green with the harvest in June; women reared in luxury cut up their dresses and made breeches for their husbands, and, with a patience and heroism that fit women always as a garment, gave their hands to work. There was little bitterness in all this. Cheerfulness and frankness prevailed. "Bill Arp" struck the keynote when he said: "Well, I killed as many of them as they did of me, and now I am going to work." [*Laughter and applause.*] Or the soldier returning home after defeat and roasting some corn on the roadside, who made the remark to his comrades: "You may leave the South if you want to, but I am going to Sandersville, kiss my wife and raise a crop, and if the Yankees fool with me any more I will whip 'em again." [*Renewed applause.*] I want to say to General Sherman—who is considered an able man in our hearts, though some people think he is a kind of careless man about fire—that from the ashes he left us in 1864 we have raised a brave and beautiful city; that somehow or other we have caught the sunshine in the bricks and mortar of our homes, and have builded therein not one ignoble prejudice or memory. [*Applause.*]

But in all this what have we accomplished? What is the sum of our work? We have found out that in the general summary the free negro counts more than he did as a slave. We have planted the schoolhouse on the hilltop and made it free to white and black. We have sowed towns and cities in the place of theories and put business above politics. [*Applause.*] We have challenged your spinners in Massachusetts and your iron-makers in Pennsylvania. We have learned that the $400,000,000 annually received from our cotton crop will make us rich, when the supplies that make it are home-raised. We have reduced the commercial rate of interest from twenty-four per cent to six per cent, and are floating four per cent bonds. We have learned that one Northern immigrant is worth fifty foreigners, and have smoothed the path to southward, wiped out the place where Mason and Dixon's line used to be, and hung our latch-string out to you and yours. [*Prolonged cheers.*] We have reached the point that marks perfect harmony in every household, when the husband confesses that the pies which his wife cooks are as good as those his mother used to bake; and we admit that the sun shines as brightly and the moon as softly as it did "before the war." [*Laughter.*] We have established thrift in city and country. We have fallen in love with work. We have restored comfort to our homes from which culture and elegance never departed. We have let economy take root and spread among us as rank as the crabgrass which sprang from Sherman's cavalry camps, until we are ready to lay odds on the Georgia Yankee, as he manufactures relics of the battlefield in a one-story shanty and squeezes pure olive oil out of his cotton-seed, against any down-easter that ever swapped wooden nutmegs for flannel sausages in the valleys of Vermont. [*Loud and continuous laughter.*] Above all, we know that we have achieved in these "piping times of peace" a fuller independence for the South than that which our fathers sought to win in the forum by their eloquence or compel on the field by their swords. [*Loud applause.*]

It is a rare privilege, sir, to have had part, however humble, in this work. Never was nobler duty confided to human hands than the uplifting and upbuilding of the prostrate and bleeding South, misguided perhaps, but beautiful in her suffering, and honest, brave and generous always. [*Applause.*] In

the record of her social, industrial, and political illustrations we await with
confidence the verdict of the world.

But what of the negro? Have we solved the problem he presents or progressed in honor and equity towards the solution? Let the record speak to
the point. No section shows a more prosperous laboring population than
the negroes of the South; none in fuller sympathy with the employing and
land-owning class. He shares our school fund, has the fullest protection of
our laws and the friendship of our people. Self-interest, as well as honor, demand that he should have this. Our future, our very existence depend upon
our working out this problem in full and exact justice. We understand that
when Lincoln signed the Emancipation Proclamation, your victory was assured; for he then committed you to the cause of human liberty, against
which the arms of man cannot prevail [*Applause*]; while those of our statesmen who trusted to make slavery the cornerstone of the Confederacy
doomed us to defeat as far as they could, committing us to a cause that reason could not defend or the sword maintain in the sight of advancing civilization. [*Renewed applause.*] Had Mr. Toombs said, which he did not say, that
he would call the roll of his slaves at the foot of Bunker Hill, he would have
been foolish, for he might have known that whenever slavery became en-
tangled in war it must perish, and that the chattel in human flesh ended forever in New England when your fathers—not to be blamed for parting with
what didn't pay—sold their slaves to our fathers—not to be praised for
knowing a paying thing when they saw it. [*Laughter.*] The relations of the
Southern people with the negro are close and cordial. We remember with
what fidelity for four years he guarded our defenseless women and children, whose husbands and fathers were fighting against his freedom. To his
eternal credit be it said that whenever he struck a blow for his own liberty he
fought in open battle, and when at last he raised his black and humble hands
that the shackles might be struck off, those hands were innocent of wrong
against his helpless charges, and worthy to be taken in loving grasp by
every man who honors loyalty and devotion. [*Applause.*] Ruffians have mal-
treated him, rascals have misled him, philanthropists established a bank for
him, but the South, with the North, protects against injustice to this simple
and sincere people. To liberty and enfranchisement is as far as law can carry
the negro. The rest must be left to conscience and common sense. It should
be left to those among whom his lot is cast, with whom he is indissolubly
connected and whose prosperity depends upon their possessing his intelligent sympathy and confidence. Faith has been kept with him in spite of ca-
lumnious assertions to the contrary by those who assume to speak for us or
by frank opponents. Faith will be kept with him in the future, if the South
holds her reason and integrity. [*Applause.*]

But have we kept faith with you? In the fullest sense, yes. When Lee surrendered—I don't say when Johnston surrendered, because I understand he
still alludes to the time when he met General Sherman last as the time when

he "determined to abandon any further prosecution of the struggle"—when Lee surrendered, I say, and Johnston quit, the South became, and has since been, loyal to this Union. We fought hard enough to know that we were whipped, and in perfect frankness accepted as final the arbitrament of the sword to which we had appealed. The South found her jewel in the toad's head of defeat. The shackles that had held her in narrow limitations fell forever when the shackles of the negro slave were broken. [*Applause.*] Under the old regime the negroes were slaves to the South, the South was a slave to the system. The old plantation, with its simple police regulation and its feudal habit, was the only type under slavery. Thus we gathered in the hands of a splendid and chivalric oligarchy the substance that should have been diffused among the people, as the rich blood, under certain artificial conditions, is gathered at the heart, filling that with affluent rapture, but leaving the body chill and colorless. [*Applause.*]

The Old South rested everything on slavery and agriculture, unconscious that these could neither give nor maintain healthy growth. The New South presents a perfect democracy, the oligarchs leading in the popular movement—a social system compact and closely knitted, less splendid on the surface but stronger at the core—a hundred farms for every plantation, fifty homes for every palace, and a diversified industry that meets the complex needs of this complex age.

The New South is enamored of her new work. Her soul is stirred with the breadth of a new life. The light of a grander day is falling fair on her face. She is thrilling with the consciousness of growing power and prosperity. As she stands upright, full-statured and equal among the people of the earth, breathing the keen air and looking out upon the expanding horizon, she understands that her emancipation came because in the inscrutable wisdom of God her honest purpose was crossed and her brave armies were beaten. [*Applause.*]

This is said in no spirit of time-serving or apology. The South has nothing for which to apologize. She believes that the late struggle between the States was war and not rebellion, revolution and not conspiracy, and that her convictions were as honest as yours. I should be unjust to the dauntless spirit of the South and to my own convictions if I did not make this plain in this presence. The South has nothing to take back. In my native town of Athens is a monument that crowns its central hills—a plain, white shaft. Deep cut into its shining side is a name dear to me above the names of men, that of a brave and simple man who died in brave and simple faith. Not for all the glories of New England—from Plymouth Rock all the way—would I exchange the heritage he left me in his soldier's death. To the foot of that shaft I shall send my children's children to reverence him who ennobled their name with his heroic blood. But, sir, speaking from the shadow of that memory, which I honor as I do nothing else on earth, I say that the cause in which he suffered and for which he gave his life was adjudged by higher and fuller wisdom than his or mine, and I am glad that the omniscient God held the balance of battle in His Almighty hand, and that human slavery was swept forever from American soil—the American Union saved from the wreck of war. [*Loud applause.*]

This message, Mr. President, comes to you from consecrated ground. Every foot of the soil about the city in which I live is sacred as a battle-ground of the Republic. Every hill that invests it is hallowed to you by the blood of your brothers, who died for your victory, and doubly hallowed to us by the blood of those who died hopeless, but undaunted, in defeat—sacred soil to all of us, rich with memories that make us purer and stronger and better, silent but staunch witnesses in its red desolation of the matchless valor of American hearts and the deathless glory of American arms—speaking an eloquent witness in its white peace and prosperity to the indissoluble union of American States and the imperishable brotherhood of the American people. [*Immense cheering.*]

Now, what answer had New England to this message? Will she permit the prejudices of war to remain in the hearts of the conquerors, when it has died in the hearts of the conquered? [*Cries of "No! No!"*] Will she transmit this prejudice to the next generation, that in their hearts, which never felt the generous ardor of conflict, it may perpetuate itself? [*"No! No!"*] Will she withhold, save in strained courtesy, the hand which straight from his soldier's heart Grant offered to Lee at Appomattox? Will she make the vision of a restored and happy people, which gathered above the couch of your dying captain, filling his heart with grace, touching his lips with praise and glorifying his path to the grave; will she make this vision on which the last sight of his expiring soul breathed a benediction, a cheat and a delusion? [*Tumultuous cheering and shouts of "No! No!"*] If she does, the South, never abject in asking for comradeship, must accept with dignity its refusal; but if she does not; if she accepts in frankness and sincerity this message of goodwill and friendship, then will the prophecy of Webster, delivered in this very Society forty years ago amid tremendous applause, be verified in its fullest and final sense, when he said: "Standing hand to hand and clasping hands, we should remain united as we have been for sixty years, citizens of the same country, members of the same government, united, all united now and united forever." There have been difficulties, contentions, and controversies, but I tell you that in my judgment

> Those opposed eyes,
> Which like the meteors of a troubled heaven,
> All of one nature, of one substance bred,
> Did lately meet in th' intestine shock,
> Shall now, in mutual well-beseeming ranks,
> March all one way.

NOTES

1. Letter to Manning M. Kimmel of Henderson, Kentucky, October 1, 1867. Kinnison Papers, Southern Historical Collection, University of North Carolina, Chapel Hill.

2. L. Moody Simms, Jr., " ' . . . in the gloomy macrocosm of Lucifer': A Mississippian Comments on the Beginnings of Reconstruction," *Journal of Mississippi History* 30 (August 1968), 194.

3. C. Vann Woodward, *The Burden of Southern History*, 3rd ed. (Baton Rouge: Louisiana State University Press, 1993), 25.

4. Patrick Henry, "Against the Federal Constitution," in *American Forum*, Ernest J. Wrage and Barnet Baskerville, eds. (Seattle: University of Washington Press, 1960), 16.

5. Quoted in James L. Golden, "The Southern Unionists, 1850–1860," In *Oratory in the Old South, 1828–1860*, Waldo W. Braden, ed. (Baton Rouge: Louisiana State University Press, 1970), 260.

6. David M. Potter, *The South and the Sectional Conflict* (Baton Rouge: Louisiana State University Press, 1968), 30–31, 78.

7. Edward Mayes, *Lucius Q.C. Lamar: His Life, Times, and Speeches, 1825–1893*, 2nd ed. (Nashville: Publishing House of the Methodist Episcopal Church, South, 1896), 183.

8. Mayes, *Lucius Q.C. Lamar*, 184–187.

9. Henry Grady, "The New South," in *American Speeches*, Wayland M. Parrish and Marie Hochmuth, eds. (New York: Longmans, Green, and Co., 1954), 450–460.

FOR FURTHER READING

Buck, Paul H. *The Road to Reunion, 1865–1900*. New York: Vintage Books, 1961, reprint of 1937 edition.

Towns, W. Stuart. "Ceremonial Orators and National Reunion." In *Oratory in the New South*, Waldo W. Braden, ed., Baton Rouge: Louisiana State University Press, 1979, 117–142.

Lucius Quintus Cincinnatus Lamar

Dickey, Dallas C. "Lamar's Eulogy on Sumner: A Letter of Explanation." *The Southern Speech Journal* XX (Spring, 1955), 316–322.

Dickey, Dallas C. and Donald C. Streeter. "L.Q.C. Lamar." In *History and Criticism of American Public Address*, vol. III, Marie Hochmuth, ed. New York: Longmans, Green, 1955, 175–221.

Lasser, William. "Lucius Q.C. Lamar." In *American Orators before 1900: Critical Studies and Sources*, Bernard K. Duffy and Halford R. Ryan, eds. Westport, CT: Greenwood Press, 1987, 251–258.

Murphy, James B. *L.Q.C. Lamar: Pragmatic Patriot*. Baton Rouge: Louisiana State University Press, 1973.

Henry Woodfin Grady

Bauer, Marvin G. "Henry W. Grady." In *A History and Criticism of American Public Address*, vol. I, William N. Brigance, ed. New York: McGraw-Hill, 1943, 387–406.

Bryan, Ferald J. "Henry Grady (1850–1889) Southern Statesman." In *American Orators before 1900, Critical Studies and Sources*, Bernard K. Duffy and Halford R. Ryan, eds. Westport, Conn.: Greenwood Press, 1987, 197–204.

Mixon, Harold C. "Henry W. Grady as a Persuasive Strategist." In *Oratory in the New South*, Waldo W. Braden, ed. Baton Rouge: Louisiana State University Press, 1979, 74–116.

CHAPTER 8

The South Looks Back: Creating the Old South and the Lost Cause

In the South, the war is what A.D. is elsewhere: they date from it. All day long you hear things "placed" as having happened since the waw; or du'in' the waw; or befo' the waw; or right aftah the waw; or 'bout two yeahs or five yeahs or ten yeahs befo' the waw or afteh the waw. It shows how intimately every individual was visited, in his own person, by that tremendous episode.[1]

Given the atmosphere described by Mark Twain, one may understand the conditions which made it easy for the former Confederates to create a mythology about their Lost Cause. As the years passed, and the reality became less vivid, but nonetheless, central to the experiences of the South, a large group of southerners consciously set about to glorify and honor the pre-war South, the Confederacy, and those who fought for it. As Clement Eaton describes it, for them and their descendants, the lost cause "passed into the realm of emotion and myth."[2] James McBride Dabbs has pointed out how the loss of the Civil War, the freeing of the slaves, the bitterness of reconstruction, and the poverty of the post-war era turned the South's mind toward the past.[3]

One of the means through which the Lost Cause was created, glorified, and sustained until well into the twentieth century was the various Confederate veteran organizations. The Confederate Survivors' Association established in Augusta, Georgia, the United Confederate Veterans formed in New Orleans in 1889, the Sons of Confederate Veterans in 1895, and on the feminine side, the United Daughters of the Confederacy that same year, all contributed mightily to the legend. These and similar groups were responsible for the building of hundreds of monuments to Confederate dead and heroes of the War; by 1914, over 1,000 monuments existed. Many of the veterans were concerned that their children and later generations would forget the battles with the "Northern aggressors" and those events which had been so vital to their lives.[4] At each of the annual reunions of the various groups, and at the dedications of these monuments, orators extolled the virtues of the Lost Cause and the Old South and created these myths as a vision of the past. Unfortunately, it was a romantic past that never really existed the way it was depicted by the orators. Their repeated expressions of how they thought it had been became gospel for the southern audiences who heard them year after year. Their attachment to the Lost Cause provided white southerners some continuity and stability in a time of rapid change.[5] That legendary reality stayed alive for decades, even after the last veterans were long in their graves, and it was doubtless one of the reasons the racial crises of the 1960s were so difficult for many southerners.[6] Those who were not able to cope with integration perceived themselves as defenders of the "Southern Way of Life," which, in large part, they viewed as the mythology described as the Old South and the Lost Cause. This southern culture was the result of the history the South had endured and which had been "sanctified by the deaths of Confederate heroes."[7] John Brown Gordon and Charles C. Jones, Jr., were among the prime movers in this crusade to make certain their fellow southerners remembered their heroes.

JOHN BROWN GORDON

John Brown Gordon was a genuine Confederate hero, possibly second only to Robert E. Lee in the hearts and minds of many white southerners.[8] He attended the University of Georgia where he was a top orator in his class and had among the best academic records of his peers. For some reason not discernable today, he dropped out during his senior year and never graduated. Until the Civil War began, Gordon worked with his father on their plantation.

Joining the Confederate forces shortly after the war began, Gordon enrolled as a captain in the Sixth Alabama and rose to the rank of Major General. He fought in many important battles of the war, among which were Malvern Hill, Antietam, Chancellorsville, Gettysburg, and Spottsylvania. He was wounded five times at Antietam, but returned to action seven months later. When Lee realized further opposition was futile, he selected Gordon to be one of three Confederate generals to negotiate with the Union at Appomattox.

After the War, Gordon returned to Georgia, settling finally in Atlanta in 1867. The Democratic party nominated him for governor in 1868, but probable fraud deprived him of the election. In 1886 and 1888 he was elected governor and Georgia voters sent him to the United States Senate in 1873, 1879 (he resigned in 1880), and 1890. Gordon served as the first commander-in-chief of the United Confederate Veterans, a post he held until his death. Throughout his post-war career, Gordon urgently and consistently promoted national reconciliation and was a leading advocate of the industrialization of the "New South." He died at his winter home near Miami, Florida, on January 9, 1904.

In this typical address to the Confederate Survivors Association, General Gordon reinforces a theme present in much of the reconciliation oratory of the era: we in the South must not forget our history and we must not allow our history to be written by the victors in the recent war. He goes on to create a picture of southern history that could have served as a model for Margaret Mitchell as she wrote *Gone with the Wind*: the plantation South.

THE OLD SOUTH[9]

Mr President, Ladies, and Brother Soldiers:

My countrymen; I thank your presiding officer for his complimentary introduction and for your generous reception.

I am physically unable to do more than seek to impress upon your minds and hearts one thought, which fills my own with anxious apprehensions. That thought is this: There is danger that the South may be inadequately represented, or wholly misrepresented in the future history of this country. Misrepresentation threatens the conquered always—the conqueror never. As remarked by me on another occasion, in the average estimation of mankind, victory vindicates, while defeat dooms to misjudgment and thoughtless condemnation. There is in this truth a philosophy as plain and profound as the laws of human nature, involving consequences so calamitous that every lover of his people should unite to avert them. Should such misfortune befall us, it requires no prophet to foretell the character and extent of those consequences. First, there would follow a decrease of our appreciation of this section and of its people; second, as an inevitable consequence, a diminution of our own self respect; next, gradual but certain retrogression and impairment of our manhood; and, finally, the loss of those distinctive characteristics which are the traditional, recognized, and chief sources of this people's greatness. No more important service could be rendered this country—not only the South but the whole country—than to clearly comprehend these dangers, and to erect firm and immovable barriers, mountain high, against these possible consequences.

Let us do our part in their erection here this morning. Let us strengthen the foundations of our future manhood and character by enhancing the self respect of southern youth. Let us ground that self respect on the facts, not on the fictions of our history. In order to contribute to this essentially patriotic end, I call your attention briefly to some of the many reasons which should forever secure for the South a measure of full justice, if not of commanding precedence in American history.

In discussing this subject I shall indulge in no criticisms of other sections. If I know the spirit of this people, or my own, we love our country—our whole country—because it is our country. We would strengthen and not weaken the bonds of cordial respect and fraternity that bind it together in a perpetual union of free and equal States. I shall utter no highly wrought eulogiums, nor even indulge in commendations of the South other than those which are pronounced by the historic records of the past. I shall not ignore the fact that this was a slave-holding section, and that it was the last home of slavery on the North American continent. But in the interest of truth, in the interest of southern youth, in the interest of the whole republic, which must live, if it lives at all, in the affections, the devotion and sterling manhood of all its sons—in the interest of all these I shall insist that, however great were the evils (and they were many) of negro slavery, it was far, very far, from being an unmitigated evil. Lamented by philanthropists, denounced by politicians, exaggerated by the uninformed, these evils have been discussed and the arguments against that institution poured into the public ear through books, in magazines, from platforms and pulpits, until the truth has been obscured, the very elect deceived, and the faith of our children in the justice and humanity of their fathers seriously threatened. For over fifty years the record of these evils, and these adverse arguments have been conspicuously placed upon one side of the balance sheet. It is a remarkable fact that the beneficent results from that institution have rarely, if ever, been fully and fairly presented upon the other. With every page of American history brimful of these beneficent results, we have been too tardy in emphasizing them to our children and to those who have ignorantly assailed us. Of course, in the brief remarks I shall be able to make this morning, I can only represent a few of those beneficial results, and with the hope that such imperfect presentation may induce others to undertake the patriotic task.

In the first place it will be admitted perhaps—but whether admitted or not, it is true—that no age or country has ever produced a civilization of a nobler type than that which was born in the southern plantation home, and which drew its nutriment and inspiration from the rural life of the southern people. It was a civilization where personal courage, personal independence, personal dignity, personal honor, and the manliest virtues were nurtured; where feminine refinement, feminine purity, feminine culture, delicacy, and gentleness expressed themselves in models of rarest loveliness and perfection: and where, in the language of a great Georgian, "hospitality was as free and boundless as the vitalizing air around us."

In the next place it will perhaps be admitted by all, that the agricultural development in certain sections of the South was almost wholly dependent upon this southern institution. Debarred by climatic influences, the white man, as a laborer, would not in centuries have subdued and brought into tillage the rich alluviums of our semitropical region. Let it, therefore, be placed to the credit of that institution that through its agency this section has, in the comparatively brief national period of one century, wrought a mighty change in the world's products, achieved an immense increase in the world's commerce, and a vast augmentation of the world's wealth and comforts.

But there is to be placed on that balance sheet a still greater credit. This institution was the instrumentality, selected by Providence, for the civilization and religious training of four millions of the African race. Who will have the temerity to deny that the native African was vastly benefited by his transfer to America and by his southern service? What friend of human progress would have deprived him in his original helplessness of the patriarchal care and kind government of the southern master, and of the holy teachings of southern Christian women upon the southern plantations, and have remanded him to native barbaric rule? Who will deny that his southern home was the school house in which he was instructed in the methods of civilized life, fitted in God's own time for freedom, and taught to aspire to usefulness, holiness, and heaven? Who will now set limits to the blessings yet in store for Africa through the elevation by southern tutelage of its Americanized children?

Such were a few of its notable and praiseworthy characteristics; but it is gone. Gone forever is that old plantation life of the South—gone with its perennial hospitality; its kindly relations of master and servant; its mutual dependence and mutual benefits; its cheerful service and freedom from care, on the one hand; and its guardianship, protection and forethought on the other; its well clad, well fed, contented Christian laborers; its quaint and merry cabin homes, and thrilling melodies, wild and weird to the stranger, but sweet, solemn and sacred to our memories still. Gone, too, forever we fear, as its marvelously interesting product—our peculiar and characteristic civilization; but that civilization has left its ineffaceable impression on the character of the people, and has infused its beneficent conservation into the life of the republic.

That southern institution, I repeat, is gone and gone forever; and no people of any section of this union would exhibit more relentless resistance to its reinstatement than would the people of these southern States. But it is a crime against the manhood of this people, and therefore against the country, to insist upon its evils and deny its benefits. The God of humanity, who permitted its establishment, sustained and guided it for a century for great purposes, has also permitted it to pass away at last and for the betterment, as we trust, of both races; but those of us who have survived it may not without criminal indifference permit prejudiced representations to become the acknowledged history of that institution in which our characters were formed. Let every fact and every phase of it be presented, and in answer to the misjudgments of the misinformed, let us point to these undeniable results and to the additional, conspicuous, and crowning fact of the general and affectionate loyalty exhibited towards the southern whites by the colored race throughout the war; to the absence of all bitterness and resentments at its close; and to the present prevailing harmony between landlord and laborer which defies all efforts at its disturbance, and is an inspiring prophecy of the future progress, power, prosperity and happiness of both races and of this entire section.

I turn next to the part borne by the South in founding, perfecting, and sustaining free government in America. Such references now cannot be untimely, because it was for this section that our dead brothers enlisted, fought, and fell. It is due to their memories, to ourselves, and to our children, that we group together and duly emphasize the remarkable contributions made by this section to the inauguration and support of republicanism in America. The bare facts, though familiar to all, if fairly presented and without embellishment, cannot fail to excite the admiration of mankind, and to reawaken our pride in the great achievements of this section. We shall thus strengthen our own self-respect, erect another barrier against the decay of Southern manhood, and increase our loyalty and devotion to our whole country.

Let us trace the South's career step by step, through every stage of American progress. What was the first official and conspicuous act leading to independence? It was the action of North Carolina, a southern colony, weak in numbers and resources, declaring herself a free and independent commonwealth more than a year in advance of the general declaration, and inaugurating her State government. This southern colony thus became the flag-bearer of the colonies, and her movement the great landmark in the early progress of our revolution.

What next? Then came doubt and apprehension; agitation and indecision among all the colonists. Who was it that then came to the rescue? Who was it that wrote the pungent resolutions embodying American menace, and, with impassioned eloquence, sent them like electric currents through all the colonies? It was an unheralded and untrained member of the House of Burgesses in the colony of Virginia.

What next? Then came additional British laws bringing increased British burdens, and independence is everywhere demanded. Who then wrote for the American people their united and defiant declaration? It was a patriotic and gifted young southerner.

Note the next step. Rebellion became a necessity. Separation was decreed and war ensued. It was still a southerner who led the raw troops of the colonies against the trained armies of Great Britain.

But the South's leadership did not end with the cessation of hostilities. When independence was achieved and the momentous problem of free and stable government was to be solved, it was again a southerner whose marked ascendancy achieved for him the proud distinction of "Father of the Constitution."

When the gigantic power of Great Britain was to be met in a second great conflict, again it was a southern commander who led the undisciplined soldiery of this newly established republic to another great victory.

When Mexico was to be met and our boundaries were to be extended, it was a Virginian and a Louisianian, both southerners, who led the American hosts through burning sands to repeated, swift, and complete successes.

Let me now briefly present the South's record in furnishing chief magistrates to the nation. For more than twenty-five years the results of our unhappy war have practically debarred the South from the Presidency, but there was a period of seventy-two years antedating that era of passion and of blood. How stands the record of Presidential services for those seventy-two years? The South furnished Presidents for forty-nine and three months; the other sections for twenty-two years and nine months. Prior to 1860 every President, without an exception, whose administration was indorsed by a second election, was furnished by these Southern States. During the entire life of the Republic but ten Presidents have been re-elected by the people. Of those ten the South furnished eight; the other sections two, and one of these was of southern birth, blood, and lineage.

But perhaps impartial history will contain no record of this section more cherished by its people than the ackowledged integrity of its public servants and the incorruptible and religious life of its citizens. It is perhaps sufficient to say for our public men that their record of incorruptibility has never been surpassed, if ever equalled, in the governmental experience of mankind. The irrefutable proof is found in the fact that from George Washington down through all our national life, with temptations ever present and opportunities abundant, no southern representative has ever grown rich in office. This is indeed high praise; but I think it just praise of our public men.

To the private citizen of the South the same general characteristics may be truthfully ascribed. It is admitted that the character of a people is not always reflected in the official lives of their representatives. It is unfortunate for the whole country that in some sections of the union neither their ablest nor their purest men have, as a rule, sought public station; but both the science and the practical administration of government have always been regarded as most inviting fields for southern intellect. The private citizen of the South is a politician in the highest sense of that term. Hence our public men have perhaps been more truly representatives of the people. It is certain that at all periods of our history, our private citizens have exacted of their public servants unsullied records and purity of public life. But whether in public or private station, the personal honor of a man was his proudest title to distinction.

If comparisons were not odious, I might be permitted to adduce in this connection an argument drawn from the United States census for 1860. The statistics of churches, of pauperism, and of crime are eloquent witnesses of the high moral and religious status of this people. The exhibit which might be presented from these official records, which are the highest evidence on such questions known to this government and established by its laws, would not only be a source of unqualified gratification to our people, but of just pride to their descendants forever. This unimpeached and unimpeachable evidence will, when fairly presented, lift this section under former conditions, to a plane of moral excellence unsurpassed, if not unrivaled, in any age.

Nor would the official record of the period during and since the war proclaim this section any less God fearing or law abiding. Indeed, the civil war with all its passions and reputed demoralization tended, it would seem, rather to elevate and purify this people. When, in its earlier stages, the sullen tramp of approaching legions and the roar of their mighty guns were heard around her borders, and when at a later period her territory was filled with hostile armies, then in all her churches and around her family altars, ignoble passions gave place to humble petitions to the Deity for His guidance and protection. Even in the camps and tents of her soldiers, prayers and praises habitually rose like holy incense, lifting them above the fear of danger and death, and fitting their devoted spirits to ascend in the battle's flame to heaven.

And after the war, with her substance wasted, her hopes blasted, and her soil still wet with the blood of her sons, even then, turning her grief-furrowed face to the God whom she had served, and without a murmur upon her lips, she cried in mingled agony of faith struggling with despair: "Though He slay me, yet will I trust in him."

A few more words and I close. The new and robust life upon which, through the ashes and ravages of war, the South has already entered, inspires our hearts with the most buoyant hopes of the future. Knee deep in these ruins, she has waded through them for a decade and erect in her conscious power, she challenged the confidence and invited the co-operation and capital of other sections; and she furnishes to-day a field for richer returns—more certain profits than any portion of our country. Her doors are thrown wide open and her heart's welcome is given to all who may find homes in her hospitable climate. Her future wealth seems assured. In another decade the roar of her great forges, the thunder of her water powers, driving her millions of spindles, will prove the century's marvel of industrial progress. But while we press to their utmost the practicable development of our admitted agricultural advantages and give encouragement to the spirit of enterprise manifested on every hand, we must permit no decrease of interest in the political welfare of the whole country. Wedded inseparably to the constitutional rights of the States, let us cultivate, by all legitimate means, a broad nationality embracing the whole union of States. Here hangs above us the flag of that union. Let us honor it as the emblem of freedom, of equality, and unity—remembering that there is not a star on its blue field which is not made brighter by light reflected from southern skies—not a white line in its folds but what is made whiter and purer by the South's incorruptible record—not one of its crimson stripes that is not deeper and richer from southern blood shed in its defense in all of the wars with foreign powers.

It is unnecessary, I feel assured, to admonish you in this connection, that the most punctilious discharge of all these obligations to our country involves no infidelity to our past or to its teachings and sacred associations. We cannot, without self-stultification and abasement, forget the men who fell in our defense in the late sectional conflict. To fail to cherish their memories in our heart of hearts to the latest generation, would be to trample self-respect, manhood, and honor under our feet.

Nor can we lose one of those peculiar characteristics of our former civilization without lowering the high order of southern character and manhood. The great problem of our future is not how to secure material prosperity. That seems already assured; but no amount of rich success, however general and brilliant, could compensate for the loss of our hitherto high standard of private and public integrity. Nor is our political status, however vital to our future, the question to us of deepest significance. No; but the great problem is how to hold to the characteristics of our old civilization, when that civilization itself is gone; how to send the current which so enriched and purified the old, coursing forever through the new life before us; how to relight the old fires upon the new altars. The more we shall be enabled to incorporate into the south's new life the chief characteristics developed by the old, the better, the higher, and the purer will that new life become.

But patriotism itself demands that we shall cherish these associations with our past; and the reason of this demand is, that a self-respecting patriot is a braver, truer, grander man than one who has lost his self-respect. If the education of the youth of the country, North and South, were guided by some such patriotic purpose, it would be well for the future of this Republic.

It was my melancholy pleasure to take part in the funeral honors paid to the North's greatest hero, General U. S. Grant. Every soldier and citizen who took part in that greatest pageant of modern times; every child who, with loving hands, placed flowers upon his bier; and every stone that shall hereafter be placed in the monument to his memory, will but add to northern manhood and northern character. So on the other hand the almost equally great demonstration in the South one year ago, over the living president of the dead Confederacy, was potential in the formation of southern character. Every bonfire that blazed on the streets of Montgomery; every cannon shot that shook its hills; every rocket that flew on fiery wing through the midnight air; every teardrop that stole down the cheeks of patriotic southern women, was a contribution to the self-respect, the character, and the manhood of southern youth.

If, therefore, an injunction could be laid upon this people which could not be disregarded, that injunction should be to cultivate the self-respect by stimulating the pride of southern youth in the past of this people. Let the proverbial respect of woman never grow less in this section, but let her purity and exalted character command now and always your chivalrous courtesy and manly deference. Let personal probity, intellectual ability, and unselfish devotion to the public weal, be the sole passports to your confidence and the price of your support to public office. Finally, let the great body of our citizens, private and official, let your teachers and your preachers, and above all your public press, unite to create and support a public opinion which shall be enlightened and inexorable, and whose resistless fiat shall forever bar the doors of this section against all commercial methods in politics, and shall make impossible among this people the triumph of mere wealth over personal, intellectual, and moral worth.

CHARLES COLCOCK JONES, JR.

Charles Jones was born in Savannah, Georgia, on October 28, 1831, the son of a prominent Presbyterian minister and planter.[10] He grew up on his father's plantation, attended South Carolina College, and graduated from the College of New Jersey (Princeton). He received a degree from Harvard Law School in 1855 and established his law practice in Savannah. In 1860 he was elected mayor of his hometown. During the Civil War, he served as a colonel of artillery.

Jones became known not as a soldier, lawyer, or politician, but as an historian and archaeologist. He published over one hundred articles, books, and speeches on various aspects of Georgia history and archaeology. Probably his most important works were *Antiquities of the Southern Indians, Particularly of the Georgia Tribes* (1873), a two-volume *History of Georgia* (1883), and *History of Savannah, Ga.* (1890).

A founder of the Confederate Survivors' Association of Augusta, Georgia, he served as its president and a chief defender of the South for years. Jones delivered the main oration at the annual reunions of the Association, one of which is included in this collection. John B. Gordon assessed this address by Jones as "really a great speech."[11] In it, Jones does his share to create and reinforce the Old South mythology and the legends of the Lost Cause as illustrated in the history of Georgia.

In 1880, the College of the City of New York awarded Jones an honorary degree, and the Oxford College of Emory University two years later bestowed upon him this honor. He died in Augusta on July 19, 1893.

ADDRESS TO THE CONFEDERATE SURVIVORS' ASSOCIATION[12]

Comrades:

According to the official returns, the aggregate wealth of Georgia, in 1860, was estimated at $672,322,777. Of this sum nearly one half was represented by negro slaves numbering 450,033 and valued at $302,694,855. During the four preceding years the taxable property of this commonwealth had increased almost one hundred and seventy-seven millions of dollars. The signs of universal prosperity were manifest, and everything betokened an era of contentment, of development, and of expanding good fortune.

While there were comparatively few who, in either town or country, could lay claim to very large estates, the planters and merchants of Georgia were in comfortable circumstances. Business operations were conducted upon a quiet, honest, and legitimate basis. Of bucket shops there were none; and gambling in cotton, stocks, grain, and other commodities was wholly unknown. Railroads were builded by honest subscriptions and, when completed, were hampered by no mortgages. Commercial transactions were entered upon and consummated *bona fide*, and did not represent operations upon paper or speculations upon margins. Men knew and trusted one another, and did not often have cause to repent of the confidence reposed. Sharp-traders were not held in good repute, and questionable methods were mercilessly condemned. Of manufacturing establishments there were few. Agriculture claimed and received the allegiance of the masses. The planters, as a class, were competent, industrious, observant of their obligations, humane in the treatment of their slaves, given to hospitality, fond of manly exercise, independent in thought and act, and solicitous for the moral and intellectual education of their children. A civilization, patriarchal in its characteristics, combined with a veneration for the traditions of the fathers and a love of home, gave birth to patriotic impulses and encouraged a high standard of individual honor, integrity, and manhood. From boyhood men were accustomed to the saddle, and familiar with the use of firearms. The martial spirit was apparent in volunteer military organizations; and, at stated intervals, contests involving rare proficiency in horsemanship, and in handling the sabre, the pistol, the musket, and the field-piece, attracted the public gaze and won the approving smiles of woman. Leisure hours were spent in hunting and fishing and in social intercourse. Of litigation there was little. Misunderstandings, when they occurred, were usually accommodated by honorable arbitration. Personal responsibility, freely admitted, engendered mutual respect, and fostered a commendable exhibition of individual manliness. Communities were well ordered and prosperous. The homes of the inhabitants were peaceful and happy.

Beyond controversy Georgia was then the Empire State of the South. At the inception of the Confederate Revolution she occupied a commanding position in the esteem of sister States with similar institutions, like hopes, and a common destiny. It may be safely affirmed that in political leadership, in intellectual capabilities, in material resources, by virtue of her situation, and in moral and physical power, this commonwealth was the pivotal state in the Southern Confederation. It was only when her borders were actually invaded, and when her integrity was seriously impaired by the devastating columns led by General Sherman, that the weakness of the Confederacy was fairly demonstrated, and the disastrous termination of the conflict was absolutely foreshadowed. . . .

The printed Journal of this [secession] Convention fills an octavo volume of more than four hundred pages, and its lightest inspection will convince the most skeptical of the magnitude and the gravity of the labors wrought by the members who composed it. Characteristic of all the deliberations of this august body are an exalted appreciation of the situation, a thorough conception of the political peril, an intelligent comprehension of the issues involved, and an earnest endeavor to anticipate every need and provide for all governmental exigencies which might arise in the changed condition of affairs.

The ordinance of secession was framed and introduced by the Hon. Eugenius A. Nisbet, an ex-Judge of the Supreme Court of Georgia, at one time a member of Congress, a gentleman of education, culture, and refinement, and a citizen honored for his purity of character, public spirit, and Christian virtues. After a protracted debate remarkable for its solemnity and power, the ordinance was passed by the convention by a vote of two hundred and eight yeas to eighty nine nays. Among those voting in the negative were Herschel V. Johnson, Alex H. and Linton Stephens, Hiram Warner, and W. T. Wofford. While maintaining the right of a State for substantial cause to secede from the Union, many of the minority contended that a fit occasion had not arisen for the exercise of that right. Before withdrawing from the Confederation, it was their belief that Georgia should wait for some overt act committed by the Lincoln administration. When, however, the ordinance was passed by the convention, recognizing the fact that their supreme allegiance was due to Georgia, those voting in the negative waived their objections and subsequently wavered not in their devotion to State and Confederacy. As a matter of history it will be remembered that when, under resolution of the convention, this ordinance of secession was engrossed and presented for signature, it was signed by every member. Six of them, however, while protesting against the action of the majority "in adopting an ordinance for the immediate and separate secession" of the State, and expressing a preference that "the policy of co-operation with sister Southern States" should have been adopted, nevertheless yielded to the will of the majority and pledged their "lives, fortunes and sacred honor" to the defense of Georgia "against hostile invasion from any source." This action on the part of the convention exerted a powerful influence in consolidating the general sentiment of the State, and encouraged other Southern commonwealths, which had not then seceded, to the prompt adoption of a similar course. The intelligence of the passage of this ordinance of secession was received by Georgia communities with the wildest enthusiasm, with bonfires and illuminations, with beat of drum, with the thunder of cannon, and with consentient acclaim.

Before the convention had concluded its labors, Georgia State forces, under the orders of Governor Brown, had taken possession of the United States forts Pulaski and Jackson on the Savannah river, and of the United States Arsenal at Augusta. With a vigor which challenges every admiration the State authorities were preparing to meet the gathering storm, the earliest thunders of which were soon to be heard in Charleston harbor. Georgia was rapidly becoming a vast recruiting camp: and the patriotic military spirit evinced by her citizens transcended all expectation. The compulsive course of this popular uprising knew no retiring ebb. Commissioners were accredited to such Southern and doubtful States as had not then seceded. Delegates were also chosen to attend the Congress which was to assemble at Montgomery, Alabama, on the 4th of February, 1861. They were empowered, upon free conference with delegates who might be present from other seceding States, to unite with them in forming and putting into immediate operation a temporary or provisional government for the common safety and defense of the commonwealths represented in that congress. It was suggested by the convention that such provisional government should not extend beyond a period of twelve months from the time it became operative, and that it should be modeled as nearly as practicable "on the basis and principles of the late government of the United States of America." Plenary powers were also confided to these commissioners, upon like consultation, to agree upon a plan for the permanent government of the confederated States. . . .

We thus perceive that the State of Georgia furnished the Vice-President of the Confederacy, a Secretary of State, a Quarter-Master General, a Commissary General, four of the twenty-one Lieutenant Generals, eleven of the one hundred and two Major Generals, and of the four hundred and seventy-five who attained unto or rose above the grade of Brigadier General, fifty-four.

To the naval service of the Confederate States Georgia contributed her full quota. The present Adjutant General of this State—John McIntosh Kell—is a worthy type of what this commonwealth did in that behalf; and, in the person of Commodore Josiah Tattnall, we proudly point to an officer whose gallantry, seamanship, and exalted characteristics commanded universal admiration. In the language of Captain Whittle, he only lacked what Decatur called *opportunity* to have inscribed his name high among the great naval men of the world. His perception was like the lightning's flash. The execution followed and with a force sufficient to overcome the resistance to be encountered. With a mind capable of conceiving the boldest designs and a courage which never faltered in their performance, it may be truly said of this Bayard of the seas he was *sans peur et sans reproche*.

So much, my friends, for the general officers who illustrated the patriotism and the valor of Georgia upon the battle fields of the Confederate revolution. Simply to name them is to point to fields of glory broader than the confines once claimed by the Southern States and to revive the recollections of grand endeavors and gallant emprises as illustrious as the annals of any people and age may boast. Among them all there was none, so far as I know, who proved recreant to the trust reposed, who faltered in the hour of peril, who failed in the exhibition of an unshaken love of country, or who neglected to manifest those traits which should characterize a military leader contending in a defensive war for the conservation of all the heart holds most dear. And some among them there were, who with superior capabilities and larger opportunities wrought memorable deeds, and achieved for themselves and nation a reputation which the bravest and the knightliest may envy.

And what shall we say of the field-officers, the staff, the non-commissioned officers and privates of the grand army which Georgia sent forth during more than four long and bloody years to do battle for the right? Their name is legion, and fearlessly did they bear themselves from the low-lying shores of the Gulf of Mexico to the furthest verge of the crimson tide breasted by the veterans of the Army of Northern Virginia—from the Atlantic slope to the uttermost limits beyond the Mississippi claimed by the Confederacy. They followed the Red Cross wherever it pointed, and the reputation of Georgia troops is intimately and honorably associated with the memorable battles fought for the independence of the South. Give me a Georgia Brigade and I can carry those heights. Such was the compliment paid at the battle of Chancellorsville by an officer who appreciated the hazard of the endeavor and understood the mettle of the men requisite for its consummation. . . .

I wish that accurate statistics were accessible, but in their absence I venture the assertion that Georgia sent not less than one hundred and twenty thousand of her sons to do battle under the flag of the Southern Confederation.

By the heavy guns at Pensacola, Mobile, and New Orleans—behind the parapets of Pulaski, McAllister, and Sumter—among the volcanic throes of Battery Wagner—at Ocean Pond and Honey Hill—upon the murderous slopes of Malvern Hill—beneath the lethal shadows of the Seven Pines—in the trenches around Petersburg—amid the smoke and carnage of Manassas, Fredericksburg, Spottsylvania, Chancellorsville, Sharpsburg, Gettysburg, Brandy Station, Cold Harbor, the Wilderness, Corinth, Shiloh, Vicksburg, Perryville, Murfreesboro, Missionary Ridge, Chickamauga, Franklin, Nashville, Atlanta, Jonesboro, Bentonville, and until the last thunders of war were hushed at Appomattox and Greensboro when, in the language of the present gallant Chief Magistrate of this commonwealth, our regiments, brigades, divisions, and army corps were "worn to a frazzle," these brave Georgians were found shoulder to shoulder with heroic companions in arms, maintaining the honor of their State and supporting the flag of their beleaguered country. You can mention no decisive battle delivered, no memorable shock of arms during the protracted and herculean effort to achieve the independence of the South, where Georgia troops were not present. Their life blood incarnadined, their valor glorified, and their bones sanctified the soil above which the Red Cross, which they followed so closely, waved long and fearlessly in the face of desperate odds. All honor to the courageous men who fell in the forefront of battle. All honor to the cause which enlisted such sympathy and evoked such proofs of marvelous devotion. Precious for all time should be the patriotic, heroic, and virtuous legacy bequeathed by the men and the aspirations of that generation. Within the whole range of defensive wars you will search in vain for surer pledges and higher illustrations of love of country, of self-denial, of patient endurance, of unwavering confidence, and of exalted action. And, as we behold among the survivors of this gigantic conflict not a few who are maimed by wounds, enfeebled by age, and oppressed by poverty, our tenderest sympathy goes out toward them, and there arises a general and an earnest desire that speedy and suitable provision should be made for every needy and crippled veteran of the grand army which Georgia sent forth to do battle for the right under the stars and bars of the Confederacy. He should at least be shielded from absolute want. By public benefaction he should be enabled to spend the residue of his days unmenaced by the calamities of hunger and cold. No more sacred duty devolves upon this commonwealth than the reasonable relief and sustentation of those who lost health and limb in defense of the general safety. With loyal hearts we elevate statues in marble and in bronze of our Confederate chieftains, and garland the graves of those who gave their lives to the Southern cause, and shall we not extend a helping hand to the living—survivors of that shock of arms—who having shared like peril, endured similar privations, fought under the same banner, and contended for the maintenance of the same principles, emerged from the smoke and carnage of that memorable strife, bringing their shields with them, but so maimed in body, and enfeebled by wounds, disease, and exposures that they are no longer capable of customary labor, or competent to engage on equal terms with their fellow men in the tiresome and life-long struggle for food, for clothing, and for shelter? To the Mother State which summoned them to the field, and to Georgians whose homes their valor essayed to protect against invasion and destruction—to her and to them only—can these disabled veterans look for that substantial aid which in this, the season of poverty, incapacity, and declining years, is essential to their well-being, and comfort. Their claim to suitable recognition in this behalf rests not upon charity, but is based upon the general gratitude and inherent right. Horatius halting on one knee was not more surely entitled to the gratitude and the help of the Roman Senate and people than is the maimed Confederate veteran worthy of sympathy, honor, and relief not only from the General Assembly of Georgia but also from the entire community. The Red Cross which he followed so long and so well belongs now only to the thesaurus of the Recording Angel. The Confederacy, once so puissant, is now simply a pure, a heroic, a glorious memory; and soon there will be numbered among the living none who bore arms in defense of the South. The time is short. Let the obligation—too long unfulfilled—be promptly and generously met. The scars which he received in protecting home and country and vested rights have won for him a claim to universal respect, a peculiar consideration which none should gainsay or lightly esteem, and a title to nobility beyond the blazon of the Herald's College.

In this epoch of commercial methods—of general and increasing poverty in the agricultural regions of the South—of absorption by foreign capital of favored localities, and of the creation in our midst of gigantic corporations intent upon self-aggrandizement—in this era of manifest modification, if not actual obliteration of those sentiments and modes of thought and action which rendered us a peculiar people—I call you to witness that there is a growing tendency to belittle the influences, the ways, the services, the lessons, and the characteristics of former years. I call you to witness that the moral and political standard of the present is not equal to that set up and zealously guarded by our fathers. I call you to witness that in the stern battle with poverty—in the effort to retrieve lost fortunes, and in the attempt to amass large moneys by speculation—in the commercial turn which the general thought and conduct have recently taken—and in the struggle by shifts and questionable devices to outstrip the profits of legitimate ventures, there has occurred a lowering of the tone which marked our former manly, conservative, patriarchal civilization. I call you to witness that many have attempted and are now endeavoring by apologizing for the alleged shortcomings of the past to stultify the record of the olden time, and by fawning upon the stranger to cast a reproach upon the friend. I call you to witness that by false impressions, and improper laudations of the new order of affairs, men in our midst have sought to minimize the capabilities of the past, and unduly to magnify the development of the present. I call you to witness that by adulation and fulsome entertainment of itinerant promoters and blatant schemers, seeking to inaugurate enterprises which are designed to benefit those only who are personally interested in them, the public has been sadly duped to its shame and loss. I call you to witness that the truest test of civilization lies not in the census, in the growth of cities, in railway combinations and the formation of Gargantuan trusts, in the expansions of manufactures, in the manipulation of land schemes and corporate securities, or in the aggregation of wealth, but in the mental, moral, political, and economic education and elevation of the population. I call you to witness that the present inclination to make one part of society inordinately affluent at the expense of the wretchedness and the unhappiness of the other, is in derogation of natural rights, impairing the equilibrium and disturbing the repose of the elements essential to the entity and the happiness of a great, honest, virtuous, and democratic nation. I call you to witness that a reign of plutocrats—a subjection of men, measures, and places to the will of millionaires and plethoric syndicates—is antagonistic to the liberty of the Republic and subversive of personal freedom. I call you to witness that this adoration of wealth—this bending the knee to the Golden Calf—this worship of mortals gifted with the Midas touch, savors of a sordid and debasing fetishism at variance with the spirit of true religion and emasculatory of all tokens of robust manhood. I call you to witness that "Mammon is the largest slaveholder in the world," and that the integrity of station and principle is seriously imperiled when subjected to the pressure of gold. I call you to witness that cardinal doctrines and exalted sentiments, when assailed, should, like troops of the line, stand fast; and at all times and under all circumstances be held above and beyond all price. I call you to witness that the alleged prosperity of this commonwealth, except in limited localities, is largely a matter of imagination. I call you to witness that, eliminating from the computation the value of slaves as ascertained by the returns of 1860, the State of Georgia is now poorer by more than twelve millions of dollars than she was twenty nine years ago. I call you to witness that behind this fanfare of trumpets proclaiming the attractions and the growth of the New South may too often be detected the deglutition of the harpy and the chuckle of the hireling. I call you to witness that the important problem involving the remunerative cultivation of the soil, and the employment of our agricultural population upon a basis of suitable industry, economy, compensation, and independence, is largely unsolved. The occupation of the planter lying at the foundation of all engagements and constituting the normal, the indispensable, the legitimate, and the honorable avocation of the masses, I call you to witness that every reasonable encouragement should be extended in facilitating his labors and in multiplying the fruits of his toil. I call you to witness that general prosperity cannot be expected while such extensive areas of our territory remain uncultivated, while so many of our farmers annually crave advances. I call you to witness that the potentialities of our former civilization, so far from being improved, have been sadly retarded by the issues of war. I call you to witness that the promises of the *ante-bellum* days, had they not been thus rudely thwarted, would have yielded results far transcending those which we now behold. I call you to witness that the grand effort now is and should be to preserve inviolate the sentiments and to transmit unimpaired the characteristics of the Old South. I call you to witness that in the restoration of the good order, the decorum, the honesty, the veracity, the public confidence, the conservatism, the security to person and property, the high-toned conduct, and the manliness of the past lies the best hope for the honor and lasting prosperity of the coming years. I call you to witness that the heroic example of other days constitutes, in large measure, the source of the courage of the succeeding generation; and that "when beckoned onward by the shades of the brave that were," we may the more confidently venture upon enterprises of pith and moment and, without fear, work out our present and future salvation.

Palsied be the Southern tongue which would speak disparagingly of a Confederate past, and withered be the Southern arm that refuses to lift itself in praise of the virtue and the valor which characterized the actors, from the highest to the lowest, in a war not of "rebellion," but for the conservation of home, the maintenance of constitutional government and the supremacy of law, and the vindication of the natural rights of man. . . .

And what, my friends, shall we say of the slave population of this commonwealth which was then confidently reckoned upon by strangers and enemies as an element of weakness? While strong men were in the tented field, our servants remained quietly at home. As was their wont, they tilled the soil, ministered kindly to the needs of unprotected women and children, and performed all customary services with the same cheerfulness and alacrity as when surrounded by the usual controlling agencies. Gentle, tractable, and docile, they conducted all domestic operations with commendable industry and regularity. Security of person and property was not invaded. The long established tokens of respect and obedience were every where observed, and our domestics, in the emergency, proved themselves in very deed the guardians of home and family. Praiseworthy was their conduct; and the Southern heart warms towards them still for their fidelity, friendship, and uninterrupted labors during this epoch of anxiety, of temptation, and of disquietude. The slaves of Georgia and of the other Confederate commonwealths cannot be too highly commended for their fidelity, quiet behavior, and valuable services during this eventful period. In localities not over-run or occupied by Federal forces they remained loyal to their owners. Few indeed were the instances of insubordination, and the history of the times furnishes no authentic cases of violence or insurrection. Because agricultural operations were so largely committed to and performed by the slave population, was the Confederacy enabled to utilize so thoroughly the white military strength of the States which composed it. Nothing attests more surely the attachment then entertained by the servant for his master and family—nothing proclaims more emphatically the satisfactory status of the relation—nothing certifies more truly the pleasant intercourse between the races, than the domestic peace which reigned within this State and the Confederacy during this season of peril and alarm. The record is unique: and yet to one accustomed from childhood to understand and appreciate the influences of that relation as developed and confirmed for generations, the result appears but a logical sequence of mutual dependence, trust, and genuine friendship.

The services of the Southern slaves were not, however, limited to the performance of domestic duties and the conduct of operations appurtenant to the plantations. Many accompanied their owners to the front, shared with them the privations of camp life, endured the fatigues of the march, were not infrequently exposed to the dangers of battle, served as cooks and hostlers, drove wagons, nursed the sick and wounded, and, in fine, discharged almost all duties other than those incident to bearing arms.

Another important station filled by the Southern slave during the war was that of a laborer engaged upon the construction of river, harbor, and city defenses, in the erection of government buildings, and in the elevation of military works at strategic points. Such service was of the highest importance. During the early months of the war it was, at various points along the sea-coast of Georgia, freely contributed by the masters of plantations. As the struggle progressed, it was made available under regulations prescribed and for compensation provided under the auspices of the Confederate government. . . .

Of the conduct of the women of Georgia during the Confederate revolution we may not speak except in terms of the highest admiration and with emotions of the profoundest gratitude. From its inception to its close their behavior was beyond all praise. Whether in lowly cottage or stately mansion there came from them no thought, no look, no message, no act, which was not redolent of love of country, full of incitement to heroic action, commendatory of all that was good and noble and virtuous, and sanctified by genuine self-denial and the exhibitions of the tenderest Christian charity. Through the long and dark hours of that protracted struggle for independence how sublime their influence, their patience, their sufferings, their aspirations, and their example! The presence of their sympathy and of their aid, the potency of their prayers and their sacrifices, the language of their patriotism and of their devotion, and the eloquence of their tears and of their smiles were priceless in the inspiration they brought and more effective than an army with banners.

And when the war was over, in tender appreciation of the brave deeds wrought in the name of truth and freedom, in proud memory of the slain, they dignified this land with soldier's monuments, gathered the sacred dust, guarded unmarked graves, and canonized those who suffered martyrdom during this eventful epoch. Than the record of the patriotism, the passion, and the generous deeds of the women of the South there is none brighter, purer, or loftier in the annals of the civilized world. . . .

Surely the memorable deeds which were then wrought, the lessons inculcated, the characters unfolded, the principles advanced, the traditions delivered, and the monuments bequeathed, should stimulate us and those who will come after us to lives of patriotism, of honesty, of courage, and of virtue.

NOTES

1. Mark Twain, *Life on the Mississippi* (New York: Penguin Books, 1984), 319.

2. Clement Eaton, *The Waning of the Old South Civilization, 1860's–1880's* (Athens: University of Georgia Press, 1968), 109.

3. James McBride Dabbs, *Haunted by God* (Richmond, VA: John Knox Press, 1972), 83.

4. Edward L. Ayers, *The Promise of the New South: Life after Reconstruction* (New York: Oxford University Press, 1992), 27.

5. Howard N. Rabinowitz, *The First New South, 1865–1920* (Arlington Heights, IL: Harlan Davidson, Inc., 1992), 174.

6. Eaton, *Waning of the Old South*, 166.

7. David R. Goldfield, *Black, White, and Southern: Race Relations and Southern Culture, 1940 to the Present* (Baton Rouge: Louisiana State University Press, 1990), 16–17.

8. Most of this biographical sketch comes from "John B. Gordon," in *Biographical Directory of the Governors of the United States, 1789–1978*, vol. I, Robert Sobel and John Raino, eds. (Westport, CT: Meckler Books, 1978), 306–307; and "John B. Gor-

don," *The National Cyclopaedia of American Biography*, vol. 1 (New York: James T. White and Co., 1898), 231.

9. Delivered before the Confederate Survivors' Association in Augusta, Georgia, April 26, 1887 (Augusta, GA: Chronicle Publishing Co., 1887). Pamphlet in University of Florida Library, Gainesville, FL.

10. This sketch is primarily taken from essays on Jones found in *Dictionary of American Biography*, vol. X, Dumas Malone, ed. (New York: Charles Scribner's Sons, 1933), 165; *Dictionary of Literary Biography*, vol. 30, *American Historians, 1607–1865*, Clyde N. Wilson, ed. (Detroit MI: Gale Research, 1984), 156–162; and *The National Cyclopaedia of American Biography*, vol. 5 (New York: James T. White & Co., 1907), 159.

11. Gordon to C. C. Jones, Jr., 6 June 1889. John B. Gordon Papers, Duke University Library Manuscript Collection.

12. Delivered by Jones in Augusta, Georgia, April 26, 1889 (Augusta, GA: Chronicle Publishing Co., 1889). Pamphlet at Louisiana State University Library, Baton Rouge, LA.

FOR FURTHER READING

Dorgan, Howard W. "Rhetoric of the United Confederate Veterans: A Lost Cause Mythology in the Making." In *Oratory in the New South*, Waldo W. Braden, ed. Baton Rouge: Louisiana State University Press, 1979, 143–173.

Foster, Gaines M. *Ghosts of the Confederacy: Defeat, the Lost Cause, and the Emergence of the New South, 1865 to 1913*. New York: Oxford University Press, 1987.

Wilson, Charles Reagan. *Baptized in Blood: The Religion of the Lost Cause, 1865–1920*. Athens: The University of Georgia Press, 1980.

John Brown Gordon

Eckert, Ralph. *John Brown Gordon: Soldier, Southerner, American*. Baton Rouge: Louisiana State University Press, 1989.

Tankersley, Allen P. *John B. Gordon: A Study in Gallantry*. Atlanta, GA: Whitehall Press, 1955.

Charles Colcock Jones, Jr.

Cass, Michael M. "Charles C. Jones, Jr. and the 'Lost Cause'." *The Georgia Historical Quarterly* LV (Summer 1971), 222–233.

Green, Claude B. "Charles Colcock Jones, Jr. and Paul Hamilton Hayne." In *Georgians in Profile: Historical Essays in Honor of Ellis Merton Coulter*, Horace Montgomery, ed. Athens: University of Georgia Press, 1958.

CHAPTER 9

Resolving the South's Problem: Defining the Segregated South

Although the word "segregation" did not enter the South's general vocabulary until early in the twentieth century,[1] the practice of separation of the white and black races already had a long history. Antebellum segregation was customary in both North and South and in some places statutes regulated the practice. All public welfare institutions such as jails, hospitals, parks, and cemeteries were segregated; most hotels and restaurants serving whites barred blacks, and theaters and opera houses relegated black patrons to the balconies. As early as 1816, the northern region of the country segregated Negroes in public accommodations, and in Savannah and Charleston, legal codes barred free Negroes from public parks.[2]

At the end of the Civil War, segregation was common practice in those institutions formed to aid the former slaves, such as poor houses and orphanages. Churches soon developed separate congregations and denominations for black and white members, and separation in what few schools there were in the devastated South was the rule.[3] In 1870 Tennessee passed a law against intermarriage, and all other southern states quickly followed suit. Five years later, the Volunteer State enacted the first Jim Crow law requiring separate cars for railroad passengers, and in 1891 a majority of the southern states had similar regulations on their books. A majority of border and southern states had school segregation laws by 1878, and all of them did by the 1890s.[4]

Northern and Republican apathy for the cause of the freed slaves encouraged the South in its quest for a methodology to control and regulate its black citizens. The Republican-dominated Supreme Court in 1883 outlawed the Civil Rights Act of a decade earlier, and in the most infamous case, *Plessey v. Ferguson*, declared the separate-but-equal policy that had evolved in the South to be constitutional. During the last decades of the century, whether through custom or by legislative enactment, the amount of segregation in the former Confederacy was "impressive," according to one historian.[5] By the first decade of the twentieth century, the pattern was solidified by law and maintained by racist white politicians who used the practice as a tool for perpetuating their political power. Not until the Civil Rights Movement a half century later were these bastions of prejudice broken down.

Why did segregation develop so strongly in the post-war South? There are many reasons and historians debate the causes and the timing of the segregationist impulse. There are, however, a number of factors that are important. The economic depression of the late 1880s and early 1890s and the ensuing revolt of the farmers against five cent per bale cotton, and the bankers and railroads they saw as the culprits in their financial distress, left many white conservative political leaders with the feeling that they were losing control of their constituents. The Democratic Party used violence, lynching, the threat of violence, disfranchisement, and segregation to regain and strengthen their hold on the southern voter. This uneasiness came on top of the southerners' feeling that the Civil War and especially Reconstruction had turned the world upside down and the cherished and well-understood "place" that everyone (white and black) had filled in southern culture was upset. A common expression heard during the era was, "the bottom rail is on top"; that was not its proper place in the minds of white southerners.[6] Among all other things, segregation brought order to race relations—order that the South had not observed since before the Civil War.

Another important factor was the rampant racism that swept the country in the last decades of the century. Many intellectuals of the era, college professors, sociologists, anthropologists, and other respectable scholars believed that the Negro race was incapable of rising much above the level of culture and civilization it had attained during slavery. Indeed, many of these "scientific racists" believed that the black man in America was ultimately destined for extinction, as he could not compete with his more advanced white brothers. Some of the books written in this period bore titles such as *The Negro a Beast* and *The Negro: A Menace to Civilization*. The demagogues who began to dominate southern politics in the late nineteenth and early twentieth centuries were able to draw from this scientific "proof" of racial inferiority arguments that merely seemed to support what their poor-white followers had believed all along. The poor-white saw himself in a bitter economic struggle with his black neighbor; it was, therefore, a short step to support the idea of separating him from any social contact whatsoever with the white race.[7]

Going hand in hand with this attitude and perspective on race was the fact that America gained an empire after the Spanish American War—an empire that included many people of color in the Caribbean and Pacific. It was the "white man's burden" to care for these less developed people, and this attitude reinforced the paternalistic treatment of blacks in the American

South, as well as Filipinos and Puerto Ricans in the nation's newly acquired possessions.

In the final analysis, perhaps the telling factor was the South's perception that the North was retreating from the defense of the southern black man and leaving the former Confederacy to deal with the freed slaves as it saw fit; as Monroe Billington put it, there was a "relaxation of the opposition."[8] Considerable evidence supports this point of view. For example, in the early 1890s, two pieces of national legislation were introduced that would have deeply affected the South's handling of the issue. The Federal Election Bill, so-called the Lodge Force Bill by southern politicians, would have required federal supervision of elections where there was evidence of voter fraud and discrimination. That bill was defeated, however, after Senate filibusters, even though it passed the House on several occasions. The Federal Aid to Education Bill, known as the Blair Bill, would have distributed federal aid to both white and black schools in the South, a measure unthinkable for white southerners. It, too, never became law even in a Republican-controlled Congress.

The "Negro problem" refers to what was to be the relationship of white to black, but not in terms of who would be on top—that was already firmly decided in the minds of the white leadership. It was a matter of how far on top the whites would be and how far apart the races would be separated. White Southerners saw segregation as "sophisticated, modern, managed race relations."[9] The policy of separate but equal treatment of the black race was "firmly entrenched in the South by the turn of the century,"[10] and it remained that way until mid-century. In practice, of course, equal treatment was never achieved and the gap between the races grew wider with each passing decade. The two speeches published here reflect the perspective of southern whites on the issue as well as the stance accepted by many southern blacks at the end of the nineteenth century.

ZEBULON BAIRD VANCE

Zebulon Vance was born on May 13, 1830, at his family home about twelve miles from Asheville, North Carolina, and before he died on April 14, 1894, he had served his native state as a member of the state legislature, United States congressman, colonel in the North Carolina Confederate forces, wartime governor, a partial term as governor after the Civil War, and finally, as a distinguished United States senator.[11]

The North Carolinian opposed secession until President Lincoln issued a call for troops, and at that point, Vance changed his position and supported North Carolina's withdrawal from the Union. After the War began, Vance fought in the New Bern campaign and in the Seven Days' battle in Virginia. In 1862 he was elected governor and served a tumultuous term in which he fought a constant battle against the Confederate government in Richmond. Vance opposed the Confederate conscription acts on constitutional grounds and created a great controversy by issuing a pardon to all North Carolina soldiers who were absent from duty with their regiments. The Richmond government considered them deserters, but Vance saw them as absentees who could be persuaded to return to their ranks. Vance was reelected in 1864 and at the end of the Civil War, federal authorities arrested him and held him for several months.

Vance was a well-known orator, and his speaking ability and reputation followed him throughout his career. He was elected Governor again in 1876, but he only served two years of the now-four year term, before he was elected to the U.S. Senate in 1879. He was reelected in 1885 and 1891 and he served in Washington until his death.

In his Senate speech on the Negro question, Vance admits slavery was wrong, but blames it on northern slave traders. His major point is that the superior white race must, in the nature of things, control the inferior race, so he tells the North to keep "hands off" and let the white South deal with the black South as they see fit.

THE NEGRO QUESTION[12]

Mr. President, one of the earliest recorded utterances of inspiration is, that the sins of the fathers are visited upon the children. This is another way of saying that the mistakes of one generation endure to plague another.

Several hundred years ago this fair land of ours, which it would seem God had specially intended for the chosen seat of liberty and the noblest development of man, was desecrated by the introduction of human slavery. The serpent thus entered into our political Eden. The great forests which covered the face of the earth called for labor to remove them, for more labor than the slowly coming immigration of the free races afforded. The morals of the age justified holding of barbarous races in bondage. The favorite place for obtaining bondsmen was the African coast. So desirable did the supplying of the newly discovered islands and continents of the West with cheap labor appear, that old John Hawkins was knighted by Queen Elizabeth, as much for his successful introduction of a cargo of slaves into the West Indies, as for his exploits against the Spaniards. Even so great and good a man as Las Casas, the Spanish apostle to the Indians, once advocated the introduction of African slavery.

First and foremost in this calamitous and iniquitous traffic was New England. In fact, so anxious were the good people of those colonies for slaves that they reduced to bondage the native Indians whom they captured in war, and, not unfrequently, those wicked people of their own race and blood who were guilty of differing from them in religious opinions.

The tobacco-growing colonies of the South soon followed suit in the importation of African slaves, and early found how profitable this cheap and involuntary labor was in the raising of their great staple. The introduction of the cultivation and uses of cotton soon gave a further impetus to slaveholding, and made the chief prosperity of all the Southern regions to depend mainly upon this enforced labor. Whilst the want of profitable returns gradually lessened the hold of the North upon slavery, its great profits constantly increased that hold upon the South.

The stony and sterile fields of New England called for manufactures and commerce. That commerce consisted very largely in purchasing slaves on the African coast, and selling them to Southern planters. Thus their interests constantly drifted the Northern and Southern people apart in regard to African slavery. After a time it ceased to exist altogether in the North, by reason of emancipation laws made to take effect at fixed periods, and by their sales to their Southern neighbors. By this time the wrongfulness of holding slaves fully dawned upon the conscience of the Northern people. Its prickings became so active that they not only deemed it a sin to hold a slave themselves, but to permit anybody else to hold one, even though there was no responsibility whatever upon them for the transgression.

They even went so far in obeying the dictates of conscience, that they did not hesitate to stand up boldly in the sight of God, with the purchase money in their pockets, and denounce the vengeance of heaven against their Southern neighbors for holding on to the negro which they themselves had sold them.

Every requisite to the effectual working of a good conscience was present. Slaveholding was not only unprofitable, as has been said, upon their soil and in their climate, but the lucrative trade of supplying the Southern planters was abolished by the constitution. In addition to this their sense of rectitude was unpardonably offended by the contemplation of the well-doing of their neighbors. Of course, men who burnt witches, banished of enslaved Quakers, and had made fortunes by the horrors of "the middle passage," could not be expected to tolerate any longer the ungodly thing which brought fortunes to Virginia and Carolina planters. With ever increasing bitterness this conscientious crusade was kept up with an extravagance of language which scrupled not to denounce the Constitution itself; which respected the slaveholders' rights under State laws, as "a league with death and a covenant with hell." The inevitable result is fresh in our recollection. It ultimately led to civil war in which more than a million lives were lost and more than three billions of property destroyed, and as much of indebtedness incurred. The slaves were set free.

Those of us in the South who had deprecated the war and deplored the agitation which led to it, as we sat in the ashes of our own homes and scraped ourselves with the potsherds of desolation, yet consoled ourselves for the slaughter of our kindred and the devastation of our fields by the reflection that this, at least, was the end; that the great original wrong committed by our fathers had at last been atoned for; that the Union having been declared indissoluble, and slavery forever abolished, the one great stumbling block and stone of offense was removed, and the people of these American States, henceforth homogeneous, could pursue their great destiny harmoniously and fraternally.

How little we knew the temper of the victors in that great struggle. We made no calculation for the fact that the necessities of party supremacy would lead men as far as even the prickings of conscience for an unprofitable sin had done. No sooner had we fairly witnessed the end of hostilities before acts of Congress were passed directing the subversion of all law and civil government in the State of the South, under cover of which they were divided into military districts, over each of which was placed a general of the Army, supported by sufficient troops. To these generals and their bayonets was committed the task of forming governments for the people of these overthrown States. This they did by holding elections under military control, by suppressing the vote of every free white man in those States, who, having at any time taken an oath to support the Constitution of the United States, had afterwards done any act in aid of the rebellion, and by thrusting with military force upon the ballot-box the entire mass of emancipated slaves, to whom the right to vote had been given by no law, human or divine, known to our federated system. By the constitution thus forced upon the Southern people the negroes were made voters and invested with the like privileges in all respects as the white people.

The Constitution of the United States had in like manner been so amended as to forbid the States from making any discrimination against the negro race, or in any manner impairing the rights which had thus been conferred upon them. Again, we in the South thought we had arrived at the end of our troubles connected with the negro question. Surely, we reasoned, as the colored man is now free, as he is made by law, State and Federal, equal with the white man in all respects, and has been given the ballot to protect himself in these rights, surely the matter will now be at rest. We can close the chasm which the agitation about him had created between us and our Northern neighbors. Again, were we sadly mistaken. After forty years of bitter agitation, four years of bloody war, and near a quarter of a century more of trial under the new order of things, the negro again "bobs up serenely," and for his sake we are to-day threatened not only with a political agitation sufficiently disastrous within itself, but with a servile war whose weapons shall be the midnight torch and the assassin's dagger, and whose victims shall be sleeping women and children. . . .

There is surely here no outrage against the negro that calls for revolution and blood. The wrong was against the white man, and was redressed by him without revolution. In obedience to the Constitution the Southern States admitted the colored citizens to a full participation in all the legal rights enjoyed by white citizens. They were placed in the jury-box, commissioned as magistrates, permitted to form companies in the volunteer militia, duly commissioned and armed. School-houses were built for them and normal schools established for the education of their teachers, whilst the school fund of the States was apportioned to their schools, in proportion to their numbers, with all possible fairness. Asylums were built for the care of their insane, deaf, dumb, and blind, wherein they receive the same treatment as the whites. The taxes for all this were levied by white legislators on their white constituents, who paid at least 95 per cent of the total out of the little which the negroes and carpet-baggers had left them. If there be any wrong, injustice, in all this, it can surely be seen only by that intellectual vision which, "reaching far as angels ken," beholds no motives for the preservation of Republican supremacy in reconstruction, but only patriotic benevolence.

Since the restoration of the South to the control of its own people the progress and prosperity of the negroes have been as great as, if not greater than, in any other country where its race exists. His increase in numbers has been phenomenal, and furnishes ample proof that he is fed, clothed, and sheltered. The decrease of the death rate, of criminal convictions, and of illiteracy, taken with the gradual and unfailing increase of his wealth, which is abundantly proven by the statistics, all give the lie flatly to the oft-repeated story of oppression and wrong under which he suffered or is said to suffer. The truth is, he began to prosper when the whites took control. Progress for him would have been as impossible under his own rule as it was for the whites. Ten years more of such government as reconstruction fixed upon the South would have made that fairest portion of the American continent a howling wilderness. In short, it would have been Africanized, a fate which even the Senator from Kansas says is "not desirable;" which, taken in connection with his opening remarks on the danger of "blood-poisoning" by the adulteration of races, means much more than appears on the surface.

The best thing, then, that could have been done for the negro was that which was done when the management of public affairs was taken from inexperienced and incapable hands and placed with the natural and competent rulers of the land. . . .

I am glad to say that North Carolina is one of the States in the South where there is least complaint of infringements of the colored man's rights, either at the ballot-box or in the courts of justice.

The State of Mississippi is one of the States of the South where the complaints on behalf of the colored man are loudest and most vehement; yet for six months past the negroes in eastern North Carolina have been voluntarily moving at the rate perhaps of three to four thousand per month to this very State of Mississippi. They are not going to Kansas or to any other Northern State, but to Mississippi, presumably for the purpose of having their votes suppressed and of being slaughtered—to Arkansas and to Texas. The fact is, they are influenced like other people, by the great economic law of supply and demand. For two or three years past eastern North Carolina has suffered from a failure of the crops, and the planters of Mississippi are offering the negroes better wages than the Carolina planters can afford to pay, and the chief agents employed by the Mississippians for effecting their contracts are intelligent educated negro men, many of them preachers.

Evidently they do not believe these stories that are served up for campaign, political purposes here. I do not wish to be misunderstood in this matter. That there are instances of mistreatment and occasionally of cruelty to the negroes now and then occurring in the South I candidly admit and regret. The millennium has not yet arrived in the land of reconstruction; the reign of perfect righteousness, of absolute justice, has not yet been established south of Mason and Dixon's line, though of course it is in full operation just north of that imaginary division. There there is no suppression of the popular vote by gerrymander or otherwise; there there is no purchase of the floating vote in blocks of five, no ejectment of colored children from white schools or colored men from theaters and barber-chairs, and where we may hope that, in the process of time and in the spread of intelligence and increased appreciation of the virtues of the negroes, one black man may soon be sent to Congress from the North; that some railroad attorney or millionaire will make room in the Senate of the United States for the colored brother; that one colored postmaster for a white town may be appointed in the North; that in the State of Kansas, the soil so prolific in friendships for the colored man, a respectable negro, duly nominated on the Republican ticket, may receive the full vote of his party, and not be scratched almost to the point of defeat by those who love him, as he was in Topeka; that one accomplished colored man may be sent abroad to represent his country in some other land than Hayti or Liberia.

Let us hope even that the great Republican party of the North may find the colored man fit to serve his country in some other region than the South and this great dumping-ground of political dead-beats, the District of Columbia, upon whose helpless people has heretofore been billeted, in all the offices from the judiciary down, every worn-out partisan for whom his people at home had no more use. Nay, under the appeals against the injustice of suppressing the colored vote which we daily hear, it would be a rapture of hope to express the belief that these great apostles of justice would restore the right of suffrage to the 225,000 people of this District, from whom it was taken on the well known ground that the negro vote was about to prove here an inconvenience. It might be replied, technically, that the injustice of suppressing votes depended upon the color of the voter, and that it was not an outrage to suppress white votes; or, again, that it was no injustice to the franchise to suppress the vote by law on account of ignorance, nativity, or poverty, as so long prevailed in Rhode Island and Massachusetts. But I positively deny that there is any systematic, authorized, or official interference with the guaranteed rights of the colored man in the South! . . .

It is natural to suppose, if they can not agree, that the stronger will have its way and dominate the weaker; but there is one proposition, Mr. President, of which you may rest assured, there is no kind of doubt: the stronger will never submit to the domination of the weaker. This might as well be set down as *res adjudicata*.

There is another fact that may be noted now in connection with it. The Senator from Kansas let fall an expression which I regretted exceedingly to hear. Prefacing his utterances that he had never known a people to endure such wrongs without revolution and blood, he said:

> The South, Mr. President, is standing upon a volcano, the South is sitting upon a safety-valve. They are breeding innumerable John Browns and Nat Turners. Already mutterings of discontent by hostile organizations are heard. The use of the torch and the dagger is advised.

This is reasonably construed as an incitation to the work of murder and arson, and although he says that he "deplores it," yet, as the excuse and justification for such a course immediately follows, it is open to the construction that it is an indirect invitation to these people to lay our homes in ashes while we sleep, and murder unsuspecting people.

The supposition that they are capable of such atrocities, it seems to me, is proof positive of their incapacity for civilized government and the extraordinary idea of justice and humanity of him who suggests it. He surely does not know anything of the inflammable nature of the negro in the South or he would not have ventured on the expression of such a threat. He furthermore told us in this connection that in case such a calamity came upon the southern people as a servile war, attended with whatever horrors it might be waged, we need look for no help from the people of our blood in the North; that we must "tread the wine press alone."

If he speaks truly in this, he passes the blackest and vilest judgement upon his own people that ever politician dared utter.

But, Mr. President, I do not believe one word of it. As the negro race that was born and reared among us did not rise up to do us harm in the hour of our extremest adversity, even for the great boon of freedom and amidst the most tempting incitements, but continued faithful to their masters and their families even within hearing of the guns that were roaring to set them free, so I do not believe that they can be thus incited to attempt it now.

They have more of State and sectional pride and of neighborly affection for the people among whom they live than the Senator is willing to give them credit for. Nor do I believe that what he has said about the feeling of the North is true; on the contrary, I believe as firmly as I believe in the gallantry, the courage, and all of the noble qualities of the great race to which I belong, that hundreds of thousands of stout hearts would come to our assistance on the wings of steam preceded by the messenger of lightning, should we unhappily ever need such help.

It might be that they would mostly be composed of what he calls the "cowardly and degraded elements," the same elements that filled your armies for the defense of the Union and which fills the ranks of the defenders of the Constitution after the Union was saved; but, for the sake of our common kindred and common glory, I believe that there would be no such feeling and no party division in such a crisis. But, Mr. President, we shall not need to call for help; we could manage such a war without assistance. Had the Senator been a participant in or a critical observer even of the last one, he would know that the eleven Southern States, which, though much divided among themselves, unaided and alone kept the whole power of the Union, with its unlimited forces and untold treasure, at bay for four long years, could easily, with the aid of the great border States, overcome seven millions of negroes. Then there would be a solution of the negro problem that would stay solved.

But a great mistake is made by those who assume that the whites exercise no influence over the negroes except by force or fraud. The black man is attached to the South and to the great body of its people. The behavior of the blacks since their freedom has in the main been good and gentle. All things considered, it has been wonderful. I believe I can say with truth that I have no personal knowledge of the occurrence of any riot or public disturbance anywhere in the South between the races that was not at the instigation of some white scoundrel; and in every case the blacks have got the worst of the fray, being deserted invariably by their cowardly white allies when the bullets began to fly. . . .

Mr. President, what is the so-called negro problem? As I understand it, it is one that can not be solved by speculation or legislation; but it is a question that will be settled by nature herself, if her laws are not interfered with by the folly and passion of men. Nature will solve it as she does waste, destruction, and all incongruities. It may be thus stated: Given a high-spirited, liberty-loving, cultivated, and dominating race, occupying a free state of their own establishment, under institutions of their own creation, full of activity, energy, and progress; with them, under the same laws, possessed of absolute legal equality, dwells an inferior race, manumitted slaves of recently barbaric origin, with no race traditions, with no history of progress, but lately invested with these unaccustomed and unearned franchises—how shall the two be made to dwell together in fraternity and progress?

This is the question. It is a principle of our law, fundamental in its nature, that the majority of those to whom the franchise is committed shall rule within limits. Is it a principle of natural law, as old as man himself, that the stronger shall rule without limit. What is strength in a state? Other things being equal numbers give strength; but in the States of the South, whose conduct is complained of, other things are far from equal. The whites where not actually in superior numbers are yet possessed of far superior knowledge, courage, skill in the use of weapons and tools, race-pride, traditions, experience of affairs, and self-control. Placing these two side by side, is it not as sure as certainty can be made that one will outstrip the other and control it? Nature would reverse all her own decisions if it were not so.

If the weaker be in the way of the stronger the former will be removed. If two men start on a journey, the pace is regulated by the slower, if they be compelled to keep together; and, however great the powers of the swifter, if compelled to wait for his feebler brother, his powers are of no more use than if he had them not. Naturally, he will drop his brother behind and stride forward. The attempt to restrain him by legislation is unnatural and he will resent it. To say that the superior race shall not by its superior knowledge and virtue rule the inferior, is to say that weakness shall control strength, that ignorance and vice shall control knowledge and virtue. To attempt by legislation to place ignorance and vice in control of knowledge and virtue because of the superior numbers of the ignorant, would be to enact that the civilization of great races shall not enjoy the power and influence with which God has endowed them; that three weak men, however ignorant and debased, shall forever control two white men, however wise and virtuous.

The mere statement of the proposition shows that it is hostile to the highest natural and moral laws which have been impressed upon man and constitute the basis of his civilization.

Mr. President, I know the negro well. I was born and reared among them, and have all my life lived in close association with them. I affirm to you, not that he is incapable of civilization, but that he is incapable of attaining to and keeping up with the civilization of the race to which we belong. At the very best, his refinement must be of a low order compared to ours. Any attempt, therefore, to force him into equality with us in the race of progress can result in nothing else but the retarding of the advancement of the Southern whites.

Those who have determined to subject, at all hazards, to negro rule those States of the South where they are in superior numbers, have simply determined that the white man's progress shall be measured by the negro's if, indeed, it does not result in explosion and mutual destruction. Fairminded men everywhere may accept this as truth. The sons of Ham have had the same opportunities that the sons of Shem and Japheth have had. No where have they improved them.

I know not whether I should give credence to the oft-repeated allegation that they are forever feeling the effect of their ancestor's curse, but this I do know, that they have been in close contact with every civilization of which we have any knowledge; with the oldest Egyptian, the Assyro-Babylonian, the Grecian, the Roman, and the modern; in each of them we read of his presence and in every instance he was a slave.

He learned nothing for the benefits of his race from his civilized masters in all these ages. He has made more progress in one hundred years as a Southern slave than he made in all the five thousand years intervening from his creation until his landing on these shores. He has no type now living on this earth equal to those of the present generation who were born and raised in the slave States of America. All of which should be considered by those who have philosophy and fairness enough to look at the matter in some other light than the necessities of the Republican party in the next campaign.

The fact dwelt upon by the Senator from Kansas concerning their behavior towards their masters during the war is fully admitted. It is a strong argument to prove either that they were unfitted for the great boon of liberty or that the horrid stories of inhuman treatment by their masters were lies. I am not only willing but anxious to have justice done them in everything, and to do all that may be required of me to aid them in the difficulties of their position; but I am not willing that they should rule me or my people. It is my pride that my State has been just to them and generous, and that in the adjusting of the new order of things after their enfranchisement I had no inconsiderable hand in providing those laws and institutions which have made them comparatively well content in North Carolina.

I believe them incapable, for many reasons, of properly controlling public affairs, but I do believe them capable of making valuable citizens under the wiser control of the whites. My solution of the problem is simply, "Hands off." Let no man be afraid that if the Northern people cease their interference the negroes will be driven to the wall. On the contrary, it is your interference that causes or aggravates whatever of trouble is inflicted upon them. . . .

So far as the evil may be capable of remedy by removal of any kind, I would suggest that it is perfectly practical to induce these people to settle in the various States of this Union which now have few or no colored people. There is ample room for them throughout the Northern and Northwestern States, each one of which could receive enough to relieve the pressure entirely upon those States in the South whose progress is about to be destroyed, and yet not inconveniently interfere with the well-being of any Northern State. Besides, if the presence of negroes in superior numbers does amount to a positive evil in the South, I submit that it is the duty of the other States to assist them in removing or so distributing the evil that it shall be harmless. If the negro is a good thing we are willing to divide him up. [*Laughter.*] There is plenty of him to go round.

Nothing is wanting to the execution of this suggestion except the consent of these Northern States. One-half of the inducements and the solicitations which they hold out to foreigners, if extended to the negroes of the South, would within ten years draw such numbers of them as to leave all the Southern States with decided white majorities; and it is well-known that there is little or no complaint of the mistreatment of negroes where there are white majorities. This would equalize the conditions of all the States. The introduction of large numbers of the colored race into every Northern State would be equivalent to an amendment to the Constitution and would restrain you effectually from the passage of any laws or the attempting of any kind of interference that would discriminate between the States of the American Union on account of their locality or previous condition of slavery. It would familiarize the masses of your people with the negro, his capacities, his habits, and his needs, and you neither would nor could then strike any vindictive blows at the Southern people without its immediately reacting upon yourselves.

As it is impossible for us to become homogeneous by all being white, this plan would make it quite possible for us to become homogeneous by all being partly white and partly colored, retaining white majorities in each State. North Carolina, Virginia, Georgia, Tennessee, Arkansas, and Texas would need not to surrender any of their colored people, and it would only require the removal of about 500,000 blacks from the States of Louisiana, Mississippi, Alabama, Florida, and South Carolina to give every State in the Union such a decided preponderance of whites as to remove all danger of negro supremacy, and all fear of trouble from this source.

What say the Republican Senators to this? Of course you will say that your doors are open now to all who may see proper to come, but that is not sufficient to induce them to remove. Are you willing to offer them some special inducement? Are you willing to vote money out of the United States Treasury to pay their expenses and to support them for a short time until they can start in their new homes? Surely, you will demonstrate your sincerity in some practical, helpful way, and not confine your benevolent statesmanship to cheap words. If you will help neither black nor white, you should, in common decency, hold your peace.

BOOKER T. WASHINGTON

Booker T. Washington was the acknowledged spokesman for black Americans during the two decades of 1895 to 1915.[13] Rising from his birth as a slave in Virginia, Washington studied at Hampton Institute where he excelled in debating and speaking activities, a background that served him well in his adult career. Graduating from Hampton in 1875, Washington returned to Malden, West Virginia, where he taught school for several years. In 1881 he was appointed head of Tuskegee Institute in Alabama, a black vocational college, where he remained until his death in 1915. His fame and reputation spread far beyond southeastern Alabama. He was an advisor to Presidents Theodore Roosevelt and William Taft, founder and president of the National Negro Business League, and the leader of black vocational education. In 1896, Harvard University awarded him an honorary Master's degree, the first black to be so honored.

While scholars have estimated that Washington gave over 4,000 public speeches in his lifetime, he is most famous for his address at the Cotton States and International Exposition in Atlanta, Georgia, on September 18, 1895. Washington was already nationally known, as he had spoken at the National Education Association annual convention in Wisconsin in 1884, and at various other venues in his efforts to raise support for Tuskegee and his campaign for black education. The Atlanta speech propelled him to the leadership of black Americans everywhere. Even W.E.B. Du Bois, who later became an outspoken critic of Washington's policies, praised the speech in a letter to the orator on September 24: "Let me heartily congratulate you upon your phenomenal success at Atlanta—it was a word fitly spoken."[14] Other blacks were not so sure, and Du Bois later became a bitter opponent of Washington. His critics saw Washington as bending too far toward accommodation with the dominant white majority and the rigid system of segregation then quickly enveloping all of southern life.

This speech clearly established Washington as the "most prominent and powerful African-American in the United States"[15] and aided him immensely in his drive to make Tuskegee a viable educational institution and black vocational education the primary vehicle for black people to rise in the American system.

ATLANTA EXPOSITION ADDRESS[16]

Mr. President and Gentlemen of the Board of Directors and Citizens:

One third of the population of the South is of the Negro race. No enterprise seeking the material, civil, or moral welfare of this section can disregard this element of our population and reach the highest success. I but convey to you, Mr. President and Directors, the sentiment of the masses of my race when I say that in no way have the value and manhood of the American Negro been more fittingly and generously recognized than by the managers of this magnificent Exposition at every stage of its progress. It is a recognition that will do more to cement the friendship of the two races than any occurrence since the dawn of our freedom.

Not only this, but the opportunity here afforded will awaken among us a new era of industrial progress. Ignorant and inexperienced, it is not strange that in the first years of our new life we began at the top instead of at the bottom; that a seat in Congress or the State Legislature was more sought than real estate or industrial skill; that the political convention or stump speaking had more attractions than starting a dairy farm or truck garden.

A ship lost at sea for many days suddenly sighted a friendly vessel. From the mast of the unfortunate vessel was seen a signal: "Water, water; we die of thirst!" The answer from the friendly vessel at once came back: "Cast down your bucket where you are." A second time the signal, "Water, water; send us water!" ran up from the distressed vessel, and was answered: "Cast down your bucket where you are." And a third and fourth signal for water was answered: "Cast down your bucket where you are." The captain of the distressed vessel, at last heeding the injunction, cast down his bucket, and it came up full of fresh, sparkling water from the mouth of the Amazon River. To those of my race who depend on bettering their condition in a foreign land, or who underestimate the importance of cultivating friendly relations with the Southern white man, who is their next door neighbor, I would say: "Cast down your bucket where you are"—cast it down in making friends in every manly way of the people of all races by whom we are surrounded.

Cast it down in agriculture, mechanics, in commerce, in domestic service, and in the professions. And in this connection it is well to bear in mind that whatever other sins the South may be called to bear, when it comes to business, pure and simple, it is in the South that the Negro is given a man's chance in the commercial world, and in nothing is this Exposition more eloquent than in emphasizing this chance. Our greatest danger is, that in the great leap from slavery to freedom we may overlook the fact that the masses of us are to live by the productions of our hands, and fail to keep in mind that we shall prosper in proportion as we learn to dignify and glorify common labor, and put brains and skill into the common occupations of life; shall prosper in proportion as we learn to draw the line between the superficial and the substantial, the ornamental gewgaws of life and the useful. No race can prosper till it learns that there is as much dignity in tilling a field as in writing a poem. It is at the bottom of life we must begin, and not at the top. Nor should we permit our grievances to overshadow our opportunities.

To those of the white race who look to the incoming of those of foreign birth and strange tongue and habits for the prosperity of the South, were I permitted I would repeat what I say to my own race, "Cast down your bucket where you are." Cast it down among the 8,000,000 Negroes whose habits you know, whose fidelity and love you have tested in days when to have proved treacherous meant the ruin of your firesides. Cast down your bucket among these people who have, without strikes and labor wars, tilled your fields, cleared your forests, builded your railroads and cities, and brought forth treasures from the bowel of the earth, and helped make possible this magnificent representation of the progress of the South. Casting down your bucket among my people, helping and encouraging them as you are doing on these grounds, and to education of head, hand and heart, you will find that they will buy your surplus land, make blossom the waste places in your fields, and run your factories. While doing this, you can be sure in the future, as in the past, that you and your families will be surrounded by the most patient, faithful, law-abiding, and unresentful people that the world has seen. As we have proved our loyalty to you in the past, in nursing your children, watching by the sick bed of your mothers and fathers, and often following them in tear-dimmed eyes to their graves, so in the future, in our humble way, we shall stand by you with a devotion that no foreigner can approach, ready to lay down our lives, if need be, in defense of yours, interlacing our industrial, commercial, civil, and religious life with yours in a way that shall make the interests of both races one. In all things that are purely social we can be as separate as the fingers, yet one as the hand in all things essential to mutual progress.

There is no defense or security for any of us except in the highest intelligence and development of all. If anywhere there are efforts tending to curtail the fullest growth of the Negro, let these efforts be turned into stimulating, encouraging, and making him the most useful and intelligent citizen. These efforts will be twice blessed—"blessing him that gives and him that takes."

There is no escape through law of man or God from the inevitable:

> The laws of changeless justice bind
> Oppressor with oppressed;
> And close as sin and suffering joined
> We march to fate abreast.

Nearly sixteen millions of hands will aid you in pulling the load upwards, or they will pull against you the load downwards. We shall constitute one-third and more of the ignorance and crime of the South, or one-third of its intelligence and progress; we shall contribute one-third to the business and industrial prosperity of the South, or we shall prove a veritable body of death, stagnating, depressing, retarding every effort to advance the body politic.

Gentlemen of the Exposition, as we present to you our humble effort at an exhibition of our progress, you must not expect overmuch. Starting thirty years ago with ownership here and there in a few quilts and pumpkins and chickens (gathered from miscellaneous sources), remember the path that has led from these to the invention and production of agricultural implements, buggies, steam engines, newspapers, books, statuary, carving, paintings, the management of drug stores and banks, has not been trodden without contact with thorns and thistles. While we take pride in what we exhibit as a result of our independent efforts, we do not for a moment forget that our part in this exhibition would fall far short of our expectations but for the constant help that has come to our educational life, not only from the Southern States, but especially from Northern philanthropists, who have made their gifts a constant stream of blessing and encouragement.

The wisest among my race understand that the agitation of questions of social equality is the extremest folly, and that progress in the enjoyment of all the privileges that will come to us must be the result of severe and constant struggle rather than of artificial forcing. No race that has anything to contribute to the markets of the world is long in any degree ostracized. It is important and right that all privileges of the law be ours, but it is vastly more important that we be prepared for the exercise of those privileges. The opportunity to earn a dollar in a factory just now is worth infinitely more than the opportunity to spend a dollar in an opera house.

In conclusion, may I repeat that nothing in thirty years has given us more hope and encouragement, and drawn us so near to you of the white race, as this opportunity offered by the Exposition; and here bending, as it were, over the altar that represents the results of the struggles of your race and mine, both starting practically empty handed three decades ago, I pledge that, in your effort to work out the great and intricate problem which God has laid at the doors of the South, you shall have at all times the patient, sympathetic help of my race; only let this be constantly in mind that, while from representations in these buildings of the product of field, of forest, of mine, of factory, letters, and art, much good will come, yet far above and beyond material benefits will be that higher good, that let us pray God will come, in a blotting out of sectional differences and racial animosities and suspicions, in a determination to administer absolute justice, in a willing obedience among all classes to the mandates of law. This, coupled with our material prosperity, will bring into our beloved South a new heaven and a new earth.

NOTES

1. Edward L. Ayers, *The Promise of the New South: Life after Reconstruction* (New York: Oxford University Press, 1992), 136.

2. August Meier and Elliott M. Rudwick, *From Plantation to Ghetto: An Interpretive History of American Negroes* (New York: Hill & Wang, 1966), 71.

3. Ayers, *Promise of the New South*, 136; Meier and Rudwick, *From Plantation to Ghetto*, 144–145.

4. Meier and Rudwick, *From Plantation to Ghetto*, 162.

5. John W. Cell, *The Highest Stage of White Supremacy: The Origins of Segregation in South Africa and the American South* (Cambridge: Cambridge University Press, 1982), 93.

6. Joel Williamson, *A Rage for Order: Black/White Relations in the American South since Emancipation* (New York: Oxford University Press, 1986), 37.

7. Cell, *Highest Stage of White Supremacy*, 116.

8. Monroe Lee Billington, *The American South: A Brief History* (New York: Charles Scribner's Sons, 1971), 371.

9. Ayers, *Promise of the New South*, 145.

10. Howard N. Rabinowitz, *The First New South, 1865–1920* (Arlington Heights, IL: Harlan Davidson, Inc., 1992), 141.

11. Most of this biographical sketch is from R.D.W. Connor, "Vance, Zebulon Baird," in *Dictionary of American Biography*, vol. XIX, Dumas Malone, ed. (New York: Charles Scribner's Sons, 1936), 158–161.

12. Speech delivered by Vance in the United States Senate, January 30, 1890 (Washington, D.C.: n.p., 1890).

13. Most of this biographical sketch is taken from Stephen E. Lucas, "Booker T. Washington (1856–1915), Educator, Community Leader," in *African-American Orators: A Bio-Critical Sourcebook*, Richard W. Leeman, ed. (Westport, CT: Greenwood Press, 1996), 341–357; and James S. Olson, "Booker T. Washington," in *American Orators before 1900: Critical Studies and Sources*, Bernard K. Duffy and Halford R. Ryan, eds. (Westport, CT: Greenwood Press, 1987), 399–405.

14. Louis Harlan, ed., *The Booker T. Washington Papers*, vol. IV (Urbana: University of Illinois Press, 1972–1975), 26.

15. Lucas, "Booker T. Washington," 342.

16. Louis R. Harlan, ed. *The Booker T. Washington Papers*, vol. 1 (Urbana: University of Illinois Press, 1972), 73–76.

FOR FURTHER READING

Meier, August. *Negro Thought in America, 1880–1915*. Ann Arbor: University of Michigan Press, 1963.

Newby, I. A., ed. *The Development of Segregationist Thought*. Homewood, IL: The Dorsey Press, 1968.

Woodward, C. Vann. *The Strange Career of Jim Crow*, 3rd rev. ed. New York: Oxford University Press, 1974.

Wynes, Charles, ed. *The Negro in the South since 1865*. University: University of Alabama Press, 1965.

Zebulon Baird Vance

Shirley, Franklin R. *Zebulon Vance, Tarheel Spokesman*. Charlotte, NC: McNally and Loftin, 1962.

Tucker, Glenn. *Zeb Vance, Champion of Personal Freedom*. Indianapolis IL: Bobbs-Merrill Co., 1965.

Yates, Richard E. *The Confederacy and Zeb Vance*, W. Stanley Hoole, ed. Tuscaloosa, AL: Confederate Publishing Co., Inc., 1958.

Booker T. Washington

Harlan, Louis R. *Booker T. Washington: The Making of a Black Leader, 1856–1901*. New York: Oxford University Press, 1972.

―――. *Booker T. Washington: The Wizard of Tuskegee, 1901–1915*. New York: Oxford University Press, 1983.

Harris, Thomas E. and Patrick C. Kennicott. "Booker T. Washington: A Study of Conciliatory Rhetoric." *Southern Speech Communication Journal* 37 (Fall 1971), 47–59.

Heath, Robert L. "A Time for Silence: Booker T. Washington in Atlanta." *Quarterly Journal of Speech* 64 (1978), 385–399.

King, Andrew A. "Booker T. Washington and the Myth of Heroic Materialism." *Quarterly Journal of Speech* 60 (1974), 323–327.

Wallace, Karl R. "Booker T. Washington." In *A History and Criticism of American Public Address*, vol. I, William N. Brigance, ed. New York: McGraw-Hill, 1943, 407–433.

CHAPTER 10

Precursors of Progressivism: Nineteenth-Century Advocates for a More Humane South

Many of the critics and historians who have written about the post-bellum South have focused on the economic problems and the need for urbanization, agricultural diversification, industrialization, and, simply put, modernization. There is no question that the post-Civil War South found itself in dire economic straits and the siren call for industrialization and a "New South" proved irresistible to many southerners.

It could be argued, however, that the South's problems were not simply economic and that the human problem should have ranked equally high on the region's agenda. Some of the dimensions of the human element included a practically nonexistant education system for either race; lynching and other brutal treatment of black men; the driving white passion to keep the black race "in its place"; ill-health, poor housing, primitive or insubstantial social services for both white and black; an inhumane prison system; narrow thinking about state rights; paranoia stemming from a regional inferiority complex; and a fear of the future coupled with an unhealthy reverance for the past. These tendencies all came together as powerful forces that constrained growth and reduced the possibilities for significant progress—economic or otherwise. The blinders worn by most of the New South advocates prevented any significant attack on these human problems. The region remained in the nation's backwater until past the half-way point of the next century, when in the 1970s and 1980s, the region became synonomous with growth and prosperity.

One of the most serious and pervasive problems facing the black man in the South in the decades after the Civil War was lynching. Used by whites as a method of Negro control (that is, "keeping the Negro in his place"), lynching took an incredible toll throughout the region. Between 1882, the first year that statistics were kept on the practice, and 1952, at least 4,739 persons were murdered nationwide at the hands of a mob. In the West lynching served as a means of vigilante control where courts and judges were few and far-between, but it was most virulent and racially-oriented in the South. During these seven decades, 82 percent of those 4,739 cases were in the South and 84 percent of the victims were black.[1]

Southern political figures, business leaders, and journalists alike all condoned the practice until well into the twentieth century. Many of the demagogues publicly affirmed their support for this extra-legal "justice." Probably the most blatant demagogic advocacy for the practice came from South Carolina's Coleman Blease, when he remarked that, "whenever the constitution comes between me and the virtues of the white women of the South, I say to hell with the constitution."[2]

Blease's irreverent disregard of the Constitution reflects the prime justification for lynching given by southern men: black rape of white women. Invariably, this charge was the rationale presented time and again in speeches, sermons, editorials, and pamphlets that supported the custom; in fact, less than one-third of those lynched were even accused of rape, and no one knows how many of these might actually have been guilty.[3]

It took a long and bitter fight for the South to renounce and give up this heinous practice. Ida Wells-Barnett and a few others started seriously challenging the habit before the turn of the century, but as late as 1948, Governor Fielding Wright of Mississippi and many other southerners denounced an anti-lynching bill proposed by President Harry Truman's Committee on Civil Rights.[4] Isolated instances of mob violence occurred even into the era of the Civil Rights crusade of the 1960s and 1970s, and some of the most visible cases of mob "justice" came during that period. Indeed, there were twelve lynchings in Mississippi as late as 1980.[5]

There were some men and women, however, in the late nineteenth century who spoke out against this stiffling culture, especially in the almost taboo area of humane treatment for the Negro. An examination of this reform rhetoric will show that there was southern dissent, even in the face of most white southerners' hardening attitudes about the role and place of the black person in the region. The idea of decent and equal treatment of the black race stood in stark contrast to the prevailing sentiment and thought in the South—and nation, for that matter. These activists founded no social action movement, and one of them felt forced to leave the region due to her outspokenness regarding racial issues. Atticus Haygood and Ida B. Wells-Barnett were precursors of those later activists who tried to redefine a new vision of the South in the Progressive years, the 1920s and 1930s, and the Civil Rights era of the 1950s and 1960s.

These speakers are clearly in the tradition of the "river of our struggle," so eloquently described by Vincent Harding in *There Is a River: The Black Struggle for Freedom in America*. Haygood can be seen as a forerunner of the twentieth century white southern liberal reformers who were not afraid to take a hard and critical look at southern culture and mores. Ida Wells-

Barnett stands as a model for the black activists of the 1960s who risked much in their quest for racial justice. These two were only a tiny spring in the late 1880s, easily dammed up by the traditional southern culture, but that trickle grew to a brook in the Progressive years and the 1920s, a creek in pre-World War II America, and a raging torrent in the 1960s.

ATTICUS GREENE HAYGOOD

A major contributor to the process of national reconciliation, Atticus Greene Haygood played a significant role in attempting to persuade the South to take a different look at the newly freed slave and to provide education and industrial training for him.

Haygood spent most of his life in Georgia, having been born in Watkinsville in 1839, licensed to preach at Oxford in 1858, and graduated from Emory College in the following year. He preached in various Georgia Methodist churches until 1870, except for two brief tours as a chaplin with the Confederate Army. He left the pastorate in 1870 when he was elected Secretary of the Sunday School and editor of all Methodist Sunday School publications for the southeast region. Shortly after moving to Nashville, Tennessee, he became editor of the Methodist Church's missionary board publications, but in 1874, his wife became ill and he resigned his positions and moved his family back to Oxford.

During his tenure as the eighth president of Emory College, Haygood struggled with problems of fund-raising and even survival for the small Methodist College. Haygood became famous in the North in 1880 after he delivered a widely disseminated sermon at Emory on the New South. In 1881 Haygood published *Our Brother in Black: His Freedom and His Future*, which added to his fame, and he was invited on a fifteen-city speaking tour in New England in which he delivered a lecture entitled, "The New South from a Southern Standpoint."

In 1882, the George F. Slater Fund, which had been established by a northern philanthropist to support education for southern blacks, appointed Haygood agent. In addition to speaking courageously in favor of Negro education to southern audiences that were not ready for that radical idea, as he does in the speech included here, Haygood also fought hard against the harsh convict lease system used by southern prisons and was a leading spokesman for improved schools for white children.

After being elected bishop of the Methodist Church, Haygood finished his career in California, returning to Georgia in 1893, where he died three years later.

THE EDUCATION OF THE NEGRO[6]

There is nothing peculiar in the subject I am to discuss at this time. The education of a Negro is the education of a human being. In its essential characteristics the human mind is the same in every race and in every age. When a Negro child is taught that two and two are four he learns just what a white child learns when he is taught the same proposition. The teacher uses the same faculties of mind in imparting the truth as to the sum of two and two. The two children use the same faculties in learning the truth; it means the same thing to them both. In further teaching and learning the methods may vary, but the variations will depend less on differences of race than on peculiarities of the individual. What is here advanced is so obviously true that any human being trying to teach any other human being that two and two are four would naturally use the same method in conveying the truth of the statement, and would certainly expect the same results when the truth was once apprehended.

All this has nothing to do with the question, Which child learns most readily? or with another question, Which child can learn most? If I were called on to answer these questions, I would say, as to the first, that the Negro child of ordinary intelligence will apprehend that two and two are four as readily as a white child of ordinary intelligence. Except in the mind of a fool there is no more in this statement to excite prejudice than if one should affirm that a Negro boy ten years old weighs as much as a white boy ten years old, or that he can jump as far.

Two Thousand Years the Start

As to the second question I would answer in perfect frankness that I do not know how much either can learn, and therefore I do not know which can learn most. If urged to answer the question, Which race, as we find them today in this country, is capable of the higher mental training and culture? I would answer that this is a very different question; for the capabilities of a race are the results not only of their original ethnic endowment, but of their ethnic history for many generations. As applied to these two races the condition of the problems of their education are not now equal, nor can they now be made equal; for the white race has fully two thousand years the start. The ethnic development of the Britons was higher before Julius Caesar than was the ethnic development of the African tribes from which our Negro fellow-citizens were taken some generations ago. Nothing should less need proving than the doctrine here set forth. Any stock-breeder can expound to you the force that is in the law of heredity. Ask the wise men who breed race-horses, Jersey cows, hunting-dogs, or even canary birds. They attach great importance to pedigree, and they can tell you why.

Nobody Knows

I do not then propose to discuss the relative capacity of the two races; my theme is a very different one. Besides, I am not prepared to discuss that question; I do not know any man who is prepared to discuss it; neither race is sufficiently educated to furnish a gauge of its possibilities. As to the Negro nobody knows, even approximately, what he can do. His experiment is just begun. Until recently he had no chance; today he has a small chance; till the gospel and common sense have conquered the prejudices of us of the white race he will not have the best conditions for showing what he can do. Considering what small chance he has had, and the short time in which he has been allowed to learn, his achievements seem to me to be most remarkable. But on this point I know very well that, as is usual where feeling enters into judgments, those who know the least from personal investigations will make the most dogmatic assertions and the most vehement denials.

The proposition which I am here to advocate is this, and this only: *The Negro in the United States ought to be educated.*

The first reason I offer is in

The Fact of His Humanity

He ought to be educated because he is a man. At this point I say nothing to those who deny the essential unity of the human race; I speak to those who do believe in that essential unity.

For one, I believe in the essential unity of the race, and I believe in the brotherhood of the race. I believe, therefore, in all brotherly help and service wherever and however I find any human being. For the very same reasons that I believe in sending the gospel and Christian civilization that goes with it to China, I believe in giving Christian education to the Negroes in America. And lest by some possibility there should be some misapprehension as to the truth I hold, let me say: I believe in giving the opportunities of Christian education to the Negroes for the same reason that I believe in giving the opportunities of Christian education to white people—that is, because they are alike human beings, and by natural, God-given right should have the best opportunity God's providence allows them for becoming all that they are capable of becoming. So long as I believe in Jesus Christ and his gospel I cannot stand upon a lower platform than this. I think I know what he would say on this subject. It is he who spoke of himself as "the Son of man," the Brother of every man; it is he who gave us the parable of the Good Samaritan and the Sermon on the Mount; it is he who lived for all men and died for all men; it is he who will tell us how to discuss and answer questions that involve the rights and needs and destinies of human beings. People who have opinions they are afraid to carry to Jesus Christ had better change their opinions. . . .

The Three Rs

As a practical question I would say: every child in this country, white and black, should have from his parents, or from the Government, an equal chance for elementary education. I believe in what Americans mean by the common school.

There should be schools enough to give to every child the rudiments of learning; if you please, the "three R's." And these should be good enough to teach the rudiments thoroughly. Such schools there must be if the children of the republic are to be educated; if they are to reach the case they must be backed by the Government. To accomplish their end wisely, justly, efficiently, there must be a fair and equitable distribution of the school funds, without distinction of race. I rejoice that every State in this Union—with perhaps one exception—does now, in principle at least, use its school fund without distinction of race, so that in the opportunities of elementary education there may be justice to both races.

What comes after this universal elementary education? The answer is simple and to me obvious. Whatever individual capacity, aided by the benevolence of good men and the wise enterprise of the Churches, makes possible. Give them all, black and white, the keys of knowledge, and then let them unlock as many doors as they can. I pity the coward who is afraid to give a human being this chance. Little danger is there that any race will rise too high, that any individual of any race will learn too much truth. There is no danger more remote than the danger of over-education; there is no danger more imminent than the danger of under-education and false education. And there is no part of the civilized world that at this time has greater need to concern itself with the social and political and moral perils that lurk in wide-spread ignorance than our own well-beloved and fair sunny South of the year 1883.

Argument on the Lower Plane

With not a few persons of good business faculty and shrewd worldly wisdom it often happens that an argument on the lower plane of policy goes much farther than an argument on the higher plane of truth and right. They are prone to forget that there is no wise policy that is against right, and that while God reigns there cannot be.

I will offer the argument on the lower plane. The Negro is here, and here to stay. He is a citizen armed with that thunderbolt of political power, the ballot. That it was given to him unwisely because untimely and without conditions that would develop in him a wise conscience as to the use of it; that as a rule he is unfit to be a voter—all this I understand fairly well. But this is not the subject to discuss at this time. He is a citizen; he is a voter. In some States he is in the majority; in every Southern State he is a tremendous power—a power, whether he uses it or designing white men use it.

It is about time to consider facts. His citizenship is a fact, and his presence here is a fact. There are now at least seven millions of Negroes in this country; nearly all of them are in the Southern States. They increase rapidly and steadily faster than the white race. Some writers have attempted, with small success, to impeach the United States census tables. This much may be said on this point; these tables are the highest authority we have on this subject.

A man who does not know that voters

Ought to Be Able to Read and Write

does not know enough to be argued with. The illiterate vote of the Southern States is simply appalling, and the illiterate vote is increasing. From 1870 to 1880 there was an increase of illiterate votes in the Southern States of nearly two hundred thousand. Figures may not be interesting to a mixed audience, but they are sometimes very instructive. I will give you a few on the illiterate vote of our section of the Union.

In Georgia the illiterate white vote in 1870 was 21,899; in 1880, 28,571; the Negro illiterate vote in 1870 was 100,551; in 1880, 116,516. In Kentucky the white illiterate vote in 1870 was 43,826; in 1880 54,956; the Negro illiterate vote in 1870 was 37,899; in 1880, 43,177. In Tennessee the white illiterate vote in 1870 was 37,713; in 1880, 46,948; the Negro illiterate vote in 1870 was 55,938; in 1880, 58,601. In Texas the white illiterate vote in 1870 was 17,505; in 1880, 33,085; the Negro illiterate vote in 1870 was 47,275; in 1880, 59,609. It has increased in every one of these States.

Encouragement for the Scared

Let those philosophers who think that "education spoils the poor for laborers" take heart. The uneducated adults among the whites and blacks in the South increase in numbers. If ignorance makes better laborers, there has been great advance in our industrial resources since 1870. There were among us nearly two hundred thousand more grown men who could neither read nor write in 1880 than in 1870. Alas! there are more illiterate women than illiterate men. Doubtless 1883 would show still farther progress—downward.

The Votes of Ignorance

Surely it cannot be necessary before this assembly to point out the perils to our institutions involved in this large and increasing illiterate vote.

How are the votes of ignorant men determined? 1. In small part by the counsels of the wise and good citizen. I say in small part, for the bad and designing demagogue has more power over the ignorant vote than has the good and unselfish patriot. 2. The votes of the ignorant are largely determined by prejudice. Out of prejudice proceed conflicts and all manner of social and political wrongs. 3. The votes of the ignorant are largely influenced by bribes, offered in one form or another. And this means fraud and corruption without end and bottomless. The worst thing about this huge illiterate vote is not the incapacity of the voters to use their ballots wisely; the worst thing about it is this: ignorance fits them exactly to become the tools of corrupt men of superior intelligence. With an illiterate vote large enough to hold the balance of power elections are for the most part dictated by demagogues and manipulated by villains. It is left to intelligent, industrious, and honest citizens to settle the costs of corrupt government.

They Say: "Teach Him Morals"

I am not unacquainted with the answer to all this as a plea for the education of the Negro. "Book learning," we are gravely informed, "is not sufficient; the Negro needs education in morals." This is true, and true as to the Negro because true as to all other men. But will sensible men seriously urge the Negro's education in morals as an objection to his education in books? Is book-knowledge, then, in itself unfavorable to good morals? Is ignorance the mother of devotion and the nurse of religion? Then recall the fierce Arabs who put the torch to great libraries, and bid them burn down your colleges and school-houses; bid them destroy your books and stop your busy press forever. Then, stop all education; stop all thinking; vegetate and die.

It is unmitigated nonsense—this miserable pretense of reasoning that since the Negro does need betterment in his morals the school-house is not good for him. . . .

Four Root Objections

The objections to the Negro's education that control men's opinions have their origin in four roots closely united.

1. In ignorance. There are not a few who are at bottom opposed to all education.

2. In stinginess. Multiplied thousands deny their own children education because it costs money. Money is their God. There are some white men in this country who by some sad mischance are both fathers of families and the owners of good properties, but they are too mean and too near barbarism to educate their children. They are traitors to their sacred trust of fatherhood and a disgrace to the human race. And as to public schools, in which the children of the poor may be taught the rudiments of education, objection, with most people, would close—if it cost them nothing. I have yet to meet one man who opposed the schools somebody else's money paid for—unless from a sentiment worse than avarice.

3. In prejudice—prejudice against the Negro because he is a Negro. Avarice is a mean spirit, but this sort of prejudice is meaner. It is cowardly and ignoble; it is, root and branch, utterly unchristian. If any think that my language is too strong, let them test their prejudices. Take them to Jesus Christ

and ask him to approve them. Test them in the light of the Sermon on the Mount and of the judgment-day. How mean they look in that light!

4. In apprehensions that appeal to two classes of fear:

(1) The apprehension that the education of the Negro will spoil him as a laborer. I know what I am talking about when I say that this fear is at the bottom of much of the current opposition to the education of the Negro. I go among the people and keep my eyes and ears open.

"Bossism"

If the argument that supports this apprehension be worth anything, it proves too much, for it is just as good as an argument against the education of the poor whites. Education will as certainly spoil them for laborers. The spirit that is capable of such an objection to the education of the poor of any race is selfish, cowardly, and essentially mean. It is worthy only of the Dark Ages. It is at bottom a plea for the tyranny of "bossism." Put into form, it says this: "I am, by virtue of money, or shrewdness, or learning a sort of 'boss' among my fellow-men; I must keep them in ignorance that I may keep them down and be better able to play the 'boss'."

But there is nothing in the argument; it is false all through. For no man is better for anything in the world to be done because he is ignorant. A trained dog is better than a wild dog. Ignorance is not a qualification for anything that God intended man to do. It is first, last, and all the time disqualification rather. Every principle of right and justice denies it; every law of political economy condemns it; the history of the human race repudiates it.

Intelligence spoils no man for anything that a man ought to do in this world. And were it otherwise, what right before God has one human being to keep another human being in ignorance in order to keep him in slavery? These questions go to the bottom, and we must go to the bottom in settling questions of rights and wrongs between man and his fellow-men. . . .

A Needless Scare

(2) With some there is opposition to the education of the Negro from a vague fear of something that is called "social equality." Just now the poor Negro is in a place where "two seas meet." There are two classes of extremists: One is in mortal terror lest the Negro should become somebody; the other is morbidly anxious that he should assert claims to what he is in no wise fitted for. If between the two he does not lose his balance he will deserve the respect of both. There never was in this world, in any nation or community, such a thing as social equality, and there never will be. The social spheres arrange themselves to suit themselves, and no laws promulgated by State or Church will change the social affinities and natural selections of men. Men choose the circles for which they have affinity, seek

the companionships they prefer, and find the places that are suited to them. . . .

Of this we may be sure: the Negro will, sooner or later, be educated. The State governments recognize him in the public school administration. Northern liberality has spent more than twenty millions of dollars in the South since the surrender of the Confederate cause for the education of the Negro. With our approval or without it this work will go on, and it ought to go on. I thank God for those who have carried it on thus far; for the liberal men and women who have given great sums of money, and for the devoted men and women who have given their personal service. That some cranks and marplots have appeared among them in the course of twenty years is no more an argument against the great work itself than is the discovery of an occasional hypocrite and scoundrel in the pulpit an argument against Christianity.

During most of the time that this work has been going on in our midst its promoters have had little countenance or encouragement from us. Many times they have been opposed and despised and made to feel our contempt.

Absurd and Childish

In all truth and common sense there is no reason for discounting, in any respect, a white man or woman simply for teaching Negroes. It is utterly absurd. I believe it to be also sinful. Let us consider our attitude on this subject for a moment. We have the Negroes to cook for us, and if they do not know how, as is often the case, our wives and daughters teach them. We employ them in all sorts of ways. When elections come on we ask not only their votes, but their "social influence." Candidates, from governor to coroner, do this earnestly, invariably, and without social discredit. We sell goods to them, we buy from them, we practice law for them, we practice medicine for them, and it is all well enough. In all business relations, except teaching, so far as I can remember our ways on this subject, whether as employers or employees, we think it all very nice, and so do our wise neighbors. How utterly and childishly absurd it is to "make and exception" if one teaches a Negro child how to spell, to read, and to write. Will some master in such fine knowledge explain just wherein it is seemly to sell goods to a Negro, or to buy from him, or to practice law for him, or to give him medicine, or even to preach to him sometimes, but a thing abhorrent to teach him whatever he can learn that we can teach? Of what shams we are guilty!

Think of people going into raptures over David Livingstone, explorer of Africa and pioneer of Christian civilization, and then turning up their noses at a teacher, not because he is ignorant or ill-bred or bad, but because, forsooth, he teaches a Negro school.

A word more I add on this point. If the best results are to be achieved, both for the white and black races, in the education of the Negro, then Southern white people must take part in the work of his education. . . .

The Only Platform

It is one of the sad things connected with the difficult problem of the two races living together in this country that not a few good people of both races have despaired of its solution. The author of the Declaration of Independence wrote, it is said, in 1782, this predication: "Nothing is more certainly written in the book of fate than that these people are to be free; nor is it less certain that the two races, equally free, cannot live in the same government."

It does not surprise me that Mr. Jefferson made both these predictions. As to the first, there was at that time in Virginia and other Southern States a strong party that favored the emancipation of the slaves. As to the second, he had studied French philosophy more than he had studied Christianity. If this country had been pagan Rome or infidel France, the first prediction would have failed—the slaves never would have been set free by the will of man. Had they been set free, the second prediction would have been fulfilled, for in a pagan or infidel country the two races could not be "equally free and live in the same government." They would not have been set free had this not been a Christian country; as it is a Christian country, the two races, "equally free" before the law, can "live in the same government," and the problem of their citizenship can be solved.

As to this whole subject, full of difficulties, as those best know who have personal relations to it, there is just one platform on which Christian people can stand. Our problem with these millions of Negroes in our midst can be properly solved, not by force of any sort from without the States where they live; no more can it be solved by repression within those States. *It can be worked out only on the basis of the Ten Commandments and the Sermon on the Mount.* On this platform we can solve any problem whatever—whether personal, social, industrial, political, national, or ethical—that Providence brings before us. On any lower platform we will fail, and always fail.

IDA WELLS-BARNETT

Ida B. Wells was born in Holly Springs, Mississippi, into a slave family in 1862.[7] She received an education at Rust College, which was an industrial school for blacks in her home town. Her parents died in a yellow fever epidemic, and she moved to Memphis, Tennessee, to teach school. She began to write for a Memphis black newspaper, *Memphis Free Speech*, but she soon found out that speech was not free for her. A series of editorials about the unequal funding for black schools in Memphis led to her being fired from her teaching position. She turned full-time to journalism, buying part of the paper, and contined to write and editorialize for it. In 1892, a mob lynched three black Memphis businessmen, and she took on the case with a vengence, claiming that the stated reason for the lynching, rape, was not the case at all, but rather, that the three had been too successful in their competition with white businesses.[8]

A mob attacked and destroyed her newspaper. She was in New York at the time, and did not return to Memphis. Soon, she was successfully speaking and writing in the North and in England, promoting the cause of antilynching. She became active in women's issues in general and especially suffrage. She founded the first Negro women's suffrage organization, the Alpha Suffrage Club, in Chicago. In her autobiography, she asserted that the Lyric Hall speech published here was the "real beginning of the Club movement among colored women."[9]

SOUTHERN HORRORS: LYNCH LAW IN ALL ITS PHASES[10]

The Offense

Wednesday evening May 24th, 1892, the city of Memphis was filled with excitement. Editorials in the daily papers of that date caused a meeting to be held in the Cotton Exchange Building; a committee was sent for the editors of the *Free Speech*, an Afro-American journal published in that city, and the only reason the open threats of lynching that were made were not carried out was because they could not be found. The cause of all this commotion was the following editorial published in *Free Speech* May 21st, 1892, the Saturday previous.

"Eight negroes lynched since last issue of the *Free Speech* one at Little Rock, Ark., last Saturday morning where the citizens broke (?) into the penitentiary and got their man; three near Anniston, Ala., one near New Orleans; and three at Clarksville, Ga., the last three for killing a white man, and five on the same old racket—the new alarm about raping white women. The same programme of hanging, then shooting bullets into the lifeless bodies was carried out to the letter.

Nobody in this section of the country believes the old thread bare lie that Negro men rape white women. If Southern white men are not careful, they will over-reach themselves and public sentiment will have a reaction; a conclusion will then be reached which will be very damaging to the moral reputation of their women."

The Daily Commercial of Wednesday following, May 25th, contained the following leader:

"Those negroes who are attempting to make the lynching of individuals of their race a means for arousing the worst passions of their kind are playing with a dangerous sentiment. The negroes may as well understand that there is no mercy for the negro rapist and little patience with his defenders. A negro organ printed in this city, in a recent issue publishes the following atrocious paragraph: 'Nobody in this section of the country believes the old thread bare lie that negro men rape white women. If Southern white men are not careful they will over-reach themselves, and public sentiment will have a reaction; and a conclusion will be reached which will be very damaging to the moral reputation of their women.'

The fact that a black scoundrel is allowed to live and utter such loathsome and repulsive calumnies is a volume of evidence as to the wonderful patience of Southern whites. But we have had enough of it.

There are some things that the Southern white man will not tolerate, and the obscene intimations of the foregoing have brought the writer to the very outermost limit of public patience. We hope we have said enough."

The *Evening Scimitar* of same date, copied the *Commercial's* editorial with these words of comment: "Patience under such circumstances is not a virtue. If the negroes themselves do not apply the remedy without delay it will be the duty of those whom he has attacked to tie the wretch who utters these calumnies to a stake at the intersection of Main and Madison Sts., brand him in the forehead with a hot iron and perform upon him a surgical operation with a pair of tailor's shears."

Acting upon this advice, the leading citizens met in the Cotton Exchange Building the same evening, and threats of lynching were freely indulged, not by the lawless element upon which the deviltry of the South is usually saddled—but by the leading business men, in their leading business centre. Mr. Fleming, the business manager and owning a half interest in the *Free Speech*, had to leave town to escape the mob, and was afterwards ordered not to return; letters and telegrams sent me in New York where I was spending my vacation advised me that bodily harm awaited my return. Creditors took possession of the office and sold the outfit, and the *Free Speech* was as if it had never been.

The editorial in question was prompted by the many inhuman and fiendish lynchings of Afro-Americans which have recently taken place and was meant as a warning. Eight lynched in one week and five of them charged with rape! The thinking public will not easily believe freedom and education more brutalizing than slavery, and the world knows that the crime of rape was unknown during four years of civil war, when the white women of the South were at the mercy of the race which is all at once charged with being a bestial one.

Since my business has been destroyed and I am in exile from home because of that editorial, the issue has been forced, and as the writer of it I feel that the race and the public generally should have a statement of the facts as they exist. They will serve at the same time as a defense for the Afro-Americans Sampsons who suffer themselves to be betrayed by white Delilahs.

The whites of Montgomery, Ala., knew J. C. Duke sounded the keynote of the situation—which they would gladly hide from the world, when he said in his paper, *The Herald*, five years ago: "Why is it that white women attract negro men now more than in former days? There was a time when such a thing was unheard of. There is a secret to this thing, and we greatly suspect it is the growing appreciation of white Juliets for colored Romeos." Mr. Duke, like the *Free Speech* proprietors, was forced to leave the city for reflecting on the "honah" of white women and his paper suppressed; but the truth remains that Afro-American men do not always rape (?) white women without their consent.

Mr. Duke, before leaving Montgomery, signed a card disclaiming any intention of slandering Southern white women. The editor of the *Free Speech* has no disclaimer to enter, but asserts instead that there are many white women in the South who would marry colored men if such an act would not place them at once beyond the pale of society and within the clutches of the law. The miscegenation laws of the South only operate against the legitimate union of the races; they leave the white man free to seduce all the colored girls he can, but it is death to the colored man who yields to the force and advances of a similar attraction to white women. White men lynch the offending Afro-American, not because he is a despoiler of virtue, but because he succumbs to the smiles of white women.

The Black and White of It

The *Cleveland Gazette* of January 16, 1892, publishes a case in point. Mrs. J. S. Underwood, the wife of a minister of Elyria, Ohio, accused an Afro-American of rape. She told her husband that during his absence in 1888, stumping the State for the Prohibition Party, the man came to the kitchen door, forced his way in the house and insulted her. She tried to drive him out with a heavy poker, but he overpowered and chloroformed her, and when she revived her clothing was torn and she was in a horrible condition. She did not know the man but could identify him. She pointed out William Offett, a married man, who was arrested and, being in Ohio, was granted a trial.

The prisoner vehemently denied the charge of rape, but confessed that he went to Mrs. Underwood's residence at her invitation and was criminally intimate with her at her request. This availed him nothing against the sworn testimony of a minister's wife, a lady of the highest respectability. He was found guilty, and entered the penitentiary, December 14, 1888, for fifteen years. Some time afterwards the woman's remorse led her to confess to her husband that the man was innocent.

These are her words: "I met Offett at the Post Office. It was raining. He was polite to me, and as I had several bundles in my arms he offered to carry them home for me, which he did. He had a strange fascination for me, and I invited him to call on me. He called, bringing chestnuts and candy for the children. By this means we got them to leave us alone in the room. Then I sat on his lap. He made a proposal to me and I readily consented. Why I did so, I do not know, but that I did is true. He visited me several times after that and after each time I was indiscreet. I did not care after the first time. In fact I could not have resisted, and had no desire to resist."

When asked by her husband why she told him she had been outraged, she said: "I had several reasons for telling you. One was the neighbors saw the fellow here, another was, I was afraid I had contracted a loathsome disease, and still another was that I feared I might give birth to a Negro baby. I hoped to save my reputation by telling you a deliberate lie." Her husband horrified by the confession had Offett, who had already served four years, released and secured a divorce.

There are thousands of such cases throughout the South, with the difference that the Southern white men in insatiate fury wreak their vengeance without intervention of law upon the Afro-Americans who consort with their women. A few instances to substantiate the assertion that some white women love the company of the Afro-American will not be out of place. Most of these cases were reported by the daily papers of the South.

In the winter of 1885–6 the wife of a practicing physician in Memphis, in good social standing whose name has escaped me, left home, husband, and children, and ran away with her black coachman. She was with him a month before her husband found her and brought her home. The coachman could not be found. The doctor moved his family away from Memphis, and is living in another city under an assumed name.

In the same city last year a white girl in the dusk of evening screamed at the approach of some parties that a Negro had assaulted her on the street. He was captured, tried by a white judge and jury, that acquitted him of the charge. It is needless to add if there had been a scrap of evidence on which to convict him of so grave a charge he would have been convicted.

Sarah Clark of Memphis loved a black man and lived openly with him. When she was indicted last spring for miscegenation, she swore in court that she was *not* a white woman. This she did to escape the penitentiary and continued her illicit relation undisturbed. That she is of the lower class of whites, does not disturb the fact that she is a white woman. "The leading citizens" of Memphis are defending the "honor" of *all* white women, *demi-monde* included.

Since the manager of the *Free Speech* has been run away from Memphis by the guardians of the honor of Southern white women, a young girl living on Poplar St., who was discovered in intimate relations with a handsome mulatto young colored man, Will Morgan by name, stole her father's money to send the young fellow away from the father's wrath. She has since joined him in Chicago. . . .

The New Cry

The new appeal of Southern whites to Northern sympathy and sanction, the adroit, insiduous plea made by Bishop Fitzgerald for suspension of judgement because those "who condemn lynching express no sympathy for the *white* woman in the case," falls to the ground in the light of the foregoing.

From this exposition of the race issue in lynch law, the whole matter is explained by the well-known opposition growing out of slavery to the progress of the race. This is crystallized in the oft-repeated slogan: "This is a white man's country and the white man must rule." The South resented giving the Afro-American his freedom, the ballot box and the Civil Rights Law. The raids of the Ku-Klux and White Liners to subvert reconstruction government, the Hamburg and Ellerton, S.C., the Copiah County Miss., and the Layfayette Parish, La., massacres were excused as the natural resentment of intelligence against government by ignorance.

Honest white men practically conceded the necessity of intelligence murdering ignorance to correct the mistake of the general government, and the race was left to the tender mercies of the solid South. Thoughtful Afro-Americans with the strong arm of the government withdrawn and with the hope to stop such wholesale massacres urged the race to sacrifice its political rights for sake of peace. They honestly believed the race should fit itself for government, and when that should be done, the objection to race participation in politics would be removed.

But the sacrifice did not remove the trouble, nor move the South to justice. One by one the Southern States have legally (?) disfranchised the Afro-American, and since the repeal of the Civil Rights Bill nearly every Southern State has passed separate car laws with a penalty against their infringement. The race regardless of advancement is penned into filthy, stifling partitions cut off from smoking cars. All this while, although the political cause has been removed, the butcheries of black men at Barnwell, S.C., Carrolton, Miss., Waycross, Ga., and Memphis, Tenn., have gone on; also the flaying alive of a man in Kentucky, the burning of one in Arkansas, the hanging of a fifteen year old girl in Louisiana, a woman in Jackson, Tenn., and one in Hollendale, Miss., until the dark and bloody record of the South shows 728 Afro-Americans lynched during the past 8 years. Not 50 of these were for political causes; the rest were for all manner of accusations from that of rape of white women, to the case of the boy Will Lewis who was hanged at Tullahoma, Tenn., last year for being drunk and "sassy" to white folks.

These statistics compiled by the Chicago *Tribune* were given the first of this year (1892). Since then, not less than one hundred and fifty have been known to have met violent death at the hands of cruel bloodthirsty mobs during the past nine months.

To palliate this record (which grows worse as the Afro-American becomes intelligent) and excuse some of the most heinous crimes that ever stained the history of a country, the South is shielding itself behind the plausible screen of defending the honor of its women. This, too, in the face of the fact that only *one-third* of the 728 victims to mobs have been *charged* with rape, to say nothing of those of that one-third who were innocent of the charge. A white correspondent of the *Baltimore Sun* declares that the Afro-American who was lynched in Chestertown, Md., in May for assault on a white girl was innocent; that the deed was done by a white man who had since disappeared. The girl herself maintained that her assailant was a white man. When that poor Afro-American was murdered, the whites excused their refusal of a trial on the ground that they wished to spare the white girl the mortification of having to testify in court.

This cry has had its effect. It has closed the heart, stifled the conscience, warped the judgment and hushed the voice of press and pulpit on the subject of lynch law throughout this "land of liberty." Men who stand high in the esteem of the public for christian character, for moral and physical courage, for devotion to the principles of equal and exact justice to all, and for great sagacity, stand as cowards who fear to open their mouths before this great outrage. They do not see that by their tacit encouragement, their silent acquiescence, the black shadow of lawlessness in the form of lynch law is spreading its wings over the whole country.

Men who, like Governor Tillman, start the ball of lynch law rolling for a certain crime, are powerless to stop it when drunken or criminal white toughs feel like hanging an Afro-American on any pretext.

Even to the better class of Afro-Americans the crime of rape is so revolting they have too often taken the white man's word and given lynch law neither the investigation nor condemnation it deserved.

They forget that a concession of the right to lynch a man for a certain crime, not only concedes the right to lynch any person for any crime, but (so frequently is the cry of rape now raised) it is in a fair way to stamp us a race of rapists and desperados. They have gone on hoping and believing that general education and financial strength would solve the difficulty, and are devoting their energies to the accumulation of both.

The mob spirit has grown with the increasing intelligence of the Afro-American. It has left the out-of-the-way places where ignorance prevails, has thrown off the mask and with this new cry stalks in broad daylight in large cities, the centres of civilization, and is encouraged by the "leading citizens" and the press. . . .

In its issue of June 4th, the Memphis *Evening Scimitar* gives the following excuse for lynching law:

"Aside from the violation of white women by Negroes, which is the out-cropping of a bestial perversion of instinct, the chief cause of trouble between the races in the South is the Negro's lack of manners. In the state of slavery he learned politeness from association with white people, who took pains to teach him. Since the emancipation came and the tie of mutual interest and regard between master and servant was broken, the Negro has drifted away into a state which is neither freedom or bondage. Lacking the proper inspiration of the one and the restraining force of the other he has taken up the idea that boorish insolence is independence, and the exercise of a decent degree of breeding toward white people is identical with servile submission. In consequence of the prevalence of this notion there are many Negroes who use every opportunity to make themselves offensive, particularly when they think it can be done with impunity.

"We have had too many instances right here in Memphis to doubt this, and our experience is not exceptional. *The white people won't stand this sort of thing, and whether they be insulted as individuals or as a race, the response will be prompt and effectual.* The bloody riot of 1866, in which so many Negroes perished, was brought on principally by the outrageous conduct of the blacks toward the whites on the streets. It is also a remarkable and discouraging fact that the majority of such scoundrels are Negroes who have received educational advantages at the hands of the white taxpayers. They have got just enough of learning to make them realize how hopelessly their race is behind the other in everything that makes great people and they attempt to 'get even' by insolence, which is ever the resentment of inferiors. There are well-bred Negroes among us, and it is truly unfortunate that they should have to pay, even in part, the penalty of the offenses committed by the baser sort, but this is the way of the world. The innocent must suffer for the guilty. If the Negroes as a people possessed a hundredth part of the self-respect which is evidenced by the courteous bearing of some that the *Scimitar* could name, the friction between the races would be reduced to a minimum. It will not do to beg the question by pleading that many white men are also stirring up strife. The Caucasian blackguard simply obeys the promptings of a depraved disposition, and he is seldom deliberately rough or offensive toward strangers or unprotected women.

"The Negro tough, on the contrary, is given to just that kind of offending, and he almost invariably singles out white people as his victims."

On March 9th, 1892, there were lynched in this same city three of the best specimens of young since-the-war Afro-American manhood. They were peaceful, law-abiding citizens and energetic businessmen.

They believed the problem was to be solved by eschewing politics and putting money in the purse. They owned a flourishing grocery business in a thickly populated suburb of Memphis, and a white man named Barrett had one on the opposite corner. After a personal difficulty which Barrett sought by going into the "People's Grocery" drawing a pistol and was thrashed by Calvin McDowell, he (Barrett) threatened to "clean them out." These men were a mile beyond the city limits and police protection; hearing that Barrett's crowd was coming to attack them Saturday night, they mustered forces and prepared to defend themselves against the attack.

When Barrett came he led a *posse* of officers, twelve in number, who afterward claimed to be hunting a man for whom they had a warrant. That twelve men in citizen's clothes should think it necessary to go in the night to hunt one man who had never before been arrested, or made any record as a criminal has never been explained. When they entered the back door the young men thought the threatened attack was on, and fired into them. Three of the officers were wounded, and when the *defending* party found it was officers of the law upon whom they had fired, they ceased and got away.

Thirty-one men were arrested and thrown in jail as "conspirators," although they all declared more than once that they did not know they were firing on officers. Excitement was at fever heat until the morning papers, two days after, announced that the wounded deputy sheriffs were out of danger. This hindered rather than helped the plans of the whites. There was no law on the statute books which would execute an Afro-American for wounding a white man, but the "unwritten law" did. Three of these men, the president, the manager and clerk of the grocery—"the leaders of the conspiracy"—were secretly taken from jail and lynched in a shockingly brutal manner. "The Negroes are getting too independent," they say, "we must teach them a lesson."

What lesson? The lesson of subordination. "Kill the leaders and it will cow the Negro who dares to shoot a white man, even in self-defense."

Although the race was wild over the outrage, the mockery of law and justice which disarmed men and locked them up in jails where they could be easily and safely reached by the mob—the Afro-American ministers, newspapers and leaders counselled obedience to the law which did not protect them.

Their counsel was heeded and not a hand was uplifted to resent the outrage; following the advice of the *Free Speech*, people left the city in great numbers. . . .

The South's Position

Henry W. Grady in his well-remembered speeches in New England and New York pictured the Afro-American as incapable of self-government. Through him and other leading men the cry of the South to the country has been "Hands off! Leave us to solve our problem." To the Afro-American the South says, "the white man must and will rule." There is little difference between the Ante-bellum South and the New South.

Her white citizens are wedded to any method however revolting, any measure however extreme, for the subjugation of the young manhood of the race. They have cheated him out of his ballot, deprived him of civil rights or redress therefore in the civil courts, robbed him of the fruits of his labor, and are still murdering, burning and lynching him.

The result is a growing disregard of human life. Lynch law has spread its insiduous influence till men in New York State, Pennsylvania and on the free Western plains feel they can take the law in their own hands with impunity, especially where an Afro-American is concerned. The South is brutalized to a degree not realized by its own inhabitants, and the very foundation of government, law and order, are imperilled.

Public sentiment has had a slight "reaction" though not sufficient to stop the crusade of lawlessness and lynching. The spirit of christianity of the great M.E. Church was aroused to the frequent and revolting crimes against a weak people, enough to pass strong condemnatory resolutions at its General Conference in Omaha last May. The spirit of justice of the grand old party asserted itself sufficiently to secure a denunciation of the wrongs, and a feeble declaration of the belief in human rights in the Republican platform at Minneapolis, June 7th. Some of the great dailies and weeklies have swung into line declaring that lynch law must go. The President of the United States issued a proclamation that it be not tolerated in the territories over which he has jurisdiction. Governor Northern and Chief Justice Bleckley of Georgia have proclaimed against it. The citizens of Chattanooga, Tenn., have set a worthy example in that they not only condemn lynch law, but her public men demanded a trial for Weems, the accused rapist, and guarded him while the trial was in progress. The trial only lasted ten minutes, and Weems chose to plead guilty and accept twenty-one years sentence, than invite the certain death which awaited him outside that cordon of police if he had told the truth and shown the letters he had from the white woman in the case. . . .

The strong arm of the law must be brought to bear upon lynchers in severe punishment, but this cannot and will not be done unless a healthy public sentiment demands and sustains such action.

The men and women in the South who disapprove of lynching and remain silent on the perpetration of such outrages, are *particeps criminis*, accomplices, accessories before and after the fact, equally guilty with the actual law-breakers who would not persist if they did not know that neither the law nor militia would be employed against them.

Self Help

In the creation of this healthier public sentiment, the Afro-American can do for himself what no one else can do for him. The world looks on with wonder that we have conceded so much and remain law-abiding under such great outrage and provocation.

To Northern capital and Afro-American labor the South owes its rehabilitation. If labor is withdrawn capital will not remain. The Afro-American is thus the backbone of the South. A thorough knowledge and judicious exercise of this power in lynching localities could many times effect a bloodless revolution. The white man's dollar is his god and to stop this will be to stop outrages in many localities.

The Afro-Americans of Memphis denounced the lynching of three of their best citizens, and urged and waited for the authorities to act in the matter and bring the lynchers to justice. No attempt was made to do so, and the black men left the city by the thousands, bringing about great stagnation in every branch of business. Those who remained so injured the business of the street car company by staying off the cars, that the superintendent, manager and treasurer called personally on the editors of the *Free Speech*, asked them to urge our people to give them their patronage again. Other business men became alarmed over the situation and the *Free Speech* was run away that the colored people might be more easily controlled. A meeting of white citizens in June, three months after the lynching, passed resolutions for the first time, condemning it. *But they did not punish the lynchers.* Every one of them was known by name, because they had been selected to do the dirty work, by some of the very citizens who passed these resolutions. Memphis is fast losing her black population, who proclaim as they go that there is no protection for the life and property of any Afro-American citizen in Memphis who is not a slave. . . .

The appeal to the white man's pocket has ever been more effectual than all the appeals ever made to his conscience. Nothing, absolutely nothing, is to be gained by a further sacrifice of manhood and self-respect. By the right exercise of his power as the industrial factor of the South, the Afro-American can demand and secure his rights, the punishment of lynchers, and a fair trial for accused rapists.

Of the many inhuman outrages of this present year, the only case where the proposed lynching did *not* occur, was where the men armed themselves in Jacksonville, Fla., and Paducah, Ky., and prevented it. The only times an Afro-American who was assaulted got away has been when he had a gun and used it in self-defense.

The lesson this teaches and which every Afro-American should ponder well, is that a Winchester rifle should have a place of honor in every black home, and it should be used for that protection which the law refuses to give. When the white man who is always the aggressor knows he runs a great risk of biting the dust every time his Afro-American victim does, he will have greater respect for Afro-American life. The more the Afro-American yields and cringes and begs, the more he has to do so, the more he is insulted, outraged and lynched.

The assertion has been substantiated throughout that the press contains unreliable and doctored reports of lynchings, and one of the most necessary things for the race to do is to get these facts before the public. The people must know before they can act, and there is no educator to compare with the press.

The Afro-American papers are the only ones which will print the truth, and they lack the means to employ agents and detectives to get all the facts. The race must rally a mighty host to the support of their journals, and thus enable them to do much in the way of investigation. . . .

Nothing is more definitely settled than he must act for himself. I have shown how he may employ the boycott, emigration and the press, and I feel that by a combination of all these agencies can be effectually stamped out lynch law, that last relic of barbarism and slavery. "The gods help those who help themselves."

NOTES

1. William I. Hair, "Lynching," in *Encyclopedia of Southern Culture*, Charles Wilson and William Ferris, eds. (Chapel Hill: University of North Carolina Press, 1989), 174.

2. Quoted in John Ezell, *The South since 1865* (Norman: University of Oklahoma Press, 1975), 375.

3. Howard N. Rabinowitz, *The First New South, 1865–1920* (Arlington Heights, IL: Harlan Davidson, 1992), 141.

4. Thomas D. Clark and Albert D. Kirwan, *The South since Appomattox: A Century of Regional Change* (New York: Oxford University Press, 1967), 292–293.

5. David R. Goldfield, *Black, White, and Southern: Race Relations and Southern Culture, 1940 to the Present* (Baton Rouge: Louisiana State University Press, 1990), 33.

6. Speech presented at Monteagle, Tennessee, on August 2, 1883. Published in *Pleas for Progress* (Nashville: Methodist Publishing House, 1889), 5–24.

7. Most of this biographical sketch is from Wanda Hendricks, "Ida Bell Wells-Barnett," in *Black Women in America: An Historical Encyclopedia*, Darlene Clark Hine, ed. (Brooklyn, NY: Carlson Publishing, Inc., 1993), 1242–1246 and Linda T. Wynn, "Ida B. Wells-Barnett," in *Notable Black American Women*, Jessie Carney Smith, ed. (Detroit, MI: Gale Research, Inc., 1992), 1232–1238.

8. Eleanor Flexner, "Ida Bell Wells-Barnett," in *Notable American Women, 1607–1950*, vol. III, Edward T. James, ed. (Cambridge, MA: Belknap Press, 1971), 565.

9. Donald L. Grant, *Anti-Lynching Movement, 1883–1932* (San Francisco, CA: R and E Research Associates, 1975), 29.

10. Address delivered at Lyric Hall in New York City, October 5, 1892. Printed as a pamphlet in November of that year; this version is from *Outspoken Women: Speeches by American Women Reformers, 1635–1935*, Judith Anderson, ed. (Dubuque, IA: Kendall/Hunt Publishing Co., 1984), 206–220.

FOR FURTHER READING

Degler, Carl N. *The Other South: Southern Dissenters in the Nineteenth Century*. New York: Harper and Row, 1974.

Williamson, Joel. *A Rage for Order: Black-White Relations in the American South since Emancipation*. New York: Oxford University Press, 1986.

Atticus Greene Haygood

Mann, Harold W. *Atticus Greene Haygood: Methodist Bishop, Editor, and Educator*. Athens: University of Georgia Press, 1965.

Towns, Stuart. "Atticus G. Haygood: Neglected Advocate of Reconciliation and a New South," *Southern Studies* 26 (Spring 1987), 28–40.

Ida Wells-Barnett

Broschart, Kay Richards. "Ida B. Wells-Barnett." In *Women in Sociology: A Bio-Bibliographical Sourcebook*, Mary Jo Deegan, ed. New York: Greenwood Press, 1991. 432–439.

Brundage, W. Fitzhugh. *Lynching in the New South: Georgia and Virginia, 1880–1930*. Urbana: University of Illinois Press, 1993.

Wells, Ida B. *Crusade for Justice: The Autobiography of Ida Wells*, Alfreda M. Duster, ed. Chicago: University of Chicago Press, 1970.

———. *The Memphis Diary of Ida B. Wells*. Miriam Decosta-Willis, ed. Boston: Beacon Press, 1996.

Index

About the Author

W. STUART TOWNS is Department Chair of Communication Arts at the University of West Florida, where he has taught since 1968. From 1975 through 1995 he was a member of the Consulting Faculty at the U.S. Army Command and General Staff College. He is the author of numerous articles on Southern oratory and communications within the military.

ISBN 0-275-96224-5

9 780275 962241